Tragedies of the English Renaissance

Titles in the Series

www.edinburghuniversitypress.com/series/rend

Tragedies of the English Renaissance

An Introduction

Goran Stanivukovic and John H. Cameron

EDINBURGH
University Press

Edinburgh University Press is one of the leading university presses in the UK. We publish academic books and journals in our selected subject areas across the humanities and social sciences, combining cutting-edge scholarship with high editorial and production values to produce academic works of lasting importance. For more information visit our website: edinburghuniversitypress.com

Edinburgh University Press Ltd
The Tun – Holyrood Road,
12(2f) Jackson's Entry,
Edinburgh EH8 8PJ

Typeset in 11/13 Sabon by
IDSUK (Dataconnection) Ltd, and
printed and bound in Great Britain.

A CIP record for this book is available from the British Library

ISBN 978 1 4744 1955 0 (hardback)
ISBN 978 1 4744 1957 4 (webready PDF)
ISBN 978 1 4744 1956 7 (paperback)
ISBN 978 1 4744 1958 1 (epub)

Contents

Acknowledgements

We would like to thank Sean McEvoy, Lisa Hopkins, Peter Sillitoe and Tiffany Stern for their advice and guidance at certain stages of our work on this book. Part of our work was supported by the Social Sciences and Humanities Research Council of Canada, for which we are grateful. We thank the librarians and staff at Patrick Power Library at Saint Mary's University for aiding our research. John Cameron would like to thank his wife Melinda and daughters Cordelia and Rosalind for their love and support.

Note on Citation

In citing early modern texts, we have modernised their spelling and typography.

Chronological Table of Key Early Modern Tragedies

The following list is designed to offer dates of publication and the first recorded performance of a specific play, followed by author(s), playing company and theatre(s). This chronology is based on those established by Andrew Gurr (1992) and Martin Wiggins and Catherine Richardson (2013, 2014, 2015).

Date	Playwright	Play	Company	Theatre
1561/1562	T. Norton/T. Sackville	*Gorboduc*		Inner Temple
1578	M. Sidney	*The Tragedy of Antonie* (closet drama)		
c. 1587/1592–3 1597–1602	T. Kyd	*The Spanish Tragedy*	Strange's Men Admiral's Men	Rose Fortune
c. 1587/c. 1588	C. Marlowe	*1 & 2 Tamburlaine the Great*	Admiral's Men	Rose
c. 1589/c. 1589–1592	C. Marlowe	*The Jew of Malta*	Strange's Men	Rose
c. 1591/1594	W. Shakespeare	*Titus Andronicus*	?Strange's Men	?Rose
c. 1591/c. 1592	Anon.	*Arden of Faversham*	Sussex's Men (1594)	Rose
c. 1592/c. 1588	C. Marlowe	*Doctor Faustus*	Admiral's Men	?Bel Savage/ Rose/Fortune

Date	Playwright	Play	Company	Theatre
1595/1597	W. Shakespeare	*Romeo and Juliet*	?Chamberlain's Men	?Theatre
c. 1596	F. Greville	*The Tragedy of Mustapha* (closet drama)		
1599/by 1602	J. Marston	*Antonio and Mellida*	Paul's Boys	Paul's
1599	W. Shakespeare	*Julius Caesar*	Chamberlain's Men	?Globe
c. 1600/1602	W. Shakespeare	*Hamlet*	Chamberlain's Men	Globe
1600/1602	J. Marston	*Antonio's Revenge*	Paul's Boys	Paul's
1600	F. Greville	*Alaham* (closet drama)		
1603	B. Jonson	*Sejanus*	King's Men	Globe
1603	J. Marston	*The Malcontent*	Queen's Revels	Blackfriars
1604	G. Chapman	*The Revenge of Bussy D'Ambois*	Paul's Boys Queen's Revels	Paul's/ Blackfriars/ Whitefriars
1603/1604	W. Shakespeare	*Othello*	King's Men	Globe
1605/?1606	?T. Middleton	*A Yorkshire Tragedy*	King's Men	Globe
1605/?1607	W. Shakespeare & ?T. Middleton	*Timon of Athens*	King's Men	Globe
c.1605/1606	W. Shakespeare	*King Lear*	King's Men	Globe
1605	E. Cary	*Mariam, the Fair Queen of Jewry* (closet drama)		
1606	W. Shakespeare	*Macbeth*	King's Men	Globe
1606/1608	W. Shakespeare	*Antony and Cleopatra*	King's Men	Globe/ ?Blackfriars
1606/1607	T. Middleton	*The Revenger's Tragedy*	King's Men	Globe
1607/1608	J. Fletcher & F. Beaumont	*Cupid's Revenge*	Queen's Revels	Blackfriars
1607/1608	G. Chapman	*Byron's Conspiracy*	Queen's Revels	?Blackfriars/ ?Whitefriars
c.1608/1609	W. Shakespeare	*Coriolanus*	King's Men	Globe/ ?Blackfriars
1610	J. Fletcher & F. Beaumont	*The Maid's Tragedy*	King's Men	Blackfriars

Date	Playwright	Play	Company	Theatre
1611	B. Jonson	*Catiline His Conspiracy*	King's Men	Globe/Blackfriars
1606/1611	C. Tourneur	*The Atheist's Tragedy*	?King's Men	?Globe
1612	J. Webster	*The White Devil*	Queen Anne's	Red Bull
1614	J. Webster	*The Duchess of Malfi*	King's Men	Blackfriars
1621	T. Dekker, J. Ford & W. Rowley	*The Witch of Edmonton*	Prince Charles'	Cockpit
1621	T. Middleton	*Women Beware Women*	?King's Men	?Globe/ ?Blackfriars
c. 1622/1621-2	P. Massinger	*The Duke of Milan*	King's Men	Blackfriars
1622	T. Middleton & W. Rowley	*The Changeling*	Lady Elizabeth's	Cockpit
1626	P. Massinger	*The Roman Actor*	King's Men	Blackfriars
c. 1629	J. Ford	*The Broken Heart*	King's Men	Blackfriars
1631	P. Massinger	*Believe as You List*	King's Men	?Blackfriars
?1631	J. Shirley	*Love's Cruelty*	Queen Henrietta's	Cockpit
1631	J. Shirley	*The Traitor*	Queen Henrietta's	Cockpit
?1631/c. 1632	J. Ford	*Love's Sacrifice*	Queen Henrietta's	Cockpit
1632/?1630	J. Ford	*'Tis Pity She's a Whore*	Queen Henrietta's	Cockpit
?1639	J. Shirley	*The Politician*	?Ogilby's Men (Dublin)	?Werburgh St (Dublin)
1641	J. Shirley	*The Cardinal*	King's Men	Blackfriars

Introduction

WHAT IS ENGLISH RENAISSANCE TRAGEDY?

English Renaissance tragedy is a kind of drama whose subject is drawn from history and which explores the evil, rage, inner conflict and fall of an individual of high estate, and in some instances the fall of persons of lower class as well. It shows the weaknesses in and limitations of such individuals that lead to their tragedy. A description of the plot of an English Renaissance tragedy, included in an undated manuscript (X.d.259) from the Folger Shakespeare Library, consisting of two leaves and dating from the 1590s, provides us with the gist of what early modern English tragedy as a genre entailed: 'A stately tragedy containing the ambitious life and death of the great Cham. The enchantments of Bagous the Brachman with the strange fortunes of Royen the captivity, release, and death of his brother Manzor the Turchestan King and happy fortunes of the Sophy of Persia with the love of Bargandell his son.' This tragedy stages the fall of a ruler from the East, the adventures and captivity of another noble figure, and a romantic plot. This description tells us that the early modern tragedy was not only a play about tragic fall and high passions, but also drama of love and adventure. A transcript of these two leaves appears in Proudfoot (1977 [1971]: 64–7).

English Renaissance tragedy explores a conflict between private life and public duty. It dramatises revenge and culminates in death, which comes at the end of the tragic hero's gradual decline from a position of good fortune and success to that of anguish and despair (McAlindon 2004: 105–6). In 1599 William Scott, who was one of the most important of English Renaissance critics, defined tragedy as 'solemnly and sadly handling great and unhappy actions, by fear and compassion to purge outrageous and cruel affections' (Scott 2013 [?1599]: 23). The high-sounding and elevated language of tragedy expressed in a range of rhetorical ornaments like bombast and metrical features such as unrhymed iambic pentameter (blank verse) intends to capture the emotional atmosphere of tragedy created by revenge, jealousy, violence and suffering, in what Michael Pincombe has characterised as Renaissance tragedy's 'characteristic range of vociferative styles', referring to the vehemence and bombast of the style of early English tragedies (2010: 5).

Tragedy is not a single dramatic kind but covers several subgenres such as homiletic tragedy (inspired by religious conflicts and divisions), biblical tragedy (based on the fall and unfortunate fate of biblical figures), historical tragedy (featuring classical and domestic historical and political figures, and the stories of their demise), domestic tragedy (presenting conflicts between middle- and lower-class individuals) and romantic tragedy (showing the ruination of romantic love). During the Renaissance the revenge tragedy was the most dominant form and explored stages in the plotting of a revenge for the murder or perceived injustice. A key feature of English Renaissance tragedy is that it was intended for stage performance, in outdoor or indoor theatre spaces. The performative nature of tragedy shaped both the language and the dramatic narrative, and the development of theatres and playing companies in London encouraged the growth of tragedy as a dramatic genre. Wherever possible, we aim to stress London's role, both as a city and as a home to public and private theatres, in shaping these tragedies in such a distinct way. Figure 1 shows a map of early modern London, produced by the German topographers Georg Braun and Frans Hogenberg. This map shows the expansion of London on the south bank of the River Thames

Figure 1 Georg Braun and Frans Hogenberg, from *Civitas orbis terrarium*, Cologne, 1572. Wikimedia Commons

outside the city's limits, where public theatres will soon emerge to meet the public's growing desire for entertainment.

Between 1572 and Shakespeare's death in 1616 the Bankside developed quite rapidly, as we can see Claes Visscher's panorama of London (Figure 2). In contrast to Braun and Hogenberg's map of the Bankside, Visscher's gives clear indication of the numerous buildings that had been built in the interim, the most famous of which being the Globe, built in 1599.

Figure 2 Claes Visscher, an imagined panorama of London, Amsterdam, 1616, print. Wikimedia Commons

SOCIAL AND POLITICAL CONTEXT FOR TRAGEDY

Tragedy flourished during the latter part of the reign of Queen Elizabeth I (1558–1603). This flourishing, which started in the late 1580s, saw a large increase in the number of theatre buildings and playing companies in London, the shift from amateur and academic to popular and professional dramatists, actors and acting companies, and a rise in the number of plays written and performed. These theatres were spread out throughout London and their location tended to reflect their status or lack thereof; likewise, theatres on the Bankside were generally less restricted by the city laws then were those located within the City of London. In time of plague during the Elizabethan period, London companies toured the provinces, so audiences in the rest of England became increasingly exposed to new plays performed in London. These changes in drama and theatre were initiated by the events that occurred in politics and society in the first half of the sixteenth century.

When King Henry VIII's (1491–1547) request to divorce Katherine of Aragon (1485–1536) was rejected by the Pope, he denied the papal supreme authority and launched religious reforms through the Act of Supremacy over the Church of England in 1534. While this act led to England breaking away from the supreme authority of the universal Catholic Church, it did not mean that the Church of England suddenly became Protestant; it remained Catholic, but not Roman Catholic. The reformation of England's Catholic church triggered a political and social process that was at once irresistible and disturbing. Henry VIII's radical act occurred at the same time as Catholic religious hegemony was being challenged across Europe in a movement that would later be called Protestantism. The king dissolved the monasteries (1536–9), but the outcome of his religious, social and political reformation remained uncertain until Elizabeth narrowly succeeded in solidifying the results of the Reformation through the 1559 parliamentary Acts of Supremacy and Uniformity. The Act of Supremacy enforced the Church of England as the supreme church in the country and the Act of Uniformity declared that worship in that church follow the Book of Common Prayer. But solidifying the Reformed church also made Elizabeth an enemy of Spain and France. Anti-Catholic feelings that dominated religious debates in Protestant society and culture therefore influenced drama as well, as Brian Cummings suggested (2002: 282). Catholic countries became convenient places for the writers of tragedy to set their narratives of vice, sin, murder, revenge and grief.

While religious cohesion in Elizabethan England was difficult to enforce as a result of such theological controversies, national unity was easier to establish. This was aided by the defeat of the Spanish Armada on 29 July 1588, an English victory that secured England's sovereignty, strengthened Elizabeth's political power and boosted the patriotic sentiments of her people. As a consequence, theatre started to flourish in conditions of peace and a promise of prosperity (Womack 2006: 19). As drama about public life, tragedy captured politics and explored personal reactions to it. What also made tragedy both a popular and important genre at this time was that it carried a strong moral lesson. It taught how to conduct oneself in the present by staging errors made by figures, often famous and frequently classical, from the past. Greek and Roman writers not only provided source material but also locations for these tragedies to play out.

Owen Chadwick has suggested that the Reformation also represented a shift in morality as well as religious belief (1988: 13). The Reformation and Humanism were crucial to drama and theatre because they displaced God and religion as theatre's main concern, liberating the language of drama from religious and moralising debates, placing man, with his desires, doubts, and agency, at the centre of plays. This liberation comes with a cost, because responsibility for one's actions assumed that an individual would accept any guilt brought on by those actions. This strong Calvinist streak in English Protestantism made it easier for other political and economic changes to take hold of society and individuals. Calvinism, which arrived somewhat belatedly in the English Reformation, nevertheless emphasised the importance of preaching God's word in every parish as well as of the concept of predestination, a biblical concept in which God determines beforehand what will happen and selects those who will be redeemed by salvation and will not fall from grace. The idea that only those who live by faith will meet salvation became not only a problem for those who accepted this proposition, but it also created the spiritual basis out of which most Elizabethan and early Jacobean tragedies sprang. Tragic heroes in English Renaissance drama are haunted by, rebel against and are ultimately brought down by the question neatly formulated by the historian of religion Diarmaid MacCulloch as: '[I]f one rejects the role of human works in the approach to God, what is the point of leading a good life?' (1990: 89). It could be said the tragic individual's fate is shaped in Elizabethan tragedy by the forces unleashed by thoughts and actions undertaken in response to this question.

Other factors, besides religion, played an important role in creating conditions for a new type of tragedy to develop in Elizabethan England. Transformations that occurred in the social history of sixteenth-century England were among the strongest of those factors external to the development of playhouses. Feudal models of agriculture and agricultural labour collided with emerging merchant capitalism, and the economic and financial concerns and ambitions of a new society intercut with the long-established adherence to the land. The desire to acquire wealth, status and fame, to pursue personal ambitions and to cope with the guilt engendered by those ambitions were sources of debate and critique, which changed English society. One can find many of the anxieties over such changes reflected in plays like Christopher Marlowe's (1564–1593) *The Jew of Malta* (c. 1589) and William Shakespeare's (1564–1616) *Richard III* (c. 1592), both of which feature Machiavellian figures who aim to upset the settled state of affairs.

Changes in religion, society and politics caused uncertainty and led to 'cultural dislocation' (Sinfield 1983: 80). This atmosphere of social dislocation produced fertile ground for tragedy to flourish. Building its dramatic narratives and plots around the clash between ardent human freedom and human sinfulness, between the spirit and the flesh, and by exploring the individual's responsibility for his or her actions, tragedy presented social debates and personal conflicts to a responsive London audience. Self-examination and reliance on one's own intellect and conscience in defending one's own spiritual and personal liberties within the larger frame of religious strife and socio-political changes in society became the key factors that shaped tragedy. As the result of this, soliloquies became the medium through which introspection became a tool for speaking not only to oneself but to the audience as well. The Reformation represented a kind of 'cultural revolution' (Simpson 2002) which had taken place in England in the second half of the sixteenth century. This can best be seen in the new tragedy that increasingly explored secular subjects dominating England's politics and society while moving further away from medieval religious drama (Happé 1999: 7). This move reflected both a Protestant impulse not to see such religious stories dramatised, and also a change in society itself with a shift towards secular drama that explored secular concerns. These two forces may not have been working in concert, but they resulted in helping to bring about English Renaissance tragedy.

Social and political currents ran alongside new cultural trends brought in by Humanism. Literature, fine arts and education embraced the spread of Humanism rooted in rediscovery of the classics. History became a valued subject, giving tragedy stories, characters and settings. In English grammar schools, translations of Greek and Roman poets, philosophers, rhetoricians and historiographers were read, memorised in parts, and commented upon in various exercises; imitations of classical, especially Roman, writers abounded. Greek and Roman writers constituted the core of the university curriculum at Oxford and Cambridge, where many playwrights, such as Christopher Marlowe and Robert Greene (1558–92), studied. Ancient Rome was held up as both a model of government and as a reminder of how uncontrolled ambition and personal passions could bring down public figures. In sixteenth-century England, republican Rome, particularly as represented in the writings of Cicero, was deemed to signify the ideal state, while imperial Rome, particularly as represented in the histories of Tacitus, signified something rather less ideal, engendering civil conflict and the horrors of war. A key instance of the conflict between these two contrasting visions of the state, embodied both within the world of the play and within one of its main characters, is Shakespeare's *Antony and Cleopatra* (c. 1607).

While the influence of the classics was immense, English Renaissance tragedy ultimately broke away from many of the rules of classical tragedy (Nicoll 1968: 45). Shaped by native dramatic tradition, literature and folklore, English Renaissance tragedy developed into a specific form. Some tragedies, like *Arden of Faversham* (1592), deal with middle-class persons; Shakespeare's *Othello* (1603) and *Romeo and Juliet* (c. 1594) and Thomas Kyd's (1558–94) *The Spanish Tragedy* (c. 1587) combine tragedy with narratives of romance, however doomed. The new tragedy developed in England blended humour and romance, suffering and evil, folklore and magic (in which some Elizabethans believed), and history and politics, and with a tragic hero usually represented, not as a completely evil creation, but as a human being with traits that the London audiences could relate to. The tragedy that developed from the late 1580s was a mix of dramatic genres, with classical and contemporary influences, and with features from the local culture and the literary heritage. This distinctly English, even London, form of tragedy would see many challenging manifestations in the years that followed.

As the ideas of Humanism permeated English arts and letters, tragedy and the Renaissance went hand in hand. Italian and French writers, philosophers and political theorists like Michel de Montaigne (1533–92) and Niccolò Machiavelli (1469–1527) were translated and commented upon, just as Italian painters and architects and Flemish and French artists arrived in England, introducing Continental art and aesthetics to an England eager to catch up with the Renaissance. Under the influence coming from the Continent, English tragedy showed how the stories and styles of tragic writing shaped by the Reformation and Humanism became altered and enriched, reflecting an English version of the Renaissance. Playwrights, both those who attended university and those who did not, were grounded in these traditions, and their tragedies reflected this.

In response to the growing number of audience members, theatres expanded rapidly between 1587 and 1595. More playwrights came to the fore as a result, all working within the same dramatic forms and styles. Elizabeth I's successor, King James I (1566–1625), was an even greater patron of the theatre. Theatres flourished under James I when he succeeded Elizabeth in 1603. When the Catholic-born but Protestant-raised Scottish king came to the throne of a Protestant and increasingly anti-Catholic England, two faiths and two crowns were brought together in one place. Although King James was not Catholic, his wife, Queen Anne, was, and her interest in theatre made some contribution to the court's investment in drama and performance in London's theatres. James's court was notorious for its ostentatiousness and wantonness and for the king's lavish spending of both the court's and the country's finances (Chambers 1951, I: 6). As a political genre focused on court and society, tragedy forcefully critiqued this change in courtly and monarchical style. In significant ways, then, tragedy written and performed in Jacobean England raises important questions about court culture and the life of courtiers during this period. The classical setting of tragedies performed in public playhouses, and of the closet dramas intended solely for private entertainment in indoor playing spaces, not only represented a vestige of tragedy's classical heritage but, more importantly, served as a theatrical veil behind which the vicious politics of courtly intrigue was thinly disguised and the malaise of Jacobean society explored in brutal detail.

In politics, however, James's reign was also marked by the peace he negotiated with Spain in 1604, which paved the way for the continuing development of the country, and by his shrewd diplomacy more generally in Europe, making him a monarch with an international outlook. Both a writer and a lover of stage performance, with a preference for masques rather than plays, James did much to patronise the theatre, most famously when he took over the patronage of Shakespeare's company, the Lord Chamberlain's Men, under the 1st and 2nd Barons Hunsdon, and made them the King's Men under himself. By making theatre companies directly serve the court and feed its appetite for arts and entertainment, James made theatre as important to his model of monarchy as politics.

Tragedy vigorously responded to all these changes that affected Jacobean England. For example, as opposed to the more individualised roles of Elizabethan tragedy, Jacobean tragedies contain more stock types, who nevertheless speak in some of the most gripping and sharp-edged language ever produced in English tragic writing. Through stories, images and stage allegories, these tragedies captured the atmosphere of James's court. With the Stuart king's accession, a community of young, ambitious and thrusting aristocrats and citizens began to emerge, and tragedy appealed to their educated tastes and social aspirations. Tragedy became more intellectual in nature, and even more classical in terms of setting and cultural and historical references, all while drawing on the realism of court intrigues and the evils of those involved in them. As private, more intimate theatres lit with artificial lighting grew in number and popularity in Jacobean England, tragedy turned inward to focus on smaller, more enclosed spaces, capitalising on the difference between darkness and candlelight to dramatise the struggle between good and evil in society and at court. Examples abound, with John Webster's (c. 1580–c. 1634) *The Duchess of Malfi* (1613) serving as perhaps the most chilling.

After James's death in 1625, significant political, religious and cultural changes occurred in England that charted the course of tragedy in the last phase of its development. For example, the reign of King Charles I (1600–49; r. 1625–49), James's son, was a period of deepening disagreement between monarch and Parliament over the role and power the Parliament should have in advising the king, who was perceived to be increasingly curbing the liberties within society, such as when he enforced religious conformity in 1633 (Butler 1984: 19–21). The growing power and role of the Puritan Protestants in Parliament meant that hostility towards theatres and actors grew. While playwrights responded with many a satiric jab against such – often hypocritical – reproofs, in plays such as Ben Jonson's (1572–1637) *Bartholomew Fair* (1614), they could not stem the rising tide of Puritanism any more than the king could. Against the background of the charged relationship between monarch and Parliament, as well as divisions among the nobility over the monarch's style of governing, the king's subjects increasingly pondered the just relationship between monarchical rule and the subject's traditional rights and liberties. In the Caroline period, tragedy drew much of its dramatic power from the politics of the court and played on the polarization between republican and royalist tendencies in English society. Tragedies of the period abound with tyrannical kings and with courtiers and citizens embroiled in self-interested schemes, and with situations in which justice is ruthlessly violated, and show the courts and city as places of enormous uncertainties, political, spiritual, personal and otherwise. However, external circumstances would soon interrupt the flourishing of tragedy.

The expansion and prosperity of London theatres ended in 1642 when they were closed in the wake of the English Civil War. Between the late 1570s and 1642, however, drama was affected not only by the emergence and disappearance of theatre buildings and acting companies, but also more profoundly by the political and cultural ebb and flow, such as the Counter-Reformation (or Catholic Reformation) on the Continent, a period that lasted from the Council of Trent (1545–63) to the end of the Thirty Years War (1648). The growing number of tragedies performed in London between Elizabeth I's and James I's deaths testifies to these forces and to the indirect role their courts had on shaping the genre. The political chasm between loyalists and parliamentarian groups calling for a reform of Parliament reached the point of civil war (Butler 1984: 22–3). Towards the end of Charles I's reign, the Puritan faction within Parliament became so strong that, in February 1641, Parliament passed a motion for the suppression of the theatres, which were closed in 1642, the year the English Civil War broke out. The closure of the theatres brought an end to English Renaissance tragedy.

DEVELOPMENT OF TRAGEDY

Classical influences

In his illuminating essay on tragedy, George Steiner offers the following definition of the genre:

> 'Tragedy' is a dramatic representation, enactment, or generation of a highly specific world-view. This world-view

is summarised in the adage preserved among the elegies ascribed to Theognis . . . 'It is best not to be born, next best to die young.' (1996: 536)

Steiner's definition is clearly indebted to Greek tragedy. This dramatic genre was most famously explained in Aristotle's (384–322 BC) classic treatise, the *Poetics*. While there is no evidence that Aristotle's *Poetics*, his work on tragedy, directly influenced Elizabethan, Jacobean and early Caroline playwrights, some tragic features described by Aristotle, like recognition (called anagnorisis), occur in many of their plays. Knowledge of the *Poetics* in the early modern period in England most influentially came from Lodovico Castelvetro's commentary in Italian, *Poetica d'Aristotele vulgarizzata et sposta* (1570). However, in those English tragedies, recognition is less a formal device than in Greek drama and more a mood, showing how a speaking part changes as the result of powerful experiences undergone at the moment of intense dramatic action and heightened emotions. Clarence's sudden realization in *Richard III* that his brother Richard aims not to save him but to have him murdered serves as a stark example of the dramatic force of such recognition. The absence of Aristotle's direct influence partly reflects the fact that the first Latin rendering of it appeared in 1623 and the first English translation (done possibly from French) in 1705.

The unfamiliarity with Aristotle's theory of tragedy, however, was offset by the presence of Greek tragedy in translations. For instance, Roger Ascham (1515–68) translated Sophocles' (c. 497–c. 405 BC) *Philoctetes* in 1543, and the plays of Euripides (c. 480–406 BC) were among the most popular of Greek drama. Translations of *Hecuba*, *Hercules Furens* and *Medea*, which appeared between 1528 and 1555, further testify to the growing popularity Euripides enjoyed in England. Despite the availability of translated Greek drama, Greek plays were much less known as stage performances than as texts in translation.

The more immediate influence on tragedy in Renaissance England, however, came from the Roman playwright Lucius Annaeus Seneca (4 BC–AD 65), who was distantly influenced

by Euripides (Rossiter 1969: 21). The impact of Senecan tragedy in England was strong but limited; for example, when performed on stage his plays were not successful. Their influence
came largely from the language and style they employed. Again,
it is translations, not performances, of Seneca that marked an
important moment in the development of tragedy as a genre
in Renaissance England. The most obvious testimony to the
popularity of Seneca in England in the middle of the sixteenth
century is evident in the number of verse translations of all ten
of his tragedies into English and in the imitations of his plays
by English playwrights. Between 1559 and 1566 most of the
individual plays by Seneca were translated into English. For
example, Jasper Heywood translated *Troades* (1559) and *Thyestes* (1560) and Alexander Neville translated *Oedipus* (1563);
John Studley translated *Agamemnon* (1566), *Medea* (1566),
Hercules Octaeus (1566) and *Hippolytus* (1566). Other plays,
such as *Hercules Furens* (1561) and *Octavia* (1566), were
attributed to Seneca during the sixteenth century. These attri-
butions are now challenged by scholars, but these plays were
also translated by Jasper Heywood and Thomas Nuce, respec-
tively. In 1581 Thomas Newton (c. 1542–1607) collected
those translations in a volume containing all ten of Seneca's
tragedies; throughout the 1580s several further collections of
his ten plays appeared. Senecan tragedy was so influential that
the first blank-verse English tragedy, Thomas Sackville (1536–
1608) and Thomas Norton's (1532–84) *Gorboduc* (1561), was
praised by Sir Philip Sidney (1554–86) precisely for the degree
to which it tried to climb 'to the height of Seneca's style' (qtd
in Vickers 2003: 381). The vogue for Seneca was such that
even Elizabeth I is attributed with a translation of the chorus
parts from *Hercules Oetaeus*. It was not until plays like *Jocasta*
and *Gismond of Salerne* became popular in the 1560s that the
Senecan mode of writing tragedies permeated the native English academic drama. *Jocasta* (1566) is partly a translation from
Lodovico Dolce's version, done by George Gascoigne, Francis
Kinwelmersh and Christopher Yelverton (the last writing the
epilogue); it was performed at the Gray's Inn. The tragedy
Gismond of Salerne (1568), written by Christopher Hatton,

Henry Noel, Roderick Stafford and Robert Wilmot, was first performed by the Gentlemen of the Inner Temple, possibly at Greenwich Palace. Productions of these two plays in the Inns of Court occurred less than two decades before English tragedies inspired by Seneca were performed, and before those performances transformed English tragedy. The importance of Seneca for the development of English tragedy primarily lies in the role the familiarity with and popularity of his plays had on creating a shift from biblical subject matter, which features in the early 'regular' (Wilson 1969: 126) tragedies written in England in the 1540s, to a new tragedy exploring themes like crime and punishment, murder and retribution, justice and freedom, chance and identity. Some of those early tragedies exploring biblical subjects include George Buchanan's *Jephtes* (1542) and *Baptistes* (*John the Baptist*, 1540), and Nicholas Grimald's *Archipropheta* (1546). As we will see, much of Seneca's impact was enhanced by being moved out of the academy and into the hands of professional playwrights who were not afraid to break the rules of their Roman predecessor. The move from inn to playhouse, from private to public, energised English Renaissance tragedy.

Although Seneca wrote his plays in Latin hexameter, English translations of his plays employed blank verse. Thus, English Renaissance tragedy took from Seneca a form of rhetorical style evident in elaborate speeches, the convention of the five-act division and chorus, pathos, moral pessimism, violent action, the domination and intensity of one passion (for example revenge, jealousy, ire), respect for the unity of time and place, which required the action of the play to be confined to one place within a short period of time, and the supernatural and ghosts. In particular, rhetoric became the most important tool that linked English Renaissance tragedy to Seneca's Rome.

Seneca lived and wrote in Rome, in an age that cultivated rhetorical ornamentation through the use of tropes and figures, such as hyperbole (the trope of exaggeration of truth). The expansion of a topic through stylistic ornamentation and persuasive deliberation as an art of speaking and of written composition was cultivated to perfection and pursued with ardour. In its rediscovery of the classical world of learning, art and literature, the Elizabethan period made rhetoric not only the key medium through which classical heritage was transposed to contemporary people but also one through which wisdom and truth were conveyed. The rhetorical skills found in Seneca's tragedies became the chief instrument through which dramatists could express the political and personal strivings of their own age.

In classical tragedy, the Renaissance dramatists had discovered the theme of human daring of the gods and the consequences ensuing from such daring, the worship of strength, superhuman ambition and rhetorical exuberance. Because it was capable of testing the limits of belief between secular and religious worlds, tragedy caused concern among authorities, best illustrated by the performance of a tragedy in Christ's College at Cambridge University in 1545. The university authorities complained that this was 'pestiferous' and 'intolerable' (Wickham et al. 2000: 25). The tragedy that found itself under attack from the university authorities was Thomas Kirchmayer's *Pammachius*, performed in the spring of 1545. Their attack was registered by Stephen Gardiner in his letter to the Chancellor of Cambridge, Matthew Parker, and to Thomas Smith, on 27 March 1545 (Wickham, Berry and Ingram 2000: 25–6). Tragedy as a genre posed a danger to the customs and beliefs of the world outside the theatre because the acting of it could move audiences to unlawful actions that conflicted with religion. From early on, performers of tragedy were seen to represent 'to the people, by their gestures, the actions of conflicting forces', as a twelfth-century text on tragedy states (qtd in Young 1933: 83), forces that threatened Christian religion and doctrine. Put simply, tragedy was regarded to be too secular in nature. This detail about the culture's anxiety over tragedy is important because it shows that Renaissance playwrights publicly exploited the potential of tragedy for religious, social and political transgression before an audience of diverse social backgrounds.

Domestic influence

During the English Renaissance a new kind of tragedy came out of this mix of late medieval tragic writing, early Tudor tragedy and the Senecan tragedy of revenge. We associate medieval tragedy with the themes of the Fall of Lucifer and the Fall of Adam, and with those exploring the conflict between human and divine will and power. The works of Dante Alighieri (c. 1265–1321) and Giovanni Boccaccio (1313–75), Italian writers of the late medieval period, left their traces in the writings of John Lydgate (c. 1370–c. 1451) and Geoffrey Chaucer (c. 1343–1400), which fed into early English tragedy. Medieval religious plays like the mid-fifteenth-century miracle play *Mankind* provided Renaissance tragedy with character types such as Vice that gave stage life to new speaking parts in Renaissance drama, such as Richard, Duke of Gloucester in *Richard III* or Iago in *Othello*.

Of critical importance was John Lydgate's *The Fall of Princes*, written between 1431 and 1439, for Humphrey, Duke of Gloucester (1390–1447), a long free-verse translation of Giovanni Boccaccio's *De Casibus Virorum Illustrium* (On the Fall of Great Men) (c. 1360); a narrative poem exploring the fall of notable individuals, it juxtaposes those from the pre-Christian era, like Julius Caesar and Alexander, with biblical figures such as Lucifer and Adam (Wickham 1966, I: 320). At the heart of Lydgate's portrayal of these figures and their fates lies the idea that an individual suffers the consequences of his actions. Lydgate treats the narratives of these falls as tragedies, saying that he took this notion of tragedy from Chaucer, especially 'The Monk's Tale':

> My maistir Chaucer, with his fresh comedies,
> Is dead, allas, cheeff poete off Breteyne,
> That whilom made ful piteous tragedies;
> The fal of pryncies he did also compleyne.
> (qtd in Wickham 1966, I: 320 n*6)

The theme of the fall of a notable and noble individual, one whose fate is determined both by his actions and by the conflict between human will and God's will, went on to become the thematic core of English Renaissance tragedy as social entertainment. Lydgate's *The Fall of Princes* cultivated a distinct 'dramatic pattern' of tragedies exploring man's world by bringing together a new story, a new language and a new kind of spectacle.

Although not a work of literary distinction, *The Fall of Princes* is, however, important for the history of tragedy, which it supplied with novel features such as the insistence on the moral weakness of character as the primary reason for the fall, the rejection of the tragic decline as the result of the working of fortune, as was the case in medieval literature, and the focus on human vices such as slander, pride, covetousness, ingratitude, murder, and tyranny that push the individual from prosperity into death (Wickham 1966, III: 221). These features of Lydgate's work influenced the subject matter and dramatic narrative of the new tragedy of the English Renaissance. In addition to exploring the sorrowful decline of great men and women, early tragedy also dramatises contempt for worldly things and expresses lament for lost glory. These motifs recurred in English tragedy as it developed into a genre centred on the destiny of those daringly testing their identity against the temptations of desire, power and knowledge (Happé 1999: 149).

Tragedy in Renaissance England begins with Thomas Sackville and Thomas Norton's *Gorboduc* (also known as *Ferrex and Porrex*), performed by a group of law students, the Gentlemen of the Inner Temple, at the Inner Temple in 1562; and Thomas Kyd's *The Spanish Tragedy*, first staged by the Strange's Men at the first Rose Theatre in the London suburb of Southwark in 1587. One of the views shared among critics is that 1561, when *Gorboduc* was first staged, marks the beginning of tragedy in England (Wickham 1981, III: 219). Both *Gorboduc*, a tragedy which one of its editors, Irby B. Cauthen, has described as 'a landmark in English drama' (Cauthen 1970: xiii), and *The Spanish Tragedy*, considered 'the most influential play during the English Renaissance' (McAlindon 2004: 151), gave later tragedies many of their structural and stylistic characteristics.

Both plays derived plot devices, stage rhetoric and storylines either directly from Seneca or from the Roman tragedy. They explored characters' psychology, introduced frequent alliteration, a patterned style of speech known as blank verse, and employed rhetoric characterised by bombast and hyperbole; they both also showed an interest in domestic politics. While *The Spanish Tragedy* is set in Spain, the dramatic allegory it presents speaks to Tudor politics. Likewise *Gorboduc* features a king from early British history while nevertheless being rooted in Tudor political theory (Cauthen 1970: xiii). This blend of classical and domestic features resulted in the emergence of two moralistic avant-garde plays exploring revenge and challenging injustice. These plays brought to English tragedy innovations hitherto not heard and seen on the English stage such as the ghost, the chorus, violent actions that take place off stage and are reported by a messenger, the five-act structure, and patterns of dialogue in which characters speak alternating lines of verse, called stichomythia. (Stichomythia was used as a stylistic device in Greek drama, from where it was taken by Roman dramatists.) Imitations of and echoes from these two plays in later tragedies became so frequent that they led to the creation of the 'sophisticated art-for-art's-sake form' (Rossiter 1959: 145) that we now call English Renaissance tragedy.

Early Tudor non-dramatic literature also left its imprint on later tragedies. Appearing alongside Lydgate's *Fall of Princes* and also inspired by Boccaccio's *De Casibus*, *The Mirrour for Magistrates* (1559, enlarged in 1587) – in which Thomas Sackville had a hand (Rossiter 1959: 145) – represents a collection of heroic complaints intertwined with prose passages, written by different authors telling stories of the tragic fall of figures from England's past (Hadfield 2001: 171). Containing nineteen tragedies, *Mirrour* has been called Tudor propaganda literature, and as a piece of secular writing it is actually thoroughly concerned with Protestantism (Waller 1986: 40). This popular work presents examples of how vices are punished; how the most powerful individuals threaten to weaken the state if justice does not prevent their evil acts from happening; and how rulers dishonour God and faith if they remain unpunished. The tragic demise of fallen kings and princes is often the outcome of a tension between Fortune and God; it is the result of a conflict between lust and will, on the one hand, and between faith and sin on the other. These themes created conditions for the outpouring of tragedy that were about to occur under the joint influence of Seneca, Kyd and Marlowe.

The role Seneca and *Mirrour* played in the development of tragedy is another proof that inclusiveness of subjects and styles represents a key feature of English tragedy. Tragedy is a mix of classical and domestic, mythological and historical, secular and religious material. Hence English tragedy is best seen as a dramatic hybrid, mixing not only these currents into one genre, but also melodrama, romance and comedy, fiction and history, and different linguistic registers and styles. Its popularity on the stage came out largely from the richness of verbal display and its powerful appeal to human morality and conduct as they are pitted against faith.

PLAYHOUSES AND PLAYING COMPANIES IN LONDON

When Elizabeth I came to the throne there were no specially built theatre buildings anywhere in England, a condition that would change radically under her rule. The degree to which things had changed in a relatively short period can be gauged by comparing *Gorboduc*, which was performed not in a theatre but at the Inner Temple in 1561, and George Gascoigne's (c. 1535–77) *Supposes*, first performed at Gray's Inn in 1566, with the performance of *Twelfth Night* at the Middle Temple in 1602; in the 1560s such performances at law courts or anywhere other than at an established theatre were simply taken as a matter of course, while by 1600 they were far more out of the ordinary. Before London theatres were established, university playing companies performed in college halls, particularly Latin plays by Seneca and Plautus (c. 254–184 BC), while travelling troupes of actors played in the yards of London inns, on wagons that were turned into make-shift stages, in churches and churchyards, in town squares and markets, at the courts of the Inns of London, in the grand banqueting halls of noble families, and in royal palaces; essentially, in any open space that could be quickly adapted into a playing space. Early playing companies were relatively small and fairly mobile, well suited for an itinerant lifestyle. The lifestyle of actors inspired misgivings in many, and in Elizabethan times both city and church authorities treated them almost as vagabonds; to many, the theatre was considered a cesspool of vice and a purveyor of subversive beliefs as well as places where rioting could easily spring up. Such fears no doubt led many London theatres, such as The Rose and The Globe, to find more hospitable grounds in the Liberty of the Clink in Southwark, an area close enough for audiences yet still outside the jurisdiction of the city authorities. Such conflicts between theatres and the City of London inspired many of the city comedies of Jonson and others, but it would find its most challenging exploration in Shakespeare's *Measure for Measure* (c. 1604).

There were seven playhouses on the outskirts of London in the last few decades of the sixteenth century. The first was built by James Burbage (c. 1531–97) in 1576 and was called simply The Theatre. Located north of the River Thames in Shoreditch, near Bishopsgate, The Theatre was constructed just outside of London. While predated by the short-lived Red Lion (1566–7) in Whitechapel, The Theatre was the first successful established theatre in London since Roman times; however, it should be noted that another theatre, in Newington Butts just east of Southwark, also has its champions as London's first established theatre. The placement of theatres outside of London was occasioned by the numerous edicts against players and playing during the 1570s. Burbage constructed The Theatre in partnership with his brother-in-law John Brayne (c. 1541–86), who had also had a hand in the construction of the Red Lion. Soon another theatre, The Curtain, would open in Shoreditch, making the area London's first theatrical district. Having cost Burbage and Brayne over 700 pounds, The Theatre was expensive for its time, and the two often found themselves in difficulties with creditors. The design was inspired by both the Inns of Court and, tellingly, the bear-baiting pits that were so common in Elizabethan London; an example of this popularity is reflected by the mistake made by Wenceslaus Hollar (1607–77) in his *Long View of London from Bankside* (1647), for he mistook The Globe and the nearby Beargarden when labelling his drawing. The building was polygonal with a thrust stage and three galleries. There was also standing room in the open yard in front of the stage. The admission prices seem to have been one penny for standing room, two pennies for the gallery, and three pennies for a stool in the gallery. The Theatre was very successful, and many different playing companies used this venue during the period. James Burbage was a member of the Earl of Leicester's Men, and it is believed that this company performed there in the 1570s. By the late 1580s and early 1590s James's son, Richard Burbage (1567–1619), who at that time a member of the Admiral's Men, brought his company to play at The Theatre, where they would play before moving on to Philip Henslowe's The Rose in Southwark.

As troubles with the City of London increased, more theatres began to move to the comparative freedom of Southwark. This was certainly the case for The Theatre. By 1597 it was yet again home to Richard Burbage (Figure 3), now a leading member of the Lord Chamberlain's Men, a company that by now also included William Shakespeare.

Figure 3 Anonymous English artist, *Richard Burbage*, 1619, oil on canvas, Dulwich Picture Gallery. Wikimedia Commons

Following the death of James Burbage in 1597, The Theatre had come under the ownership of Richard and his brother Cuthbert (c. 1565–1636), who now began to encounter difficulties with their landlord, Giles Allen. The original lease was only for twenty years, and so by 1596 the future of The Theatre was under genuine threat. A long and drawn-out series of legal battles ensued involving the Burbages, Allen and Brayne's widow, resulting in The Theatre being forced to stand empty, a situation that occasioned a satirical poem by Everard Guilpin, who writes of 'the unfrequented Theatre, / [which] Walks in dark silence and vast solitude' (qtd in Wickham et al. 2000: 375). Burbage's company had to play at the nearby Curtain Theatre as they awaited an outcome that increasingly seemed likely not to go in their favour. With tensions mounting and hopes faltering, the Burbages concocted a daring plan that has since become famous in the annals of theatre history. Taking advantage of a legal loophole that acknowledged Allen's ownership of the land but not of the property on it, the Burbages oversaw the complete dismantling of The Theatre in December 1598. Despite the protestations of Allen, Margaret Brayne and her business partner, Robert Myles, the Burbages' plan was a complete success. The material from The Theatre would later be moved to Southwark in 1599, where it would be renamed The Globe.

Despite the great importance of The Theatre and the even greater importance of The Globe, there were other theatres of great standing during this period. In Southwark, near the site of The Globe but on the Bankside district, lay a theatre of central importance for theatre scholars: The Swan. Formerly owned by the Monastery of Bermondsey but left to the Crown following the dissolution of the monasteries, the site was purchased by Francis Langley (1548–1602) in 1589 and a theatre constructed on it in the mid-1590s. Despite its use by the Earl of Pembroke's Men, its possible use by the Lord Chamberlain's Men in 1596, and its notoriety as the stage that saw the performance of the infamous *Isle of Dogs* (1597) (Crawforth et al. 2015: 104), its chief importance to scholars lies with the fact that it was captured in a drawing, 'the only surviving record of the interior of an Elizabethan theatre' (Cooper et al. 2006: 100). 'Surviving' may not be the most accurate verb, for what we have is not the original drawing by Johannes De Witt, the Dutch traveller who attended a play at The Swan in 1596, but a later copy of the drawing by Arendt van Buchell. The drawing teaches us much about the dimensions and properties of the Elizabethan theatre, which will be explored in detail below.

Only several hundred yards away from the original site of The Theatre in Shoreditch, The Curtain was established in 1577; by a strange, or perhaps fortuitous, coincidence, the name derived not from theatre curtains but from the theatre's closeness to the nearby field of Curtain Close. While little is known about its earlier years, The Curtain is perhaps best known as the principal home of the Lord Chamberlain's Men during the 1590s, a time when the Burbages fought to maintain ownership of The Theatre and when, most importantly, Shakespeare began to write and see performed some of his best-known earlier plays, such as *Romeo and Juliet*. It has even been conjectured by some – and hotly contested by others (Craik 1995: 4–5) – that the reference by the Prologue in *Henry V* to the 'wooden O' refers not to The Globe but to The Curtain. After the Lord Chamberlain's Men moved on to The Globe, by 1603 The Curtain became the principal playhouse of the Queen Anne's Men. Nevertheless, the ties between The Curtain and the Lord Chamberlain's Men were strong, so strong that members (later of the King's Men) still had shares in it as late as 1624. Interest in The Curtain was reignited in June 2012 when its remains were discovered in Shoreditch, a discovery that will no doubt enhance our understanding of London theatres during the English Renaissance.

Another important theatre rediscovered in modern times (1989) was The Rose, located in Bankside, Southwark, built in 1587 by the grocer John Chomley and by Philip Henslowe (c. 1550–1616), a complicated character who has been of inestimable service to scholars of the period. Henslowe's importance is twofold, for not only was he heavily involved in the London theatre from the 1580s until his death in 1616, but he also kept detailed notes of his involvement in what has come to be known as *Henslowe's Diary*. While not a diary in the modern sense, *Henslowe's Diary* records items such as accounts, payments to writers and players, payments for expense such as costumes, the takings for various plays, 'his financial relationship with companies of players, principally the Admiral's Men, and accounts relating to the building and maintenance of the theatres in which he was interested (Henslowe 2002: xviii–xvix). This work has allowed scholars to date works, to chart their success, to discover material details of the London stage, and to catch a glimpse, however small, of the actual theatres of Shakespeare's time. By 1592 The Rose had become the principal home of the famous tragedian Edward Alleyn (1566–1626), who, in combination with the Lord Strange's Men and the Admiral's Men, began to perform in the roles that would make him the greatest tragedian of his day (Figure 4). Praised by Ben Jonson for giving life to so many poets by giving life to their works (Jonson 1996: 62) and by Thomas Heywood (c. 1570–1641) for outdoing the shapes of Proteus and the tongue of Roscius

Figure 4 Anonymous English artist, *Edward Alleyn*, 1626, oil on canvas, Dulwich Picture Gallery. Wikimedia Commons

(Stapleton 2013: 152), Alleyn was best known for his leading roles in Christopher Marlowe's *Tamburlaine* (c. 1587), *The Jew of Malta* (c. 1590) and *Doctor Faustus* (c. 1592); he was also Henslowe's son-in-law, a relationship that helped him take on an increasingly profitable role in the business end of London's theatres, such as The Rose and The Fortune.

At the time of Alleyn's involvement with The Rose, the theatre was heavily extended by Henslowe to better accommodate the London crowds Alleyn was expected to draw. However, as Andrew Gurr notes, the enlargement of The Rose 'presents many puzzles' (1992: 128). The degree to which Alleyn's fortunes were tied to The Rose's can be attested by the fact that the theatre seems to have gone into decline at the time of his initial retirement in 1598 (he would briefly return to the stage in 1604). Henslowe and Alleyn began to direct their attentions from The Rose to The Fortune, a new theatre located back in Shoreditch, at around this time. Ironically, while The Theatre had moved to Southwark, at least in part in response to the rise of theatres such as The Rose in that district, the new Fortune Theatre was built in Shoreditch in 1600 as a response to the vacuum left by The Theatre's change of residence. The Rose itself began to fall into disuse, and while it did briefly house the Worcester's Men in 1602, by the time its lease ran out in 1605 it had been essentially abandoned. Like The Curtain, The Rose has had an interesting modern history; attempts to develop on the original area of the theatre were halted in 1989 by the theatre community, a move that resulted in the site being preserved, excavated by archaeologists from the Museum of London, and finally opened to the public in 1999.

Henslowe and Alleyn's new theatre, The Fortune, was originally financed largely by Alleyn himself, who also arranged a thirty-year lease and the hiring of Peter Streete (1553–1609), the same builder who had designed The Globe in 1599. Frustratingly, his contract instructs him to design a theatre in imitation of The Globe without clarifying the exact dimensions or details of the theatre itself; of course, Streete would have already known such details, but such information would be of invaluable use to scholars of the period. Nevertheless, the contract and Alleyn's papers have given us tantalising clues, clues that also suggest much about how theatres had changed in dimension and size during the 1590s (Orrell 1997: 54–7). The year 1621 would prove eventful, for that was the year that, as The Globe had done eight years previously, The Fortune burned to the ground. Edward Alleyn would see to the rebuilding of the theatre, completed in 1623, only this time of brick and with a sturdier roof of lead and tile. By this time Alleyn had largely removed himself from the business of theatre, and so at his death in 1624 The Fortune passed on to Richard Gunnell (d. 1634) who also had a hand in the playhouse built at Salisbury Court in 1629. Until 1631 the principal players were the Palsgrave's Men, but after their move to Salisbury Court The Fortune played host to members of the King's Revels. Less is known about the later years of The Fortune, and some have argued that it 'never fully recovered' from the 1621 fire (Foakes 2003: 41); nevertheless, it did continue to put on comedies and even managed to run afoul of the authorities for performing a religious ceremony on stage in 1639. This rebelliousness would continue even after the Civil War, for plays were temporarily performed there after the official banning of all plays in 1642; unfortunately, such obstinacy in the face of Puritan opposition was not enough, and by the time of the Restoration what remained of The Fortune would have to be sold for scrap material.

As important as all of these theatres were, however, they have all been eclipsed by those patronised by Shakespeare's company: The Globe and Blackfriars. As mentioned above, The Globe was built in 1599 following a dispute between the Burbages and their landlord in Shoreditch, one that precipitated the move to Southwark. Built on land owned by Thomas Brend (c. 1516–98) and his son Nicholas (c. 1560–1621), the theatre's specific location was confirmed only in 1989 as near Anchor Terrace on Southwark Bridge Road, 'bounded to the north by Park Street (previously known as Maid or Maiden Lane), to the west by Anchor Terrace . . ., to the east by Porter Street and to the south by Gatehouse Square' (Blatherwick 1997: 69). In addition to being the theatre that saw the production of so many of Shakespeare's plays, The Globe is especially important for being owned by the actors who played in it, for the principal shareholders were all members of the Lord Chamberlain's Men. For example, Richard Burbage and his brother Cuthbert each owned 25 per cent of The Globe, while Shakespeare, Thomas Pope, John Heminges and Augustus Phillips all owned 12.5-percent shares. The distribution of these shares changed over the years, but the important thing was the control that the players now enjoyed, for this distinguished the Lord Chamberlain's Men from other playing companies; while still reliant on patronage, the company managed to achieve a level of financial independence rarely seen during the period.

With a stage roughly twelve metres wide and nine metres deep that held up to 3,000 spectators, The Globe was larger than The Theatre, and while much ink has been spilled on the exact features and dimensions, scholarly consensus remains unlikely. Wenceslaus Hollar's *Long View of London*, as Figure 5 shows, has proved invaluable, both for our image of the old theatre and for the overall look of Shakespeare's Globe (featured in the far left corner on the south bank of the Thames).

Figure 5 Wenceslaus Hollar, a panoramic view of London, Antwerp, 1647, etching. Wikimedia Commons

Hollar's etching likewise proved invaluable when builders sought to restore the modern Globe, which opened in Southwark in 1997, near the original location, as shown in Figure 6.

However, it should be noted that discrepancies and grey areas remain, with Hollar's image of a round theatre coming into conflict with the polygonal theatre most likely to have been built; likewise, the stage design of Shakespeare's Globe has had to rely on the drawing of The Swan, by a visitor to London, Johannes De Witt, shown in Figure 7.

Figure 6 The Globe, London. Wikimedia Commons

Figure 7 Arendt van Buchell, copy of Johannes de Witt's drawing of
The Swan, by 1596. Wikimedia Commons

Located at the base of the stage was the pit or yard, an area for spectators to stand and watch the performance. These spectators, or groundlings, would later be mocked by Hamlet as wanting to see 'nothing but inexplicable dumb shows and noise' (*Hamlet* 3.2.10–11). One wonders how the audience would have responded to such mockery, but it must be stressed that the stage itself invited this kind of interaction with spectators. The Globe's apron stage allowed for actors to respond more directly to audiences, for audiences to respond more directly to actors, and for playwrights to anticipate and incorporate such responses in the drama. One thinks of Iago's query, following his duping of Cassio, 'what's he then that says I play the villain?' (*Othello* 2.3.321), as yet another example of such interaction, one that shows Shakespeare anticipating curses from the audience over Iago's villainy and writes, in response, a metadramatic answer to such curses. This metadramatic element is explicit in The Globe motto, *Totus mundus agit histrionem*, or 'the whole world plays the actor'. One also thinks of Laurence Olivier's 1944 film version of *Henry V*, with audience members both on the stage and on the floor engaging in the action and mockingly repeating key speeches back to the players.

Although it is a belief that has been contested, *Henry V* is widely seen as being the first play to be performed at The Globe, in 1599 (Woodcock 2008: 12). The other contender is *Julius Caesar*, a play much easier to accurately date as a result of being recorded by Thomas Platter (c. 1574–1628), a Swiss visitor to London who saw the play on the 21 September 1599, enjoyed it thoroughly and remarked on the English 'custom' of ending plays, even tragedies, with a dance (qtd in Dillon 2007: 52). For many, The Globe has come to be seen as *the* theatre of the English Renaissance. It would remain the key theatre for the Lord Chamberlain's Men (later the King's Men), although the company would also make use of the indoor Blackfriars Theatre. Unfortunately, tragedy befell The Globe on the 29 June 1613, when the theatre burned to the ground as a result of misfired cannon used during a performance of *Henry VIII*. Because Shakespeare is frequently believed to have abandoned the stage at this point for retirement in Stratford-upon-Avon, the burning of the Globe is sometimes seen to signal the end of an era. While understandable, this supposition ignores the fact that The Globe was soon rebuilt, remaining the home of the King's Men for many years to come; likewise, the King's Men would continue on after Shakespeare's death in 1616, with John Fletcher (1579–1625) taking over as principal playwright, to be followed by Philip Massinger (1583–1640) after Fletcher's death. The Globe would not officially close until 1642 when it, along with all theatres in London, was closed by Puritan edict. The structure itself was demolished in 1644, but the idea of The Globe lived on and would come to life with the opening of Shakespeare's Globe in 1997.

The American director and actor Sam Wanamaker (1919–93) was the driving force behind the creation of Shakespeare's Globe, which explains why, when another theatre built along similar lines as the Blackfriars was opened on the same site as The Globe in 2014, it was called the Sam Wanamaker Playhouse. Since there is no surviving image of the Blackfriars, we can resort to Inigo Jones's sketch of The Cockpit Theatre, also known as The Phoenix (Figure 8), to illustrate what an indoor theatre in which tragedies were performed looked like.

While neither as widely known nor as widely loved as The Globe, the Blackfriars was truly significant, not only for the King's Men but for the direction that London theatres, and English Renaissance tragedy, ultimately would take. Like The Swan, the Blackfriars owed its existence to the dissolution of the monasteries for it was formerly the site of a Dominican monastery, hence the name. For much of the late sixteenth century, the theatre was home to the Children of the Chapel, one of the many troupes of child actors, such as Paul's Children, that served as competition for the adult playing companies. Such companies became known for their roles in stage satires by John Lyly (c. 1553–1606) and later Ben Jonson, John Marston (1576–1634) and George Chapman (c. 1559–1634) and would thus play a key role in the War of the Theatres. In 1596 James Burbage purchased the priory's former dining hall along with the rooms below it. At roughly 15 metres wide and 30 metres long, Burbage desired two galleries to comfortably seat a large number of spectators. The theatre soon fell into trouble with both authorities and local residents. Blackfriars Theatre was located in the west of the city.

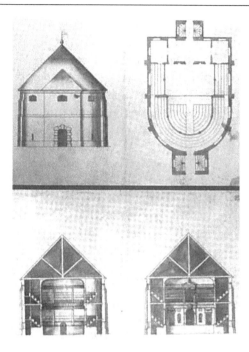

Figure 8 Inigo Jones, drawing of The Cockpit, also known as The Phoenix, c. 1617. Wikimedia Commons

Unlike The Globe, it was in a fashionable neighbourhood likely to attract wealthy customers but also likely to gain powerful enemies. At one point even the patron of the Lord Chamberlain's Men, 1st Baron of Hunsdon (Henry Cooper 1547–1603), took part in a petition against the company. Mired in litigation and forbidden to play at Blackfriars, the Lord Chamberlain's Men was forced to watch other playwrights and companies play at their theatre, which became a breeding ground for experiments in drama and for new talents such as John Fletcher and Francis Beaumont (1584–1616). Tragicomedies by these playwrights first began to appear at this theatre, which also broke new ground in the use of music and – impossible for The Globe – artificial light. All of these innovations began to attract much wealthier patrons than the theatres in Shoreditch or Southwark, a fact that was not lost on Burbage and the Lord Chamberlain's Men.

By the time the Lord Chamberlain's Men received royal patronage and became the King's Men, things had begun to change for the company. Increased revenue, increased social prestige and recognition from the Crown also upped the ante for Shakespeare's company. Such a rise also led to more court performances, which was reflected in the nature of tragedy; critics have noted the importance of the court performances for contextualising plays such as, for example, *Measure for Measure* (c. 1604) and *King Lear* (1606). This rise also led to the company's ability to be more resilient in the face of pressure from without. These factors contributed to the King's Men finally being able to move into the Blackfriars in 1608, which they began to use for performance the following year. The advantages of the new theatre were many: although it was a smaller theatre, entry prices were more expensive, which meant that more money could be made with fewer patrons; these patrons were generally more desirous for theatrical innovation, which allowed for greater dramatic experimentation; the indoor theatre itself also allowed for new advances, as visual and aural effects could be used to a much greater degree to enhance the intimacy of performance. An indication of the new playing conditions for such indoor theatres is provided by the title page of William Alabaster's tragedy *Roxana*, which was first performed in 1595 but was printed in 1632. In the middle frame of the section at the bottom of this 1632 title page (Figure 9) we can see the audience seated very close, and around, the stage, and above the stage looking down on the action. This change in performance style and audience proximity to the stage greatly enhanced the intimacy of the performer–spectator relationship, an enhancement that dramatist such as Shakespeare, in *Othello*, and Webster, in *The Duchess of Malfi*, would exploit to great effect.

Finally, the indoor theatre also allowed for playing all year round, resulting in the King's Men playing The Globe during the summer months and the Blackfriars during the winter. Extremely successful, some estimates suggest that the new theatre brought in twice the revenue of The Globe. However, the change in venue meant a loss of the more popular elements of

Figure 9 Title page of William Alabaster's *Roxana*, 1632. Wikimedia Commons

the theatregoing audience. There were benefits, then, but one can begin to see a reversal of the move from inn to playhouse mentioned above, from public to private, from playhouse to court. As we discuss in later chapters, court and closet drama would begin to take precedence over earlier public forms, which would have a great impact on the tragedy that would be produced.

Such a widespread and diverse collection of playhouse and playing companies emerging in such a short period of time suggest something new about Renaissance London, something that was contributing to a unique form of tragedy, different from that found on the Continent and distinct to the city. The growing number of theatre buildings and internal organizations of the acting companies in London in the late 1580s and throughout the 1590s played a significant role in the rise of a new kind

of tragedy. With the rise in competition for commercial success between individual playhouses and among theatre companies, especially the three largest and most fiercely competitive,
the Chamberlain's Men, Admiral's Men and Pembroke's Men,
demands for new plays grew so significantly that playing companies and playhouses relied not only on plays that could be
performed throughout the year but on playwrights producing
plays based on such formulas that would secure commercial
success. Numerous fashions, for historical dramas, Roman
plays, city comedies, tragicomedies and so on, all went through
various phases of holding the London audience's attention, and
London playwrights tried their best to capitalise on such fashions while they lasted. In particular, tragedy became a popular
kind of drama because its subject matter centred on a daring
individual and on the exploration of the emotional, psychological and social consequences of the fall from virtue, fame
and status. Such explorations responded well to the opportunities and challenges posed by the new relationship between the
individual and the social and political world of an increasingly
post-feudal, proto-capitalist, Protestant England. An example
of this can be seen in Hamlet's frequent comparisons – culmi-
nating in the closet scene – between his father, Old Hamlet,
and his uncle, Claudius, comparisons that frequently reflect not
differences between two characters but between two wholly
different world-views. The conflicts between those world-
views helped to set the stage, literally and figuratively, for the
tragedies of the English Renaissance, works that, as Sir Philip
Sidney argued, teach 'the uncertainty of this world, and upon
how weak foundations gilded roofs are built' (Sidney 1973:
363). As an institution whose presence both within and outside
the boundaries of London walls grew, theatre made tragedy one
of their main sources of public and private entertainment, one
of frequent and lucrative financial gain. The popularity of tragedy as a kind of drama and the specific features of individual
plays cannot be separated from the technical characteristics of
the stage on which these tragedies were performed, from the
physical conditions of specific venues within which these stages
existed in Renaissance London, or from the internal structure

and operations of London theatre ventures and playing companies that performed in them. Regardless of their classical sources or Continental settings, these tragedies were shaped by the conditions of Renaissance London; in short, these were London tragedies.

In our study of English Renaissance tragedies, we begin with a discussion of those plays inspired by Seneca, such as Thomas Kyd's *The Spanish Tragedy*, which explore the complications of revenge, an exploration that will be taken up and complicated further in the revenge tragedies of Shakespeare, Marston, Webster and Ford. Another central concern of tragedy is that of the tragic protagonist, and many English Renaissance tragedians, challenged by Marlowe's overreachers like Tamburlaine, dramatised the rise and fall of overambitious and self-aggrandising individuals. In addition to indiscriminate revenge and unbridled ambition, English Renaissance tragedies also explore themes of love and jealousy, as we will see in Shakespeare's *Romeo and Juliet* and *Antony and Cleopatra*, and Ford's *'Tis Pity She's a Whore*. Among other tragic forms, the domestic tragedy, such as *Arden of Faversham* and *Othello*, represents a particular development of English Renaissance tragedy. Despite being set outside of England, *Othello* is a domestic tragedy in the sense that the play is concerned with staging the effects of jealousy on marriage and within a single household. It also, by making use of Italian and Mediterranean settings, can be connected to other English Renaissance tragedies often set in foreign locations which nevertheless tackled English society and politics.

CHAPTER I

The Emergence of Elizabethan Tragedy and the London Stage

The second decade of Queen Elizabeth I's reign saw the defeat of the Spanish Armada in 1588. It also witnessed the first performances of Kyd's *The Spanish Tragedy* and Christopher Marlowe's *The Tamburlaine the Great*, Parts One and Two, tragedies which had already 'provide[d] some justification for starting "Elizabethan" drama' (Rossiter 1950: 61) as a distinct form of tragic theatre. *The Spanish Tragedy* introduced to the London stage the figure of a tragic revenge hero caught in a complex plot involving murder and intrigue. This move shaped both the protagonist as revenger and it influenced the tale and plot structure of other tragedies whose authors looked back at Kyd's success as a model. *Tamburlaine* popularised another novelty to the London tragic stage, the unrhymed iambic pentameter line, blank verse, which Ben Jonson would refer to thirty years later as Marlowe's 'mighty line' (Jonson 2012: 183). The innovations brought in by these two playwrights marked a new development in Elizabethan tragedy. Marlowe and Kyd wrote plays which were, as Martin Wiggins says, 'on the cusp of seismic shift' (2000: 32) in drama, a major shift from the rhetorically stiff drama of the 1570s to the new tragedies of the late 1580s and 1590s. Both Marlowe's and Kyd's tragedies 'sounded new' (Wiggins 2000: 33) because they were not written in rhyming couplets, like Nicholas Udall's *Ralph Roister Doister* (1551–3) and *Gammer Gurton's Needle* (1575), believed to by William Stevenson, which was the usual verse form. The unrhymed iambic pentameter, popularised by Marlowe and Kyd, added a much more striking and immediate quality to their writing.

Some forty years after protest letters had been written by individuals and the Privy Council to Matthew Parker, the Archbishop of Canterbury, against the production of tragedies at universities, because such plays were 'poison' (Wickham 2000: 28), the genre of tragedy moved from being attacked by the religious authorities to a type of play that burgeoned with the growth of London's theatre scene. The impact of Marlowe's *Tamburlaine* plays on the course of development of the English tragic theatre shows this. It is precisely because tragedy as the genre was under so much religious scrutiny and attack that it started to resist certain Christian teachings, particularly those concerning revenge 'against God's word that earthly revenge is wrong and justice sits only in heaven' (Gurr 1988: 139). Seneca, appropriated by Kyd, paved the way for this kind of earthly revenge.

Translations of Seneca's plays such as *Troades*, *Thyestes* and *The Lamentable Tragedy of Oedipus* were not only crucial to the introduction of tragedy in both theatre and dramatic literature, but also heralded the use of the word 'tragedy' in Elizabethan England. In the 1560s, when *Oedipus* was translated and entered in the Stationers' Register as a 'lamentable history', the word 'tragedy', as Jonathan Bate suggests, 'was not yet familiar descriptive shorthand for a kind of play' (Bate 2008: 400). Some of the plays which we now consider lost were labelled 'tragedy' in their titles, such as the multi-authored, popular *The Tragedy of Tancred and Gismund*, performed in April 1568, and *The Tragedy of the Destruction of Thebes*, produced at Oxford University in May 1569 (Wiggins 2012: 23, 38). Following the success of *The Spanish Tragedy*, tragedy flourished in London theatres, and it also created an appetite for tragedy that would soon be seized upon by the commercial theatre. By the late 1580s the label 'tragedy' was used widely, so that one of the first popular tragedies of the late Elizabethan period, Part One of Christopher Marlowe's *Tamburlaine the Great*, was known as *The Tragicall Conquests of Tamburlaine the Scythian Shepherd* (Wiggins 2012: 374). The title page of the 1590 quarto edition gives the title *Tamburlaine the Great, Diuided into two Tragical Discourses* and represents one of the rare instances of the word 'tragedy' appearing on the title page of printed drama in the late 1590s (Leech 1970: 6). By the first half of 1592, when 'THE TRAGEDIE of Arden of Feuersham & Blackwill', a play which we now refer to as *Arden of Faversham*, was entered in the Stationers' Register and thus licensed for performance, and then published in the same year, the term 'tragedy' had become associated with the idea of stage performance.

LOVE AND DOMESTIC TRAGEDY: *ARDEN OF FAVERSHAM*

Theatre historians and drama critics have long debated the authorship of *Arden of Faversham*, with Kyd and Marlowe sometimes suggested as possible authors. Some scholars have even contended that William Shakespeare might have written it. In a concerted effort to offer a new idea of Shakespeare's body of plays, the editors of the recently published third edition of the complete Oxford Shakespeare have added *Arden of Faversham* to Shakespeare's canon of work, treating the play as a collaboration between Shakespeare and an anonymous author (Taylor 2016). It remains to be seen whether this attribution, which sometimes has been made and often contested, will stand the test of time. What is more certain is that this tragedy was continuously performed from the late 1580s through to the 1630s. This popularity suggests that the 'issues and implications of the play [were] directly relevant to their own time' (White 1982: xxii). But this popularity also shows that tragedy started to dramatise not only historical subject matter but also the crisis of love and marriage in the domestic context of contemporary England.

It is not certain with which playing company *Arden of Faversham* was connected. However, Roslyn Knutson notes that, although *Arden of Faversham* was performed before 1593, a tentative case can be made to connect this play with the Chamberlain's Men after 1594 and the Pembroke's Men in 1593 (Knutson 1999: 349). The connection of *Arden* to the Pembroke's Men, however, as Karl P. Wentersdorf has documented (1977), is easier to establish. If the play was owned by the Pembroke's Men at that time, this may help to explain why it is so hard to nail down the location at which *Arden* was performed as the company rarely had a stable location to perform and it spent much of 1592 touring the country as a result of the plague. Perhaps the Pembroke's Men choice of a play with a local setting, that is, a setting in the country, may have even be influenced by this touring in the provinces. Possibly there was a bigger audience in the provinces for English settings and characters, and the story of the real murder of Thomas Arden only strengthened the case for the play's popularity among the spectators. *Arden of Faversham* is a rare example of a play with scenes in both London and the provinces, which may have helped the play's popularity in both the provinces and London. This makes *Arden of Faversham* a London tragedy. And this association of London with the domestic tragedy in both the anonymously published *A Warning for Fair Women* (1599) and *Arden* shows a close connection of tragedy with the city and of tragedy with reality.

Arden of Faversham remains popular today with both amateur and professional theatres around the world. For example, in 2014, the Royal Shakespeare Company staged this play at the Swan Theatre in Stratford-upon-Avon, and in 2015 the Artists' Collective Theatre from Calgary in Canada produced the play. It also continues to generate much critical discussion, such as among feminist critics who write about the autonomous actions of the main female protagonist, and among critics who are interested in the tension between romantic relationship and marriage, on the one hand, and affective male friendship, on the other. This tragedy of jealousy and desire introduced to London theatres a thriller-style suspenseful plot based on a passionate love-triangle, involving Thomas Arden, his wife Alice, and her lover Mosby. The tragedy anticipated characters

whose emotions and psychologies were closer to real-life people than those who speak in rhetorical clichés and set speeches,
and whose dramatic lives are destined by fate, as in most imitations of Senecan plays. The number of London theatres grew
substantially after the demolition of The Theatre, which stood
in Shoreditch from 1576 and 1599, and the construction of The
Globe in 1599, and the establishment of private, more intimate
theatres. '[T]he little world of London', then a 'microcosm of
England' (Rossiter 1962: 162), had become a place for tragedy, and *Arden of Faversham* is one of the first tragedies to
consider both London and the English provinces as sites for
tragedy. *Arden of Faversham* was based on a real event that
took place in the town of Faversham in Kent, where, while playing a game of backgammon at his home, on 15 February 1551,
Thomas Arden was murdered by paid assassins hired by his
unfaithful wife, Alice Arden. This murder was narrated in detail
in Raphael Holinshed's *Chronicles of England, Scotland and
Ireland*, first published in 1577, and in several other sources
that chronicled historical events in England. The origin of this
tragedy in one of the main sources for early English history, a
source that Shakespeare and others would rely heavily upon
in their history plays, makes *Arden of Faversham* a chronicle
play and a play performed in London around the same time
as some of the early English history plays by Shakespeare.
This makes *Arden of Faversham* 'an alternative history of
England' (Helgerson 1997: 134) because its story is based on a
local and domestic conflict of ordinary people that took place
some forty years earlier, not events and persons from a distant
past and place. This emphasis on the recent and the domestic
secures *Arden of Faversham*'s novel place on the London stage,
so much so that, as Martin Wiggins has stated, 'English drama
had seen nothing like it ever before' (2008: vii). In the play,
Arden is convinced that his wife Alice has been unfaithful, and
he wants to find out whom she has cheated with. Alice is having a passionate affair with Mosby and she wants to leave her
unsatisfying marriage with Arden, and is thus plotting to have
him murdered. Yet more than this clandestine love affair is the
reason for murdering Arden, as Mosby's ambition to acquire

wealth is an additional motivation for the murder of Arden. For example, Mosby relates to Arden:

Master Arden, being at London yesternight,
The Abbey lands whereof you are now possessed
Were offered me on some occasion
By Greene, one of Sir Antony Ager's men. (Sc. 1, 292–5)

If this tragedy shows that Mosby is in love with Alice, it also shows that Mosby is implicated in a business transaction that interferes with Arden's economic interest. Cuckoldry and economy thus jointly drive the fast-paced plot of this play to its tragic end. A jealous husband, a hoarder of wealth and a financer, Arden ends up being both an aggressor and a victim. The play complicates this ethical and psychological situation by also presenting a close bond which Arden has with his friend, Franklin. An early domestic tragedy, *Arden of Faversham* is also a tragedy of revenge which shows that revenge is, in Andrew Gurr's words, 'a complex phenomenon psychologically as well as morally' (1988: 139).

Because the play is not set in the classical Rome of the academic Latin tragedy performed at the universities and the Inns of Court, *Arden of Faversham* is not one removed in time and space. It introduced to the commercial stage of London theatres a national tragedy and domestic drama of love, desire, betrayal and violence that takes place in an English home and on the streets of London. Unlike most tragedies of revenge staged between *The Spanish Tragedy* and plays like *The Revenger's Tragedy* and *Hamlet*, which were set in the more or less unspecified moment in the past and at a foreign court, *Arden of Faversham* is a distinctly English play, with the plot and action shared between Faversham and London. Critics who have focused on the fact that the murder was committed in the Ardens' home, which the play locates in Faversham near an inn named Flower-de-Luce, have located the crime in a 'local extra-urban site' (Greenberg 2015: 155 n. 50), suggesting that the provincial household is the centre of action in a domestic tragedy. Catherine Richardson has pointed out that the representation of the household, and

the connection between family, domestic life and household in
Arden of Faversham, emphasise the link between 'the household
and the community' (2010: 21) as a central motif in this and
other domestic tragedies. The role London plays in this tragedy
is not just to provide a contrast to life as lived in the provinces
but also to reveal the aspects of Arden's character which com-
plicate the audience's sympathy with him as a victim of cuckoldry. In his household, he is a jealous husband. In the outside
community, he is a ruthless and scheming businessman, and,
as Alice complains to Greene, a source of marital discontent as
well. In London, Arden keeps bad company and lodges at one
of London's most prestigious addresses at that time, Aldersgate
Street ('He is now at London, in Aldersgate Street' (Sc. 2, 99),
says Greene to Shakebag). Greene, robbed of his land by Arden,
tells Alice:

> Pardon me, Mistress Arden; I must speak
> For I am touched. Your husband doth me wrong
> To wring me from the little land I have
> My living is my life; . . .
> Desire of wealth is endless in his mind,
> And he is greedy-gaping still for gain.
> Nor cares he though young gentlemen do beg,
> So he may scrape and hoard up in his pouch.
> But seeing he hath taken my lands, I'll value life
> As careless as he is careful for to get;
> And tell him this from me: I'll be revenged'
> (Sc. 1, 469–80)

The play complicates revenge not only by adding another
character with his own motivation for revenge, but also by
destroying Arden, a manipulator of those with money, as a
mere victim of cuckoldry. By making Arden unsympathetic
and by giving at least some credence to the grievances of his
enemies, the tragedy also further troubles both our sympa-
thies and the issue of revenge.

In revenge tragedies like *Hamlet*, the connection between
revenge and the Protestant idea of responsibility placed on the

individual for his actions reveals the extent to which 'the rise of reformed religion and the development of revenge tragedy are virtually synonymous in early modern England'; even if in this revenge tragedy it is political, not social or economic status, that motivates revenge (Streete 2010: 209). Yet *Arden of Faversham* shows that revenge comes from a combination of motives such as love, money and social status. Alice wants to get out of an unsatisfying marriage; her lover Mosby is after wealth and economic status, which he would acquire if Alice became a widow. So Alice tells Greene 'in secret' about her marriage with Arden:

> I never live good day with him alone.
> When he is at home, then have I frowned looks,
> Hard words, and blows to mend the match withal.
> And though I might content as good a man,
> Yet doth he keep in every corner trulls;
> And weary with his trugs at home,
> Then rides he straight to London; there, forsooth,
> He revels it among such filthy ones
> As counsels him to make away his wife.
>
> (Sc. 1, 492–501)

The play presents the Ardens' household as a space of domestic oppression and of danger, bordering on violence, and one in which both privacy and the wife's safety are compromised. Despite his standing in the town, Arden is a failed master of his household. As a 'failed patriarch' (Richardson 2010: 23) who is part of a community of the 'filthy ones', the morally compromised dregs of the society, Arden is, in the tragedy, set up as a victim of revenge. And the revenge carried out against him is not a random act driven by his opponents, Mosby, Alice and maybe Greene as well. Rather, Arden brings revenge upon himself through his own actions. Private and economic reasons interconnect in pushing these characters to seek revenge against Arden, who is compromised by the extremes of his character and his extravagant London lifestyle.

Mosby's predicament illustrates most glaringly the extent to which *Arden of Faversham* captivated its audience, which saw, perhaps for the first time, a new play which exposed on the stage the vagaries of their own private lives. This can be seen in a rhetorically elaborate and ornamented speech in which Mosby bares his inner dilemma to another character. This forces Mosby to confront how the new economic conditions following the dissolution of land ownership, which came with the Reformation and involved the selling off of ex-monastic lands, has skewed his emotional and domestic relationships. In a speech that shows most of the characteristics of a soliloquy (in which a speaking part reveals a character's private thoughts to an audience), Mosby says to Alice:

> I have neglected matters of import
> That would have stated me above thy state,
> Forslowed advantages, and spurned at time.
> Ay, Fortune's right hand Mosby hath forsook
> To take a wanton giglot by the left.
> I left the marriage of an honest maid
> Whose dowry would have weighted down all thy
> wealth,
> Whose beauty and demeanour far exceeded thee.
> This certain good I lost for changing bad,
> And wrapped my credit in thy company
> I was bewitched.
>
> (Sc. 8, 83–93)

At this point, the play makes a powerful statement about how a mixture of economic greed and social prejudice leads to delusion and failure in Reformation society in which responsibility for one's actions falls on the individual. Mosby's wasted ('Forslowed') economic opportunities cause him to abandon a more beautiful and chaste wife whom he loves more than Alice and compromise his own worth in an affair with Alice. As many men of his time did, Mosby links women to witchcraft, as when he later confronts Alice for casting spells on him ('I will break thy spells and exorcisms', Sc. 8, 95), absolving himself from any responsibility that might have led to his demise. The end of the play stages Alice's conflicting passions as she admits being betrayed by Mosby's false love but at the same time reaffirming hers for him. Tragedy, rooted in performing high passions intended to move spectators, comes to a high point when Alice replies to Mosby:

> Ay, now I see, and soon to find it true,
> Which often hath been told me by my friends,
> That Mosby loves me not but for my wealth,
> Which too incredulous I ne'er believed.
> . . .
> I will do penance for offending thee
> And burn this prayerbook, where I here use
> The holy word that had converted me.
> See, Mosby, I will tear away the leaves,
> And all the leaves, and in this golden cover
> Shall thy sweet phrases and thy letters dwell,
> And thereon will I chiefly meditate
> And hold no other sect but such devotion.
>
> (Sc. 8, 106–9; 115–22)

This is a voice of a dramatic character with distinct individual characteristics. Alice's speech anticipates a new kind of tragedy of revenge that will dominate the London stage and that will culminate with *Hamlet*. As a protagonist, Alice has achieved self-realisation, because she understands that she has been used by Mosby to achieve his goal of acquiring Arden's wealth. But when she also tells the audience that this self-realisation does not cancel her love for Mosby, she removes herself from the action of revenge and makes an indirect comment on the tragedy of revenge – that her revenge is not what she desires – and this makes her both a distant observer as well as a victim of tragedy. Alice's independent action shows a broader concern of this tragedy with actions and feelings that are free from social norms. As Viviana Comensoli observes, 'The play exploits the prevailing ideology of private life in part by subjecting to close scrutiny its insistence upon uniformity and hierarchy' (1999: 85). By having Arden murdered, Alice also acts against her period's attitude towards divorce, which would have given the husband the right to leave his wife and marry another woman, a view most strongly expressed by the Puritan cleric John Rainolds in his tract defending divorce, *A Defence of the Judgment of the Reformed Churches*, published in 1609:

> And how can he [a cuckolded husband] choose but live still in feare & anguish of minde, least shee add drunken[n] esse to thirst, & murder to adultery. I meane least she serve him as *Clytemnestra* did *Agamemnon* as *Livia* did *Drusus*, as *Mrs. Arden* did her husband.
>
> ([1597] 1609: N1ʳ)

As Catherine Belsey writes in her critical assessment of Alice's role in the play against the background of divorce law in the period, 'The divorce debate polarized already conflicting definitions of marriage' because the 'Anglican position was that marriage was indissoluble' (1985: 140). Alice acts against this cultural and religious doctrine. Her unfaithfulness shows that this tragedy undermines the cultural view, expressed in Rainolds's tract, that gives only the husband the power to act. From Belsey's feminist perspective, Alice's act and expression of liberation do not come without a price. 'There is an indication in *Arden of Faversham*', says Belsey, 'that in opting for Mosby in place of Arden, a freely chosen sexuality based on concord in place of the constraints of the institution of permanent marriage, Alice Arden may be committing herself to a form of power more deadly still' (1985: 144). Alone on the stage, speaking to the audience, Mosby says:

> You have supplanted Arden for my sake,
> And will extirpen [remove] me to plant another.
> 'Tis fearful sleeping in a serpent's bed,
> And I will cleanly rid my hands of her.
>
> (Sc. 8, 40–3)

Alice may have freed herself from the matrimonial chains with Arden, but the culture of man's rule over wife will catch up with her: fearing that Alice might be unfaithful to him too, Mosby will enact Rainolds's advice to the husband to rid himself of a wife suspected of unfaithfulness.

Alice's speech anticipates independent female tragic women like the Duchess of Malfi or one of the queens, Anne or Margaret, from *Richard III*. Her intensely personal rhetoric shows the power of tragedy both to express heightened emotions in uninhibited language and to display a struggle between passion and social status. Because of its bold treatment of a story which circulated in the culture, *Arden of Faversham* occupies an important place among London tragedies in the late Elizabethan period.

TRAGEDY AND THE PERFORMANCE OF POWER: CHRISTOPHER MARLOWE'S *TAMBURLAINE THE GREAT*

Almost a year after *Arden of Faversham* introduced the domestic tragedy of love to theatregoers in the provinces, a different kind of new tragedy triumphed in London: a tragedy of ambition set outside England and written in an extravagant language. With Christopher Marlowe, as Peter Sillitoe has remarked, tragic drama performed in London witnessed 'a sudden improvement in . . . quality and impact' (2013: 15). The impact of blank verse came from its skilful use in the play's 'intoxicating' (Mulryne and Fender 1968: 55), ornate and exaggerated language, which Marlowe cultivated to great effect. This kind of verse was not unique to Marlowe's drama, but it popularised for the English stage a kind of dramatic poetry rarely heard before. The impact of Marlowe's rhetoric was such that Ben Jonson, a fellow London playwright, remembered 'Marlowe's mighty line' (2012: 638) many years after the playwright was dead, having been killed in a tavern in Deptford on 30 May 1593. When the first Admiral's Men performed the two parts of *Tamburlaine* at The Rose in Southwark, the play became an instant hit. It remained, as Tom Rutter writes, 'arguably the single most widely imitated play of the early modern stage, one whose distinctive style many dramatists tried to recreate' (2012: 12). Despite some of its structural shortcomings, like the episodic composition of the play and the sometimes monotonous bombastic pitch of some of its rhetoric, the *Tamburlaine* plays represent, in the words of Ian McAdam, 'one of the most important historical moments in the history of English theater' (1999: 73). McAdam's detailed analysis of Tamburlaine focuses on a discussion of the ironic conflicts within Tamburlaine's character as part of a larger debate about the development of subjectivity, especially masculine subjectivity, in Marlowe's plays. Yet what makes *Tamburlaine* one of the most important plays in the history of early modern theatre is that its appearance on the English stage influenced several later tragedies. The theatre provided an ideal home for the dramatic form and style of Marlowe's plays. Marlowe found his home in tragedy; comedy, of which he was capable but only as part of the language of tragedy, was not the genre that interested him. His career as a tragic dramatist ran parallel to the expansion of public theatres on the Bankside; suddenly there were numerous venues at which plays were performed, and London's commercial theatres were hungry for new stage drama.

It may be a mere coincidence of theatre and drama history that Marlowe wrote *Tamburlaine, Part One*, in the same year, 1587, that The Rose was probably built. The Rose became the most popular playing space in Southwark. We know, however, that the repertoire of this smallest of London's public theatres was dominated by Marlowe's plays until the playwright's untimely death (Eccles 1990: ii). Excavations of The Rose in the 1989 revealed that the stage was very small, which, as the theatre historian Christine Eccles has argued, afforded the 'intimate relationship between . . . both actor and audience' (1990: iii). The Rose may have been small in scale but its three galleries rising close to the small stage produced an intimacy which aided the development of *Tamburlaine*'s popularity. In addition to these physical conditions of the theatres itself we add the fact that one of the few leading tragic actors of that time, Edward Alleyn, started playing at The Rose just as Marlowe's play was performed, and Tamburlaine was one of the roles that he played with great success. The success of the *Tamburlaine* plays was therefore a combination of a set of circumstances that came together at the right time: the right actor for a part was ready to play that part in a newly built theatre; Philip Henslowe, who was The Rose's manager, was eager to cash in on new drama and was therefore ready to take on Marlowe's new play.

Scholars have entertained the question of what is new about *Tamburlaine, Part One*. They have offered two responses. Firstly, the play is one of a growing number of plays in this period, which 'debunked or demystified power' and which overturned 'social, cosmic, [and] ethical' (Holbrook 2015: 99) hierarchies. Secondly, by showing the fall of the 'mighty Tamburlaine' (3.3.96), *Tamburlaine, Part One*, dramatises the main topic of medieval notions of tragedy, which is the demise of a powerful character whose prerogative is undercut by mortality. Yet towards the end of Part One, Zenocrate's words reveal that the strength of tragedy lies in its impact on the audience:

> But see, another bloody spectacle!
> Ah, wretched eyes, the enemies of my heart,
> How are ye glutted with these grievous objects,
> And tell my soul more tales of bleeding ruth!
>
> (5.1.339–42)

Zenocrate's words make for a 'morally edifying ending' (Rutter 2012: 25) of the play. They also illustrate that tragedy is a bloody spectacle that satisfies the audience's hunger for 'more tales of bleeding ruth'. While Part One of *Tamburlaine* staged a tragedy which pleased audiences by showing how transient and fragile earthly rule is, it also invited them to see Marlowe's drama as 'daring gods out of heaven' (Hopkins 2008: ch. 5). This phrase captures Marlowe's own rebellion against God. It is not just the character of Tamburlaine with which, as Emily Bartels says, Marlowe's play has 'astounded' (2008: 22), but the style and quality of Marlowe's dramatic poetry that has contributed to this shock effect as well. On the stage of the first, small Rose Theatre, Marlowe's bombastic verse could be spoken more directly to the audience; as noted above, it was the language and its power that Jonson still remembered thirty years on.

In the early scenes of Part One of *Tamburlaine the Great*, this language, full of astonishing linguistic energy and visual power, undermines the period's ideologies and doctrines. It is

also packed in one of the first impressive speeches heard from
the stage, as Tamburlaine threatens Theridamas, one of the
Persians:

> In thee, thou valiant man of Persia,
> I see the folly of thy emperor.
> Art though but captain of a thousand horse,
> That by characters graven in they brows
> And by thy material face and stout aspect
> Deserv'st to have the leading of an host?
> Forsake my king, and do but join with me,
> And we will triumph over all the world.
> I hold the Fates bound fast in iron chains
> And with my hand turn Fortune's wheel about,
> And sooner shall the sun fall from his sphere
> Than Tamburlaine be slain or overcome.
> Draw forth thy sword, though mighty man-at-arms,
> Intending but to raze my charmed skin,
> And Jove himself will stretch his hand from heaven
> To ward the blow and shield me safe from harm.
> So how he rains down heaps of gold in showers
> As if he meant to give my soldiers pay!
> And, as a sure and grounded argument
> That I shall be the monarch of the East,
> He sends this Sultan's daughter, rich and brave,
> To be my queen and portly empress.
> . . .
> Those thousand horse shall sweat with martial spoil
> Of conquered kingdoms and of cities sacked.
> Both we will walk upon the lofty cliffs,
> And Christian merchants that will Russian stems
> Plough up huge furrows in the Caspian Sea
> Shall vail to us as lords of all the lake.
>
> (1.2.166–87; 191–6)

These lines present Tamburlaine as a ruthless ruler from Asia,
the kind of potentate that was not unfamiliar to English tragedy.

For example, George Peele's tragedy *The Battle of Alcazar*, performed possibly at The Rose in 1589, and the lost anonymous *The Sultan* in 1580 (Wiggins 2000: 33) testify to the popularity of plays featuring rulers from the East on the English stage. Paradoxically, the extreme power wielded by such Eastern rulers had the potential for radically undermining the stability of the monarchy in the West. Tamburlaine breaks up an alliance between a soldier and his king, threatening the stability of a state built on such an alliance. He displays desire for power over the world beyond measure, imagining himself taking the power of Fortune, the classical goddess of opportunity, by which he overturns the period's belief in the supreme power of Fortune to direct the course of human life and actions. Marlowe also radically tampers with the way by which classical mythology would have been understood by his contemporaries. He has Jove, the god of heaven, appear transformed into a golden shower, not to Perseus' mother, Danaë, as in the classical myth, but to Tamburlaine's soldiers. This overturning of the familiar myth with which the schooled members of the audience would have been familiar continues the line of Marlowe's unorthodox treatment of familiar themes.

The exaggerated language which Marlowe uses to express Tamburlaine's dazzling hunger for empire is encapsulated in elaborate verbal images conjuring up other worlds beyond England. But this language also plays into the audience's anxiety about the conquest by the Turks, who were threatening Western Christianity by advancing from the East. This anxiety is also reflected in contemporary anti-Turkish invective. While Marlowe experimented with his mighty line by pushing the limit of the visual image within a language of verbal excess and ornament, he is both 'unmooring of the ideologies of his time', concerning 'language, class, and ethnicity' (Burnett 2004: 127) – he is putting a Scythian shepherd risen to become an Islamic warrior at the centre of a stage in Christian London – and portraying Tamburlaine, an omnipotent warrior, as an object of irony. God and monarchs are also targets of his attacks. Peter Holbrook says: 'When Tamburlaine attacks God he attacks kings, and

vice-versa, since kings derived their sovereignty from the divine
... In this sense religious blasphemy and political opposition
are indistinguishable' (Holbrook 2015: 103). Holbrook draws
attention to an important role the Elizabethan tragedy was starting to play in England. The tragedy of Tamburlaine was not only
a source of pleasure because it showed the audience that justice
could be redeemed and evil punished, but also because of the
subversive innovation of its language.

In the *Tamburlaine* plays Marlowe experiments with the
language of tragedy to construct a protagonist endowed with
both an impressive rhetorical power and force of personality
while also responding to his period's political and imperial
undertakings. As Harry Levin states: '[I]n the late 1580's and
1590's, an epoch of rising empires and falling dynasties, Marlovian tragedy voiced aspirations which were collective as well
as individual' (1965: 55). Acted out on the stage, those aspirations are undercut, as Marlowe demonstrates in Part Two of
Tamburlaine.

Marlowe 'may not have originally envisaged' writing the second part, says Tom Rutter (2012: 25). Yet Tamburlaine does
not die at the end of Part One, which may have left it easier for
Marlowe to write Part Two following the success of Part One.
From the opening lines in Part Two, stating that Tamburlaine
'brings a world of people to his field/From Scythia to the oriental plage/Of India' (2 *Tamb.* 1.1.67), to his last dying words,
'Tamburlaine, the scourge of God, must die' (2 *Tamb.* 5.3.248),
the tragedy shows Tamburlaine's progressive defeat and loss
of power ironically undercut by his self-reflective aggrandise-
ment. Some modern critics maintain that the important political role Marlowe's hyperbolic language performs is to scrutinise
critically, rather than merely glorify, the heroic individual. For
example, Simon Shepherd states that the *Tamburlaine* 'could be
seen as an ironic investigation of the construction of heroism, in
particular exploring the idea that rhetoric creates personal reputation' (1986: 67). Marlowe's rhetoric, however, both creates
and destroys that reputation. Tamburlaine's rhetoric of imagining the razing of the built-up centres of civilisation resonates

chillingly in the twenty-first century marred by the devastation of many cities in the East:

> I will, with engines never exercised,
> Conquer, sack, and utterly consume
> Your cities and your golden palaces,
> And with the flames that beat against the clouds,
> Incense the heavens and make the stars to melt,
> (2 Tamb. 2.4.192–6)

The fall of the tragic hero is that much bigger because of Tamburlaine's inflated language. Marlowe presents Tamburlaine's heroic greatness by having him tell Zenocrate to 'behold' him 'Raving, impatient, desperate, and mad,/Breaking my steeled lance with which I burst/The rusty beams of Janus' temple doors' (2 *Tamb.* 2.4.111–14). Marlowe's powerful use of language captures Tamburlaine's exaggerated idea of heroism as everlasting, and questions the notion that earthly power and ambition are permanent. Tamburlaine says:

> But I perceive my martial strength is spent;
> In vain I strive and rail against those powers
> That mean t'invest me in a higher throne
> As much too high for this disdainful earth
> (2 Tamb. 5.3.119–22)

Its long rhetorical speeches and the exaggerated style push the *Tamburlaine* plays towards the formal rhetoric of classical tragedy. Marlowe turned his classical education into the subject of his drama. But because the audience of early modern theatres came from all social ranks, except the very poorest, and who therefore had different levels of education, or no education at all, such mesmerising rhetoric was in itself a spectacle that the theatre capitalised on and encouraged. The *Tamburlaine* plays enriched, deepened and amplified both the sound and the story behind dramatic rhetoric, and introduced to the London theatre the kind of dramatic language that would give it authenticity.

TRAGEDY AND THEATRICALITY: WILLIAM SHAKESPEARE'S *RICHARD III*

It was several years until a successful dramatic figure like Tamburlaine could find its match on the London stage. Either in 1592 or 1593 the Lord Chamberlain's Men performed *The Tragedy of King Richard the Third*, probably first acted at The Theatre, a tragedy that the *Tamburlaine* plays anticipated. *Richard III*, as Simon Palfrey has recently remarked, is 'Shakespeare's great exercise in the Marlovian manner' (2014: 75–6). Both playwrights wrote a tragic part at the centre of the play, who dominates the action by devising one bloody spectacle after another. Both Tamburlaine and Richard are compulsive talkers using elaborate rhetorical, ritualistic-sounding language, delivering more lines than any other speaking part in their respective plays. The opening long monologue, or exposition, in *Richard III* may have been written in the shadow of Marlowe's *The Jew of Malta*, performed in 1589, in which Barabas addresses the audience in a similar direct manner and with a similar rhetorical flexibility and irony, as he narrates the past and present events that will direct his actions. If we think of Shakespeare's *Titus Andronicus* (1592) and *Richard III* as his first tragedies, we should note that a major change in tragedy had already occurred before Shakespeare came on the scene, such was the impact which Kyd's and Marlowe's plays had on the tragedy of the 1590s.

Richard III belongs to the time in Shakespeare's career when the influence of Seneca was still evident, as in *Titus Andronicus*, the style of which can be related to that of *Richard III*. With *Richard III*, revenge as an element of tragedy acquires a new form. *The Spanish Tragedy* became the chief example of revenge drama, and *Arden of Faversham* extended that example to the English domestic tragedy and considered several protagonists with different motives. *Richard III*, however, shows how 'the sense of normal life has been disrupted by something horrible and otherly', as John Jowett, the editor of the Oxford Shakespeare edition of the play, maintains (2000: 25). Writing from a similar perspective, Nicholas Brooke says that 'The dominant role of Richard can be assimilated if he is seen as the instrument of divine retribution on a guilty society' (1968: 49). But the play is not only a study of one man's thirst for power. *Richard III* dramatises the ruthlessness of the personal ambition at the climax of the Wars of the Roses, and the death of those wars, symbolically, with Richard's death on the battlefield at the Bosworth Field. Like Tamburlaine's quest for power, Richard's proves equally hollow.

The extraordinary verbal capacity displayed by Richard III on stage required an actor of great skill and verbal craft. Richard Burbage was such an actor. Burbage was one of the leading actors of his time and one of the founding members of the Lord Chamberlain's Men in 1594, and, as Stanley Wells suggests, he 'could encompass the irony of Richard III' (2015: 19). The actor Anthony Sher described Richard III as 'a terribly taxing part, vocally, mentally, physically', when he prepared to play the role of Richard with the Royal Shakespeare Company in 1984 (1986: 39). Dressed in a black costume and using elbow-high crutches, Sher played Richard III by moving like a spider, echoing old Queen Margaret who insultingly referred to Richard III as 'that bottled spider' (4.4.76). In a short but powerful metaphor, Shakespeare encapsulates the ugliness, poison, danger and quick movement of Richard. Wells concludes that Richard's 'hyperactive mental activity', which Sher displayed on stage, is one way of drawing our attention to the fact that tragedy is the result of individual strategy and agency. Actors who have presented Richard's 'disturbing vitality' (Brooke 1968: 49) on stage have reflected on the demands that this play puts on them, confirming that the play is a complex piece of tragic theatre as well as striking evidence of the creative imagination of early Shakespeare. For example, Anton Lesser, who played Richard in Adrian Noble's production of *The Plantagenets* at the Royal Shakespeare Theatre in 1988, says about *Richard III*: 'On its own the play inevitably requires a central pyrotechnic performance of great magnetism and theatrical invention' (1993: 141). Shakespeare's innovation in making English history the subject of his early tragedies was one of the great inventions of his dramatic art that added novelty to the English theatre and a new dimension to English tragedy.

Richard III opens with one of the most memorable stage entrances in early modern English drama. Richard, Duke of Gloucester, not yet Richard III, tells the audience:

> Now is the winter of our discontent
> Made glorious summer by this sun of York,
> And all the clouds that loured upon our house
> In the deep bosom of the ocean buried.
> Now are our brows bound with victorious wreaths,
> Our bruised arms hung up for monuments,
> Our stern alarums changed to merry meetings,
> Our dreadful marches to delightful measures.
>   . . .
> But I that am not shaped for sportive tricks,
> Nor made to court an amorous looking-glass,
> To strut before a wanton-ambling nymph,
> I that am curtailed of this fair proportion,
> Cheated of feature by dissembling nature,
> Deformed, unfinished, sent before my time
> Into this breathing world scarce half made up,
>   . . .
> . . . since I cannot prove a lover
> To entertain these fair well-spoken days
> I am determinèd to prove a villain,
> And hate the idle pleasures of these days.
> Plots have I laid inductious, dangerous,
> By drunken prophecies, libels, and dreams
> To set my brother Clarence and the King
> In deadly hate the one against the other;
>   (1.1.1–8, 14–21, 28–35)

These lines, taken from one of the longest monologues that Shakespeare wrote, reveal much about the protagonist. For example, Henry Goodman, the actor who played Richard III in the 2003 production of the play directed by Sean Holmes at the Royal Shakespeare Theatre, sees Richard as 'a king, a man – son, brother, husband – crucially isolated, alienated, frustrated, and dysfunctional in all those areas of his life' (2004: 202). Most of these elements of Richard's character are already revealed in the opening speech. While his fellow soldiers revel in the victory and peace by indulging in sensual pleasures, Richard's bodily deformity prevents him from a similar indulgence. He voices his frustration for not being able to prove himself a man. Although the historical Richard and the events the play stages belonged to the late medieval period, not the late sixteenth century when Shakespeare's play was performed, Shakespeare's Richard voices the modern period's concern that the time of the performance of this tragedy was weakened or emasculated by peace. To compensate for this unsettling peace in which he cannot realise himself as a lover, Richard devises a plot to overthrow his brother and reveals himself explicitly as a villain. The critic A. C. Bradley has remarked that Richard and Macbeth 'are the only heroes who do what they themselves recognize to be villainous' (1966: 15). As we can see in Richard's expository speech, such moments of self-awareness represent elements that are also revealing of Richard's self-awareness of the theatrical role he plays, as he creates and propels the plot. This connection between Richard's part and the sequence of tragic events that he sets in motion illustrates Bradley's point that one of the major novelties that Shakespeare introduced to early English tragedy is that human action, not external forces like Fortune or God's will, are the primary movers of tragedy. Thus Bradley says that 'The calamities of [Shakespearean] tragedy do not simply happen, nor are they sent; they proceed mainly from actions, and those the actions of men' (1966: 15). However, the actions of men constantly come into conflict with external forces as revealed by prophecy. The play, for instance, refers to dreams and prophecies as premonitions of tragic events. The outcome of such supernatural foreshadowing is a test to the limits of an individual's responsibility for tragedy. So Richard says to Buckingham:

> As I remember, Henry the Sixth
> Did prophesy that Richmond should be king
> When Richmond was a little peevish boy.
> A king – perhaps, perhaps.
>
> (4.2.96–9)

Part of the play's retribution is that this prophecy will come true at the end of the tragedy, when Richard dies in battle and Richmond is crowned king. However, whatever role prophecy may play, the characters themselves are the final arbiters. Bradley expands his important point about the specificity of Shakespearean tragedy, and states: 'What we do feel strongly, as a tragedy advances to its close, is that the calamities and catastrophe follow inevitably from the deeds of men, and that the main source of these deeds is character' (1966: 7). When Bradley writes about 'character' he has in mind a set of effectively ahistorical personal dispositions, not the historical development of the concept of individual agency in drama. As Hastings says: 'I think there's never a man in Christendom/Can lesser hid his love or hate his love or hate than he' (3.4.56–7). Richard shows that, although his emotions are obvious and visible, others are seduced by his skilled operation of language. When Richard tells Buckingham and the audience, 'I am unfit for state and dignity' (3.7.187), nobody catches his irony. Although Bradley also recognises that a Shakespearean tragedy is 'a story of exceptional calamity leading to the death of a man in high estate' (1966: 6–7), his assessment of tragedy as drama deriving from the actions of men relates tragedy more immediately to the audiences that are called on to consider it a moral for their own actions. This aspect of tragedy may appear less transparent in a historical drama like *Richard III*, but it will be more evident in a play about love and the family's role in it when we come to *Romeo and Juliet*.

As a playing part intended to be performed in an unroofed public theatre, Richard represents a significant shift in the development of tragic characters. On the one hand, Shakespeare resorts to earlier national dramatic tradition in making a royal figure from English history close to a figure from folklore drama. Thus, Janet Hill suggests that Richard's 'insistent friendliness towards the playgoers' is important because it shows that Shakespeare is probably modelling him 'on the guild plays' devil figure' (2002: 121), a proposition also made by Robert Weimann who argues that Richard is modelled on the figure of Vice from the miracle plays (1997: 149). Shakespeare in fact makes this connection explicitly, when Richard, Duke of Gloucester (still not King Richard III) tells young Prince Edward: 'I say, "Without characters fame lives long" *(Aside)* Thus like the formal Vice iniquity,/I moralize two meanings in one word' (3.1.81–3). This connection with the Vice figure, and the tradition of theatre from the past, not only gives meaning to his performance but also demonstrates to the audience how self-conscious he is about his performance. This also shows that in some crucial aspects, like character and story development, late sixteenth-century tragedy derived from an earlier theatre tradition.

On the other hand, Shakespeare also creates Richard as a master player who is a man of 'now', always ready to guide the audience through the tragic action that he is directing and playing a part in. This aspect of Richard's role fits with the public theatre's apron stage that allows for a more immediate and intimate contact with the audience to whom Richard could speak more directly. In that sense, the opening lines also show, as Alexander Leggatt has observed, that 'Richard's capacity for long-range planning and his mastery of the political situation go along with an extraordinary theatrical control' (1988: 32). Richard is not the only character in the play that describes its actions within the play in terms of theatre and acting. Buckingham is another one:

> I can counterfeit the deep tragedian:
> Speak, and look back, and pry on every side,
> Tremble and start at wagging of a straw,
> Intending deep suspicion. Ghastly looks
> Are at my service, like enforced smiles;
> And both are ready in their offices
> To grace my stratagems.
>
> (3.5.6–12)

The tragedian that Buckingham presents himself to be is modelled on Richard. Richard's gestures, facial expressions, backward glances and language reflect his role as a performer of tragedy and as a part within tragedy.

Richard's desire for power is stronger than his erotic desire, which is evident in the scene in which he seduces Queen Anne. Words like 'poison' and 'infect' (1.2.142–7), and their derivations, complement the exchanges between Richard and Anne in the course of his seduction of her; and Richard the seducer is called 'foul toad'. This reference to an ugly animal belongs to the repertoire in which the play renders Richard's masculinity in terms of predatory animals, including, most frequently, the boar, which was also the symbol on Richard's coat-of-arms. Queen Margaret calls him an 'abortive, rooting hog' (1.3.228); a messenger reports that Richard 'Had dreamt tonight the boar had razed his helm' (3.2.9); in the same scene, Hastings reveals his fear over Richard's danger, counselling his peers 'To fly the boar before the boar pursues us' (3.2.26), and develops the metaphor of a victim or prey trying to escape the wild boar's chase. In both Acts 4 and 5, the boar is connected with Richard's bloodthirsty intentions (4.5.2) and (5.4.130). These associations between Richard and the boar have been connected with his aggressive masculinity. Criticism puts emphasis on Richard's masculine behaviour, not his sexual power, which, for example, allows Rebecca Bushnell to argue that Richard is a tragic hero to whom Shakespeare avoids attributing 'that most common of tyrannical vices, which is lust' (1992: 351).

In one of the most comprehensive essays on the relationship between Richard's deformity and masculinity as also a larger comment on how masculinity was understood and described in early modern culture, Ian Frederick Moulton has argued that 'Shakespeare's characterization of Richard III functions as both a critique and an ambivalent celebration of excessive and unruly masculinity and, in so doing, highlights the incoherence of masculinity as a concept in early modern English culture' (1996: 255). Moulton shows that Richard's 'aggressive masculinity is reflected in his utter contempt for women', which is most evident in his seduction of Queen Anne. Moulton's research of historical, cultural and dramatic evidence from 1–3 Henry VI casts a particular light on Richard's destructive masculinity and his tragic demise. Moulton thus concludes that 'In the absence of strong masculinity royal authority, English manhood, unruled and untamed, turns to devour itself. It is this unregulated, destructive masculine force that is personified in the twisted and deformed body of Richard III' (1996: 258).

Richard III is a play that, in addition to inciting passions from the audience watching the spectacle of the fall of a mighty and dangerous hero, illustrates how tragedy functioned as both a spectacle that imparted a moral stance and also functioned as Elizabethan propaganda. In the last speech of the play, against the background of Richard's slain corpse, Richmond's lines:

> Smile, heaven, upon this fair conjunction,
> That long have frowned upon their enmity.
> What traitor hears me and say not 'Amen'?
> England hath long been mad, and scarred herself:
> The brother blindly shed the brother's blood,
> The father rashly slaughtered his own son,
> The son, compelled, been butcher to the sire.
> . . .
> Now civil wounds are stopped, peace lives again.
>
> (5.6.20–6; 40)

show the moral and propagandist role early Shakespearean tragedy played. These lines expose the futility of the Wars of the Roses. Shakespeare also celebrates the peace ushered in by the Tudors, to the welcoming ears of his late Elizabethan audience.

Critics who study the cultural impact of the Elizabethan theatre and its role as a political institution in early modern English society argue that early English tragedians were central to this role assumed by that theatre. For example, Steven Mullaney writes:

> When [James] Burbage dislocated theater from the city, he established a social and cultural distance that would prove invaluable to the stagecraft of Marlowe and Shakespeare: a critical distance . . . that provided the stage with a culturally and ideologically removed vantage point from which it could reflect upon its own age with more freedom and license than had hitherto been possible. It was

a freedom, a range of slightly eccentric or decentered perspectives, that gave the stage an uncanny ability to tease
out and represent the contradictions of a culture it both
belonged to and was, to a certain extent, alienated from.
(Mullaney 1988: 30–1)

Mullaney's account of the crucial role theatres played from their
new liminal locations outside the City of London is central to
how we understand the development of tragedy. As Mullaney
points out, theatres 'dislocated' outside the city limits became
spaces of freedom and radical resistance to orthodoxy. Thus
tragedy, which started to flourish in those theatres, became a
genre particularly invested with displaying, commenting on and
overturning contradictions of the age that produced them. The
Elizabethan tragedy had more firmly become a kind of drama
that robustly reshaped perceptions of the world its spectators
lived in. It did so with politics and history, as well as with love
and desire.

TRAGEDY AND THE PASSION OF YOUTH:
SHAKESPEARE'S *ROMEO AND JULIET*

The table of contents in the 1623 Folio shows that Shakespeare wrote more comedies than tragedies. Under the head-
ing 'TRAGEDIES' we find eleven plays, compared to fourteen
comedies and ten histories. As a writer of tragedies, Shakespeare
developed more slowly than as a writer of comedies. Yet, as
the example of *Richard III* shows, his early tragedies started
as a skilful and sophisticated response to the new language and
metrical form of Marlowe's and Kyd's tragedies. But then, probably in 1595, Shakespeare wrote a tragedy whose many new
elements showed a fresh turn in his tragic writing. Shakespeare
introduced a variety of character types from different social
classes and wrote a tragedy, not about historical figures from the
classical or national past, but about people in domestic conflict.
This character diversity, in particular, was unlike anything the
new English tragedy had explored. Unlike his earlier, and indeed

most of his later, tragedies, in which action is built around a single remarkable protagonist, in *Romeo and Juliet* Shakespeare introduces a pair of equally matched protagonists. With this structural invention, Shakespeare enriched his tragedy using an element that is typical of his comedies. For example, in *The Comedy of Errors* (1594), in adapting his source from Roman comedy, he doubles the number of masters and their servants.

In 1597 a quarto edition of a play was published advertising 'an excellent conceited' tragedy of Romeo and Juliet that had been often performed 'with great applause' (Chambers 1951, I: 338). *Romeo and Juliet* was most likely first performed at The Theatre and then at The Curtain. The two advertisements indicate that this well-crafted play was an immediate success. Richard Burbage, who played the part of Richard III, acted in the role of Romeo when the Lord Chamberlain's Men took on the play for their repertoire. This instant success was unusual because it was uncommon for 'two young and inexperienced people' (Brown 2001: 79) to be at the centre of a tragedy, because tragedy typically required a hero of noble stature and high consequence, with some exceptions like *Arden of Faversham*. Shakespeare may have written this play just around the time when London theatres reopened after they had been closed during the plague that struck the city in 1593–4. The plague lingers in the background of this intense love story in the form of several references to pestilence. After a period when London was beset with such pestilence, a tragedy of love, passion and the erotic vibrancy of youth came as a refreshing new direction. But the tragic irony of this play in which love and death intermingle is, as Jonathan Bate has observed, that 'the houses of both Capulet and Montague escape the plague, yet still the children die first. The final scene takes place in an ancestral tomb, but those who lie dead are the flower of a city's youth – Mercutio, Tybalt, Paris, Juliet and her Romeo' (2008: 13). Life has returned to a city after the plague, but the dead bodies of the city's young are a chilling reminder of the human losses the city has suffered during the plague.

Romeo and Juliet was an innovative tragedy in terms of its theme, composition and quality of language. Jill Levenson, the editor of the Oxford edition of this play, summarises the novel nature of this tragedy, when she says that 'With *Romeo and Juliet* tragedy entertains not only new subject matter, but also conventions of plot, character, and style from a totally different theatrical mode which flourished during the 1590s' (2000: 50). Tragedy of the 1590s was dominated by the style and type of character that were launched by Marlowe's extremely popular tragedies. Elaborate and bombastic rhetoric, and tragedies centred on a hero dominated by a single ambition, drive and passion, were the basic features of the tragedies written and performed before *Romeo and Juliet*. Gurr has pointed out that 'The durability of the Marlowe style and repertoire is a testimony to the strength of the citizens' enthusiasm for the playhouses most accessible to London's working population' (1988: 151). *Romeo and Juliet*, however, breaks away from this theatrical mode.

In order to distinguish himself in the cutthroat theatre scene of the 1590s London, Shakespeare experimented ambitiously. He chose to dramatise the kind of marriage that became a new fashion in his culture, which promoted a free choice of a mate based on love that went against the authority of parents to choose a mate for their sons and daughters. In other words, Shakespeare dramatises a marriage of love rather than a marriage of convenience. When Juliet rebels against her father's plan for her to marry Paris, one of Verona's most eligible young men, according to Capulet ('Verona brags of him/To be virtuous and well-governed youth', 1.4.180–1), and uninhibitedly offers herself to Romeo ('Take all myself', 2.1.92), Shakespeare verbalises the extreme of independence and freedom that his culture experienced. This rebellion itself was a novelty for the English stage, because, before *Romeo and Juliet*, as Northrop Frye has observed, '[t]ragedies based on the rebellion of youth against age are not frequent in the drama of Shakespeare's time: even the Duchess of Malfi is killed by brothers' (Frye 1991: 46).

About two years before Shakespeare wrote *Romeo and Juliet*, his contemporary George Whetstone published a prose treatise on the subject of love in which he directly and extensively addresses the subject of free choice when choosing a marriage partner. Whetstone argues that

> The office of free choice, is the root of foundation of Marriage, which consists only in the satisfaction of fancy: for where the fancy is not pleased, all the perfection of the world cannot force love, and where the fancy delights, many defect are perfected, or tolerated among the married.

Having promoted the idea that what we might refer to in modern terms as 'having a crush on someone' and love are the prerequisite of marriage, Whetstone than critiques the father's meddling in choosing a marriage partner for his daughter and opposes forced marriage, in terms that surprisingly foreshadow the story and plot of *Romeo and Juliet*. Whetstone continues:

> I cry out upon enforcement in marriage, as the [most] extreme bondage that is: for that the ransom of liberty is the death of the one or the other of the married. The father thinks he hath a happy purchase if he get a rich young ward to match with his daughter; but God he knows, and the unfortunate couple often feels, that he buys sorrow to his child, slander to himself, and perchance the ruin of an ancient gentleman's house, by the riot of the son of law, not loving his wife. (1593: U1^r and E3^{r-v})

The new ideology of marriage which Whetstone promotes covers some of the same ground which Shakespeare dramatises in *Romeo and Juliet*. The old Capulet's forced marriage of Paris to Juliet is presented in the play as a kind of enforced bondage from which Juliet liberates herself by stepping into the plan prepared by Friar Laurence that leads to her death. Sorrow and death of a child are precisely what Whetstone warns the imaginary father his forced marriage can lead to. When Whetstone foresees even the ruin of the father's house as the result of forced marriage we cannot help but notice that Shakespeare's tragedy averts this calamity by sacrificing the two young people in order to save the two households from ruin. This is how he deepens the tragedy of Romeo and Juliet, which ends with an intense awareness of all that has been lost. As the Prince says towards the end of the tragedy: 'All are punished' (5.3.295). The tragedy of Romeo and Juliet is governed by the fate and stars, which is suggested by the Chorus's reference to 'A pair of star-crossed lovers' (line 6) and which is alluded to in Capulet's line 'Earth-treading stars that make dark heaven light' (1.2.25). This is what the audience would have expected of a tragedy, because they lived in an age that believed in fate and astrology's ability to direct the course of human life. As Romeo says when he unsuccessfully fights against that fate, 'I deny you stars!' (5.1.24). Yet what makes *Romeo and Juliet* an especially novel tragedy is that Shakespeare challenges conventional expressions of belief in tragic fate with a more realistic conception of tragedy, which has roots in the new ideology of a free choice of a marriage partner. These two systems of belief clashed on the tragic stage and thus inspired audiences to engage with their own world at more than one level, and to draw their own conclusions about human fate.

In *Romeo and Juliet* the language of courtship and love captures the liberty, sensuality and passionate fervour of youth. Shakespeare may even be self-conscious of the novelty of the language he is using, as when the Chorus to the play instructs the spectators to 'with patient ears attend' (Chorus, 13). Shakespeare focuses attention on language as the main medium for constructing meaning in the play, and this focus encourages his audience to listen attentively to each line as it is spoken on the stage. This language is less rhetorically contrived and more lifelike. The lovers speak in dialogues that probe into the nature of their love, and the play transforms Fortune into the mere opposition of the everyday circumstances which end up being obstacles to the young lovers' happiness, and which push the plot towards its tragic ending. Friar John is unable to deliver Friar Laurence's message from Verona to Romeo in Mantua that Juliet will be alive in the tomb, because the authorities in Mantua suspect him of being a carrier of the plague. In Mantua, as in the London of Shakespeare's day, pestilence ended lives and thwarted desires. Such circumstances contribute to the life-like nature of this tragedy, and, as Holbrook observes, show that 'humans are creatures of space and time and vulnerable to fortune' (2015: 21).

In our modern world, there is a sense that courtly love is an outdated literary concept, yet when Romeo asks 'Is love a tender thing?' (1.4.23), he asks a question that mattered a lot in the sixteenth century and that Shakespeare's culture examined critically and extensively in different kinds of writing. Ian Moulton has recently argued that:

> Whatever its current status, love more certainly was a critical concept in the sixteenth century. It was a topic of lengthy, serious, and widely circulated philosophical treatises and medical texts, as well as countless books offering practical advice about marriage, courtship, and sexual relations. And this is to say nothing of its ubiquity as the subject for lyric poetry, stage plays, and fictional narratives. (2014: 5)

Moulton's point that marriage, courtship and sexual relations were at the centre of critical writing about love is important because it helps us understand *Romeo and Juliet* as a cutting-edge play, a play that engages precisely with the three elements central to the important topic of love. The play thus provided an important contribution to debates about love in late Elizabethan England. It may be that for that reason, and because it features young people as protagonists, the play may have been particularly popular with young and educated audiences, especially, as Gurr writes, since 'In the 1590s the Shakespeare company [Lord Chamberlain's Men] became notably popular with the Inns of Court students for its plays about love.' To these 'Romeo-quoting students' (1988: 149, 151), as Gurr calls them, Shakespeare's first major tragedy presented a powerful version of love expressed in extravagant language, one that comes at a deathly price.

Romeo and Juliet experience this new freedom afforded to them by the culture that energises the play. Mercutio, however, fantasises about love and desire in a speech about the queen of fairies, Queen Mab, and says:

> . . . I see Queen Mab hath been with you.
> . . . she gallops night by night.
> Through lovers' brains, and then they dream of love;
> On courtiers' knees, that dream on curtsies straight;
> O'er lawyers' fingers, who straight dream on fees;
> O'er ladies lips, who straight on kisses dream,
> Which oft the angry Mab with blisters plagues,
> Because their breath with sweetmeats tainted are.
> . . .
> This is the hag, when maids lie on their backs,
> That presses them and learns them first to bear
> Making them women of good carriage.
>
> (1.4.51, 68–74, 90–2)

Mercutio has just told Romeo that he had had a dream the previous night (Romeo: 'I dreamt a dream tonight'/Mercutio: And so did I' 1.4.44–4), and he has proceeded to tell him his dream. Mercutio maintains that the way to explain love is best done in a dream because love itself has no form and is everywhere. Mercutio, as A. D. Nuttall has stated, is also 'conversely intent on showing the absurdity of love, that it is all illusion' (2007: 108). But in telling his dream Mercutio maintains that love is not absurd, but omniscient, unselective of its targets, random and hard to explain in any other terms but those of fantasy. He uses only terms that befit a narrative of a dream, but the quality of love which he talks about is not much different from love that defines the love of Romeo and Juliet. He continues his thought, which he begins with: 'If my heart's dear love – ' (2.1.158). Juliet picks this up, saying:

> I have no joy of this contract tonight:
> It is too rash, to unadvised, too sudden,
> Too like the lightning which doth cease to be
> Ere one can say 'It lightens'. Sweet, good night.
> This bud of love, by summer's ripening breath,
> May prove a beauteous flower when next we meet.
>
> (2.1.160–5)

Direct and transparent description of love as a sudden and rash force complements Juliet's similes and simple metaphors, which stand in sharp contrast to the elaborate metaphors and mini allegories that Mercutio devises. When she speaks about love figuratively, her favourite rhetorical figure is hyperbole, a figure of exaggeration: 'My bounty is as boundless as the sea,/My love as deep' (2.1.176–7). Some of these lines read like they were taken from a Petrarchan sonnet, which was particularly fashionable at the time when Shakespeare wrote *Romeo and Juliet*, and the vogue was at the height just at the time when the play was performed. By the late 1590s the sonnet fashion had started to peter out.

We can think of this interesting way of turning the sonnet's lyrical form into dramatic lines as Shakespeare's attempt to contrast the stylistic and structural formulas of the sonnet to a new language of love free from constraints of the conventions of literary love, and to use the closed form of the sonnet (it consists of fourteen lines) to illustrate the restrictions of love as emotion and of the language of love, before Romeo and Juliet's nuptial night. Breaking away from love that is not experienced to that which is experienced means also leaving the sonnet behind and speaking in the language of sexual consummation. The love duet of Romeo and Juliet before is presented as a sonnet:

Juliet:	Good pilgrim, you do wrong your hand too **much**,
	Which mannerly devotion shows in <u>this</u>,
	For saints have hands that pilgrims' hands to **touch**,
	And palm to palm is holy palmers' <u>kiss</u>.
Romeo:	Have not saints lips, nor holy palmers **too**?
Juliet:	Ay, pilgrim, lips that they must use in <u>prayer</u>.
Romeo:	O then, dear saint, let lips do what hands **do**;
	They prey, grant thou, lest faith turn to <u>despair</u>.

(1.4. 210–17)

After the first quatrain with the rhyming scheme a b a b (much/touch and this/kiss) and the second quatrain with the same rhyming scheme (too/do and prayer/despair), this dialogue will end up in full Petrarchan sonnet mode with interlaced key words, dominated by the word 'lips' and leading to a kiss. This is a strategic move, as Shakespeare dramatises that the power of breaking away from clichés, and after a kiss, this love will lead to erotic pleasure, which moves beyond the Petrarchan and sonnet tradition in the play. Romeo's pronouncements like 'Love is a smoke made with the fume of sighs . . ./Being vexed, a sea nourished with loving tears' (1.1.186, 188) illustrate his adherence to the Petrarchan manner of speaking about love, which Romeo first associates with Rosaline who is the object of his Petrarchan adoration but for whom he has no real feeling: 'This love feel I, that feel no love in this' (1.1.178). Romeo is often portrayed as an immature young lover early in the play. But this young lover is also thinking about 'love's transgression' (1.1.181), in the sense of violation of the laws of love. Romeo is transgressing by forgetting about Rosaline, the image of Petrarchan love which leaves him cold.

Romeo and Juliet is one of Shakespeare's unabashedly erotic plays. The language of eroticism abounds. References to eroticism provide a natural contrast to love expressed as an idea; they give fleshy vivacity to this plot of courtship and assure that love is not merely understood in terms of transcendence and clichés but as an emotion leading to sexual consummation. Nurse takes pleasure in remembering her own lusty youth and projecting the same for Juliet, when time comes: 'Thou will fall backward when thou has more wit' (1.3.44), implying she will lie on her back during sexual intercourse. Mercutio, whose hyperactive imagination matches his hyperactive erotic drive, does not miss an opportunity to speak sexually. His instructions to Romeo have phallic connotations: 'If love be rough with you, be rough with love;/Prick love for pricking, and you beat love down' (1.4.25–6). His curious comment, 'O Romeo, that she were, O that she were/An open-arse, or thou a popp'rin' pear' (2.1.37–8), has invited provocative critical interpretation. Bruce R. Smith was among the first critics to comment on the peculiar sexual innuendo in these lines, saying that, 'It is not Juliet's pudenda that Mercutio jokes about but Romeo's', leading him to conclude that this is an image of anal sex, between men (1994: 64). Mercutio exhibits particular interest in sexual language, and the following lines allude to the effect of sexual over-activity on the male member: 'Sure wit, follow me this jest now till thou hast worn out thy pump, that when the single sole of it is worn, the jest may be remain, after the wearing, solely singular' (2.3.59 –61). To our modern ears these lines may seem a bit too convoluted and opaque to be connected with male sexual activity. But in a culture in which the language of sexual acts and sexuality was not as transparent as in our modern times, as drama critics we rely on the dramatic context to decode such meanings. Therefore, because of Mercutio's obsession with sexual jabs and puns, and because these lines are distinctly convoluted to avoid addressing the issue, their sexual undertones seem to be implied rather than directly expressed. In contrast to the opacity of Mercutio's lines, Juliet's question 'Let me be satisfied, is 't good or bad?' (2.4.36) is clear; she wants to hear from the Nurse that it is Romeo who was the young man she met at the Capulets' ball. But the ambiguity of the word 'satisfied' leads us to think that that sexual satisfaction is also implied in this word. At another point in the tragedy, Juliet will be equally bold in wishing to be sexually satisfied, when in the first balcony scene she says: 'O that I were a glove upon that hand' (2.1.67), where the allusion to sexual penetration is suggested.

But Romeo is also transgressing, as Jonathan Goldberg provocatively argues, by acknowledging 'the affection, the love of Benvolio for him' (1994: 222). The affection is there, but it reflects Romeo and Benvolio's friendship. In Shakespeare's time, affective friendship included a different set of terms of expression and gestures of closeness and intimacy. This ought not to be confused with homoerotic attachment, as Alan Bray has pointed out, despite acknowledging that there 'there is always a potential ambiguity about intimacy between men' and then hastening to add that 'in early modern England such intimacy was peculiarly ambivalent' (1990: 19). Shakespeare's text leaves us to grapple with that ambivalence, and that provides an opportunity for a stage production to fill a performance with inventive solutions.

The play contrasts the language of the vitality of eroticism with the poetry of the macabre, death and tragedy. There is something eerie and sinister in the lines in which Friar Laurence takes time to explain the effect of poison on Juliet:

> The roses in thy lips and cheeks shall fade
> To wanny ashes, thy eyes's windows fall
> Like death when he shuts up the day of life.
> Each part, deprived of supple government,
> Shall stiff and stark and cold appear like death;
> And in this borrowed likeness of shrunk death
> Thou shalt continue two-and-forty hours,
> And then awake as from a pleasant sleep.
>
> (4.1.100–6)

Details of this image give the death theme immediacy in material terms because they make death, even the process of dying, palpable and visible. It is not just an instance of Shakespeare's macabre style of writing. This kind of eerie image Shakespeare expands when Juliet faces 'the horrible conceit of death and night' (4.3.36) in the tomb of her ancestors.

This connection between sexuality and death is not accidental, because both themes feature so prominently in *Romeo and Juliet*. A critic concerned with gender and sexuality, Jonathan Dollimore has regarded this tragedy as 'a play about the paradoxical binding together of desire and death' (1999: 108) and has documented clear instances of this, from the Prologue to the final line by Juliet, 'Thus with a kiss I die' (5.3.120). Dollimore develops this point and argues, provocatively, that, '*Romeo and Juliet* is also an adult fantasy *about* adolescent desire. It's no secret that adolescent sexuality contains a powerful erotic charge for the adult, regardless of sexual orientation' (1999: 108). Dollimore's point opens up space for further critical debate about the relationship between death, tragedy, loss and desire in this play both because the language and dramatic narrative invite this discussion and because the openness with which Shakespeare addresses these connections must have come as a refreshingly new way of bringing tragedy down from the pedestal of life of the heroic and the noble to the natural and the carnal. This attentiveness to details of sexual language that

he does not explore in *Richard III* is not to be found in the tragedies of his predecessors. It has taken criticism a long time to start
addressing the issue of sexuality and desire in *Romeo and Juliet*;
wider cultural and social change made this issue more salient in
late twentieth-century criticism. For example, this is evident in
a book devoted solely to the subjects of 'love and sexuality'
in English Renaissance drama, in which Shakespeare's plays feature prominently, but which makes no mention of *Romeo and
Juliet* (Rose 1988).

Approached in the light of New Historicism and cultural
materialism, critical practices which regard theatre as a cultural
institution in which social power is on display, where it circu-
lates, and where it is also produced, tragedy is seen as a powerful moral force. English tragedy showed the other side of the
actions, beliefs and ideas that the culture upheld, as it demon-
strated how to translate the symbolic action of tragedy into an
event that stimulated new thinking. Louis Montrose elaborates
on this idea and offers a particularly illuminating assessment
of the relationship between early modern theatre and its social
role. He says that

> the symbolic actions performed in the theatre had the
> immediate, if frequently transitory, capacity to stimulate
> the intellect and to promote the emotional well-being of
> their actual and vicarious participants. [Plays] were com-
> mercial entertainments, pleasurably purveying informa-
> tion, counsel, and fantasy. (1996: 40)

This passage summarises much of the stage and verbal power
because of which the four tragedies discussed in this chapter
remained popular for so long, with the *Tamburlaine* plays performed almost continuously until the closing of the theatres in
1642. Although our record about the early modern audience's
response to the plays performed is sparse, we can reasonably
believe that the longevity of these plays on the stage is enough of
an indicator to suggest that by way of their symbolic actions they
stimulated the intellect, inspired imagination, tapped into the
fantasies of audiences, staged emotions, and remained a source
of pleasure. In doing that, these four tragedies fulfilled their roles

as socially engaged drama within a theatre as an institution of social commentary and critique. *Romeo and Juliet* is a good example of a play which illustrates how Shakespearean tragedy is less concerned with showing a character to be either morally good or evil. *Romeo and Juliet* illustrates that Shakespeare imagines his tragic characters to be neither wholly good nor wholly evil; as we will see with other English Renaissance tragedy, such as *Hamlet* and *Antony and Cleopatra*, the forces that make the characters in these plays impressive are inextricable from the forces that undermine them. As Paul Hammond notes

> the work of tragedy is to estrange such a selfhood from the world around it, and from itself. That which impels the protagonist, and seems to be a source of strength – love, ambition, duty – turns against him to undo him, is seen as excess or as error, and is called by names such as *hubris, hamaritia,* or *furor.* (2009: 199)

Such estrangement will continue in the tragedies that follow as protagonists constantly find themselves at odds with both their surroundings and themselves.

CHAPTER 2

Late Elizabethan Tragedy

The 1580s was a pivotal decade in the history of early English drama, marked by two important events. In 1583 the Queen's Men was established, which was 'at the time the most illustrious company of actors ever assembled in England' (McMillin and MacLean 1998: 1). This move was intended as an attempt to regulate public entertainment, especially in terms of controlling the subject matter of plays. It also meant that such entertainment was given royal protection against frequent complaints coming from the City (Chambers 1951: I, 28). The clash between the authorities' attempt to police stage entertainment in the City and the expansion of such entertainment across the River Thames meant that tragedy was adapted to different kind of playing venues.

REVENGE TRAGEDY AFTER SENECA: THOMAS KYD'S *THE SPANISH TRAGEDY*

Sometime around 1587 (Wiggins 2012: 369), Thomas Kyd wrote *The Spanish Tragedy, or Hieronimo is Mad Again*, a play that would play a formative role in the development of revenge tragedy in England. Kyd's tragedy was still popular in 1614, when Ben Jonson remembered it in the Induction to his comedy *Bartholomew Fair*, where he says: 'He that will swear *Jeronimo* or

Andronicus are the best plays yet, shall pass unexcepted at, here, as a man whose judgment shows it is constant, and hath stood still, these five and twenty, or thirty years' (Jonson 1967: 11). Jonson may be said to 'mock [the] consistency of taste' (Marino 2011: 91), remembering playgoers shouting to see plays that they had enjoyed for at least two decades. Jonson's frustrated comment could also be read as an acknowledgement of the fact that precisely this taste in tragedy had not lost freshness and importance for drama. *The Spanish Tragedy* inevitably raises questions about the identity of late Elizabethan tragedy and the resilience of its features in tragedies of the Jacobean period as well.

Although there is truth in the claim that 'English Renaissance culture was in many ways different from ours, but not so different as to prevent us from recognizing the kinds of conflicts its tragedies explore, or deprive those tragedies of any direct impact on the conflict we ourselves face' (Watson 1990: 301), any familiarity with the vision of life that a play like *The Spanish Tragedy* presents is grounded in the historical conditions which shaped the theatre for which Kyd wrote his play. In fact, the durability of this tragedy in its own time, which so irked Jonson, had more to do with how Kyd's play reimagined the English tragic drama within both the theatre scene and the Reformed culture of early modern England, than with the kind of internal, ethical and emotional struggles experienced by its protagonists. As Gregory Colón Semenza has summarised, the popularity of this play is most evident, not only in adaptations, imitations and allusions, but in the way that *The Spanish Tragedy*

> frees later tragedians from the generic imitations and epistemological determinism of classic, Aristotelian tragedy; it advances the genre, that is, precisely by rejecting its most basic rules and assumptions about the mimetic function of drama. In doing so, it establishes a dramatic mode consistent with the increasing epistemological indeterminism of post-Reformation European thought and, in the process, establishes its most basic tool – theatrical self-awareness and/or self-scrutiny – as the basis of the early modern, and perhaps the modern, theatrical experience. (Colón Semenza 2010: 153)

As Colón Semenza points out, this lack of determinism sprang directly from the Reformation itself, as it unmoored established religious and political ideas across the Continent and England. If there was a moment in the history of English drama that marks a clear separation between the Aristotelian, more Continental ideas about tragedy and the English example of the genre, that moment fully arrived with *The Spanish Tragedy*. With Kyd, tragedy became increasingly separated from the notion that it represented an imitation of action which presents only a downfall of a noble from a distant past and started to be concerned with showing misfortunes of fictional personages from the contemporary period. The play is both a tragedy of love, of Bel-Imperia's attempts to satisfy her love for a heroic man; of a father who has lost his son, Horatio, married to Bel-Imperia; and a revenge drama which sacrifices the woman, who avenges Don Andrea, her dead lover, and takes the men accused of murder and vengeance, Lorenzo and Balthasar, to hell.

The Spanish Tragedy is best known for the ways in which it transforms the legacy of Senecan drama into dynamic stage action. Kyd turned the ceremonial rhetoric of Senecan drama, detached from feeling, into a heightened language of emotion, and connected the protagonist's individual will to an elaborately planned revenge. One of the key differences between Senecan tragedy and English tragedy lies in its handling of stage violence. While Senecan tragedy is content with reporting the horrible acts of violence, the English tragedy shows such acts on stage. Macabre effects (like Hieronimo's severed tongue) and killings suggest nostalgia for the world of Senecan drama, which Kyd's play transforms and enlivens. Kyd turned such elements of drama into stage effects whose visual and verbal power in creating stage spectacle was enhanced by the smallness of The Rose Theatre where *The Spanish Tragedy* was first performed. Revenge in Kyd is not merely a motif around which tragedy unfolds. Rather, it is both a protagonist and a spectator of its own rough justice, because Kyd personifies Revenge as a self-aware stage character reflecting on its own deeds.

The metatheatrical element of tragedy, tragedy that looks back at its own creation of language and action, shows that Kyd is sensitive to the close relationship between the genre and the theatre that produces it. In a well-known soliloquy, Hieronimo acts tragic action at the moment when he delivers it on stage.

> What outcries pluck me from my naked bed,
> And chill my throbbing heart with trembling fear,
> Which never danger yet could daunt before?
> Who calls Hieronimo? Speak, here I am.
> I did not slumber, therefore 'twas no dream,
> . . .
> But stay, what murderous spectacle is this?
> A man hanged up and all the murderers gone,
> And in my bower to lay the guilt on me.
> This place was made for pleasure not for death.
>   *He cuts him down*
> Those garments that he wears I oft have seen –
> Alas it is Horatio, my sweet son.
>
>   (2.5.1–5, 9–14)

The metadramatic element of this speech, which Kyd immediately enhances by using rhetorical questions, prepares for the dramatic discovery of Hieronimo's dead son. The power of recognition, which the macabre stage effect produces, makes the reality of death more obvious; it puts it centre stage and dispels any illusion that alternative reality, like dreams or hallucinations, could capture emotions fully. The audience is made even more aware that it is watching a theatre of revenge on stage in the next scene, when Don Andrea sits down with Revenge to observe the doing of revenge, while Revenge delays the process. Don Andrea says:

> Brought'st thou me hither to increase my pain?
> I looked that Balthazar should have been slain;
> But 'tis my friend Horatio that is slain,
> And they abuse fair Bel-Imperia,
> On whom I doted more than all the world,
> Because she loved me more than all the world.
>
>   (2.6.1–6)

In moments like this, Kyd's tragedy dispels any notion that the audience is watching anything but a play that is self-aware of its power to create an illustration of the spectacle of death: Don Andrea, in the role of spectator, is literally on stage, being watched by theatregoers watching him watch the theatre of death and revenge, staged by Revenge, playing before his eyes, and before the eyes of playgoers. This scene shows how Kyd utilises resources of the theatre well in order to craft meaning out of his drama. He draws attention to the affective power of the theatre to engender high emotions and cause suffering and pain ('Brought'st thou me hither to increase my pain?'), and to show that tragedy creates new rules about itself in the process of being acted on stage. This creation is not surprising given that English tragedy was so new at this time, and Kyd is literally creating it during the course of the play. The relationship between theatre and tragedy is even more evident in Revenge's answer to Don Andrea:

> Thou talk'st of harvest when the corn is green:
> The end is crown of every work well done;
> The sickle comes not till the corn be ripe.
> Be still, and ere I lead thee from this place,
> I'll show thee Balthazar in heavy case.
>
> (2.6.7–11)

Revenge's reply indicates that Hieronimo's emotional reaction should not be treated as *pathos*, as creating affect, but only as an element in the chain of actions leading to retribution. Revenge's role here is to check the hero's own actions and motivations, to direct the course of tragedy, and to energise the action by no longer being merely the subject of rhetoric but a participant in the plot. *The Spanish Tragedy* was obviously one of the most innovative new tragedies of the late Elizabethan period, and one of the bloodiest and most influential.

REVENGE TRAGEDY AFTER KYD: SHAKESPEARE'S *HAMLET*

The relationship between Kyd's *Spanish Tragedy* and *Hamlet* is both obvious and complicated. The ghost, the Machiavellian villain (King Claudius, Hamlet's uncle), the revenge, the play-within-the-play – they all come from Thomas Kyd. This relationship is also 'close and profoundly important', states Philip Edwards, the Cambridge Shakespeare editor of the play (Edwards 1985: 3). However, Edwards contends that 'How far that relationship developed through Shakespeare reworking of a Kydean *Hamlet* is impossible to say' (Edwards 1985: 3). Brian Vickers has even argued that it is possible to attribute to Shakespeare with some precision a few 'quite short samples' (Vickers 2012: 1) in the 1602 edition of Kyd's texts, which would have occurred at the time when *Hamlet* was a new play. There were earlier versions of the Hamlet story available to Shakespeare, like the twelfth-century story of Amleth available in Saxo Grammaticus' *Historiae Danicae*, first printed in 1514. Hamlet is a successful revenger in Grammaticus, but Shakespeare changes that to achieve a tragic ending, to make a cruel, bitter, bleak, more painful and cathartic ending, an ending that complicates the nature of revenge in ways not found in the Danish original. Denmark had significance for the Elizabethans because Anne of Denmark had become the wife of King James VI of Scotland, Elizabeth I's most likely successor, in 1589. There was also a French version of this old Danish story written by François de Belleforest and published in his *Histoires tragiques*, translated into English only in 1608. Another possible source may be an earlier lost play now referred to as the *Ur-Hamlet*, but the author of this play is not known.

Before *Hamlet* was first performed at The Globe, probably in 1600, three years before Queen Elizabeth I's death, the tragedy of Hamlet was mentioned by Thomas Nashe in the Preface to Robert Greene's prose romance *Menaphon* (1589), in the context of a remark about the excessive popularity of Seneca in Elizabethan theatre. Seneca's popularity in England was so widespread that Nashe could not resist mocking that tradition's excesses: 'English Seneca read by candlelight yields many good sentences, as "Blood is a beggar", and so forth; and if you entreat him fair in a frosty morning, he will afford you whole Hamlets, I should say handfuls, of tragical speeches' (Nashe 1972: 474). The target of Nashe's attack is the kind of Senecan tragedy which recycles clichés of style and language and presents them as new drama. Although Nashe's remark does not tell us much about which *Hamlet* play he refers to, the ironic edge of his remark makes *Hamlet* the subject, or at least an illustration, of the criticism which targets the rhetorical excesses of the Senecan style of writing then prevalent in English tragedy.

Hamlet was a bold theatrical experiment mostly because of the abundance of new language the force of which transformed the scenes of bloodshed and themes of 'thwarted love' (G. R. Hibbard 1994: 49), the mother–son relationship, trials of friendship, and suspicion of political authority, into a fast-moving plot which emphasised the possibilities of Senecan drama to engage with political, personal, emotional and intellectual aspects of a tragic life and fall. *Hamlet* thus matches perfectly Sir Philip Sidney's description of the genre of tragedy in *An Apology for Poetry* (1595), for it

> opens the greatest wounds, and shows forth the ulcers that are covered with tissue; that makes kings fear to be tyrants, and tyrants manifest their tyrannical humours; that, with stirring the affects of admiration and commiseration, teaches the uncertainty of this world, and upon how weak foundations guilded roofs are built. (Sidney 1973: 117–18)

In *Hamlet*, Shakespeare transforms and plays with the conventions of revenge tragedy freely in part because the Elizabethan audience, as Germaine Greer has remarked, knew those conventions 'as well as we today grasp the complicated rules of spy fiction' (Greer 1991: 57) or, we can add, any other genre of popular culture. By introducing new layers of meaning, new ethical problems and stage props (such as the wall hanging in the scene in Gertrude's bedroom behind which Polonius hides at the moment when Hamlet kills him), Shakespeare counts on his audience recognising when novelty adds new layers to a convention. Criticism has addressed many of these elements of *Hamlet* as well as others depending on the changing trends and critical tastes. Most recently, for instance, *Hamlet* has been the subject of criticism about the relationship between drama, stage performance and the print circulation of 'political knowledge' about the condition of England. This approach turns

Hamlet into a performance of everyday politics that is itself like a Senecan play. In this way, Senecanism comes across not as an antiquated mode of expression on stage but as a modern and readily available way of turning politics into performance. Thus, *Hamlet* 'offered such [political] knowledge for consumption to a paying, not-professional audience' and, in doing so, *Hamlet* was one of the plays which 'repurposed' such political knowledge 'from professional tools into the matter of political conversation among those excluded from political activity' (Kiséry 2016: 7). Suddenly, revenge is no longer a recycled convention taken from Seneca, but a new way of showing how politics actually occurs both outside theatres as well as on stage.

Revenge in *Hamlet* turns a tragic hero into an unstoppable thinker, one who thinks not only about how to perform revenge, but, more importantly, what to think of the world and people around him. Hamlet delays because he thinks too much about too many matters at the same time. Thinking about the revenge which the Ghost compels Hamlet to perform, and keeps reminding him to do, gets in the way of thinking about what it means to love – a woman, mother, father, friend – what it means to know and to live. Ironically, it is this thinking that Hamlet so castigates himself for that makes him such a compelling character. This makes *Hamlet* a tragedy different from Kyd's drama, where language and action leading to revenge move together, and a new kind of tragedy in which drama is in the language itself. *Hamlet* controls the tragic hero's affective impulse for revenge by turning revenge into a subject of a moral debate in accordance with the learning and instruction in the humanist culture familiar to Shakespeare, and thus to Hamlet, a student from Wittenberg, once an eminent centre of humanist education on the Continent. Delaying revenge may be less an effect of a personal disposition than a reflection of Hamlet's facility with the knowledge and arguments of humanist training, adapted to a new sixteenth century's thinking about the Christian attitude towards revenge. Alan Sinfield has addressed this point clearly when he says of Hamlet that, 'Having studied at an international university in Germany, Hamlet has a different sensibility from that of his father, an old-fashioned warrior who wagered his kingdom in combat with Fortinbras, King of Norway, whom he slew' (2005: xxv). One cannot imagine old Hamlet hesitating, even for a moment, to avenge himself upon an enemy. The linguistic novelty of *Hamlet* in evident in the large number of new words, phrases and combination of words which Shakespeare invents and reimagines in *Hamlet*. For example, the Ghost has just entered the stage and the audience hears Hamlet say the following:

> Let me not burst in ignorance, but tell
> Why thy canonized bones, hearsèd in death,
> Have burst their cerements, why the sepulcher,
> Wherein we saw thee quietly inurned,
> Hath oped is ponderous and marble jaws
> To cast thee up again.
>
> (1.4.25–30)

Shakespeare invented the words 'cerements' and 'inurned', the first meaning 'grave-clothes', that is waxed cloth in which the dead were wrapped, and the second, 'buried, entombed' (Hibbard 1994: 182). Shakespeare places these invented words in an emotionally charged and evocative language that creates an image of death that is almost alive: death that tears the burying cloth of the dead; tombs that burst open and gape, their marble jaws open, like a hungry animal. Shakespeare stuns his audience into seeing and hearing new words and images that captivate the senses and imagination. The play brims with instances like these, containing many words used only in *Hamlet* or words that nobody had ever heard before in a particular combination with other words. For example, Frank Kermode has stressed Shakespeare's wide use of hendiadys (a rhetorical figure by which a single idea is expressed using two words connected with 'and') in *Hamlet*. More than this, Kermode sees in *Hamlet* 'a new way of representing turbulent thinking', 'a new rhetoric', one that 'register[s] the pace of the speech, its sudden turns, its backtracking, its metaphors flashing before us and disappearing before we can consider them' (2000: 16). This compulsive innovation makes *Hamlet* an explosive and avant-garde tragedy. A tyrannical or weak ruler who is the main source of evil and corruption and has to be eliminated by the sole initiative and acts of a revenger is the main element of many revenge plays at the time when Shakespeare wrote *Hamlet*, and *Hamlet* is no exception to this generic requirement of Senecan tragedy. Hamlet's dilemma is also the theatre's dilemma: how to stage the downfall of a tyrant in a culture in which one of the most heinous crimes against the state and its stability was to kill its ruler. Hamlet's behaviour has been described as 'eccentric' (Sinfield 2005: xii), because he represents a new kind of avenger who is also a thinker relying on conscience to guide his purpose, not an avenger within the fading custom of honour-driven revenge. The novelty of Hamlet's approach to revenge is made all the clearer when he is contrasted with another revenger in the play, Laertes, who rather than thinking is willing to act.

Another novelty in *Hamlet* is a shift from making Vice, a medieval type, the allegory of revenge, as in Kyd, and the primary agent of tragedy, to rooting tragedy in a combination of the political circumstances, individual actions and deliberations of a modern humanist person. The Ghost in *Hamlet*, which comes out of 'a pagan revenge tradition' (Bevington 2011: 61), sets the tragedy in motion and plays an important role in its development, but its legacy as the main agent of tragedy is balanced with personal and political causes in the play.

The connection between performance and revenge, between theatre and tragedy more broadly, which Kyd made obvious by making Revenge both an actor and spectator of its bloody actions, is further extended in *Hamlet*, both in the play-within-the-play showing the murder of Gonzago (3.2) and at the level of Hamlet's identification with a tragic figure who is also a performer. *Hamlet*, in fact, extends one of Senecan tragedy's main features: self-conscious meta-theatricalism. *Hamlet* ensures that theatre audiences witness revenge as play-within-the-play, as a spectacle that both entertains and horrifies them, just as the play-within-the-the-play in *Hamlet* both horrifies and entertains the onstage players observing the meta-theatrical murder of Gonzago. After Hamlet has explained to his mother, Queen Gertrude, the meaning of, and the reason for wearing, his 'inky cloak' (1.2.77), he proceeds to tell her that his 'moods, shows of grief'. . ./are actions that a man might play;/ But I have that within which passeth show –/These but the trapping and the suits of woe' (1.2.84–6). Hamlet's 'inky cloak' symbolises his grief as much as it can be a reference to his status as a student wearing a black gown, as was the custom. A. C. Bradley and other proponents of character criticism explain moments like this as showing 'Hamlet's melancholy' and 'his own inability to understand why he delays' (Bradley 1904: 101). Seen in this way, Hamlet is a character with a psychological trait in realist drama. Yet Hamlet tells us that subjectivity is performance; it is a stage act whose power of conviction depends on how spectators interpret the relationship between outward appearance and the affect (moods and grievances) that underpin appearance. If we view Hamlet in terms of the way that he tells us he behaves, as a man playing a part, and therefore as an avenger who is also an actor, we then see his delay as a way of acting the part of an avenger. While much of Act 2, scene 2 reads like Shakespeare's dramatic essay on the power of theatre to move to action and the crucial role 'common players' (2.2.344) or actors have in translating text into action on stage, this scene also illustrates what tragedy may have meant to the Elizabethans. The First Player's demonstration to Hamlet how the players should stage the Greek tragedy of blood and tyranny featuring the clash between Pyrrhus and Priam brings the live tradition of academic classical drama on stage within another play. When this classical tragedy ends up inciting and literally crafting a new tragedy within Shakespeare's play, we see how theatre itself acts as a producer of tragedy. At this point in *Hamlet*, the audience watches the process of shaping a new tragedy out of old tragic stories and actions. The amount of space Shakespeare gives to describing and polishing tragic action within his own play suggests that late Elizabethan tragedy is drama that is being created as it is being performed on stage.

Tragedy was a highly regarded genre in the Greek and Roman theatrical tradition. Yet *Hamlet* raises questions about what tragedy's effect and role might be in its own time, especially in relation to how tragedy affects an individual living in different aesthetic and cultural conditions in the early seventeenth century. Hamlet addresses this topic in one of his major speeches:

> Now I am alone.
> O what a rogue and peasant slave am I!
> Is it not monstrous that this player here,
> But in a fiction, in a dream of passion,
> Could force his soul so to his whole conceit
> That from her working all his visage waned,
> Tears in his eyes, distraction in's aspect,
> A broken voice, and his whole function suiting
> With forms to his conceit? And all for nothing.
> For Hecuba?
> What's Hecuba to him, or he to Hecuba?
>
> (2.2.537–47)

Hamlet is emboldened by the Player's readiness and determination to act out believable emotions while only being part of a fiction presented on stage. He also questions what tragedy means to the audience of his time. He does this by asking his audience to observe that tragedy manifests itself in the process of acting; tragedy is a performance in which a performer can be distant from the essence of, but at the same time engaged with, the part he – an adult male actor or a boy playing a female part – is presenting. Hamlet's example of the Player acting the part of Hecuba suggests that the rediscovery of Greek tragedy in the Renaissance was beginning to have a strong influence on the English theatre. This raises the question: 'What is tragedy?' What is it about, what does it consist of, why does it matter, and to whom does it matter? For Shakespeare, tragedy brings satisfaction and resolution of doubt, as well as the fulfilment of revenge. Shakespeare does that not only because of his inventive language and fast-paced plot, but because he sees his own tragedy as transforming a long tradition of the genre, from classical to his own modern times.

One way of thinking about how Shakespeare crafts tragedy in *Hamlet*, how he intensifies some and subdues other elements of tragedy, and how he paces the tragic action in its rush towards the resolution, is to consider the relationship between some of the play's main characters. For example, Gertrude strikes us as a key character in this tragedy only if we think of her in the context of psychoanalytic criticism that explores the fraught relationship between her and her son, Hamlet. Otherwise, she does not have a central presence in the play, nor does she speak much. Her relationship with Hamlet is complicated by his griev-ance against her second marriage, to his uncle Claudius, fol-lowing the murder of Hamlet's father. 'Mother, you have my father much offended;' (3.4.11), Hamlet tells her, bursting into her bedroom. Her reply, however, tempers the blame: 'Come, come, you answer with an idle tongue' (3.4.12). But the serious-ness of Hamlet's blame has to do with the fact of inheritance, as he says to Horatio at the very end of the play, when outlining Claudius's crimes:

> He that hath killed my king and whored my mother,
> Popped in between th'election and my hopes,
> Thrown out his angle for my proper life,
> And with such cozenage – is't no perfect conscience
> To quit him with this arm?
>
> (5.2.65–9)

Hamlet first accuses Claudius of murder, and then of whoring his mother, but it is important that he closes on the issue of theft (which is how C. T. Onions glosses 'cozenage'), for Claudius has taken what is rightfully Hamlet's in terms of inheritance. This shows that Gertrude's incest may not matter nearly as much as Claudius's theft. Lisa Jardine has persuasively argued that, his-torically, Gertrude's second marriage was problematic primarily from the perspective of 'the complexity of kin and inheritance obligations' (1996: 46), and less so over the issue of incest, for such marriages did sometimes take place. In the Elizabethan period, marriages like Gertrude's were considered incestuous, but only because a woman was marrying her late husband's kin. In other words, this was not seen as a marriage within her own family. Therefore, the culture was ready to turn the blind eye to such marriages (Jardine 1996: 45). Hamlet's concern is as much

political as it is moral. He worries that his mother's second marriage will deny him his inheritance. Therefore, her 'offence' is a
cause for Hamlet's private grievance but not a crucial motivat-
ing factor of Hamlet's tragedy.

The way Shakespeare erases Gertrude from the play at the
moment of her own death, by committing the mistake of drink-
ing from the poisoned cup intended for her son, reinforces
Gertrude's insignificance in the tragic action of the play. This
can be illustrated down to the cues included in the text when
Gertrude dies. Simon Palfrey and Tiffany Stern have examined such repeated cues in detail and have shown how they
shape meaning in *Hamlet*. Repeated cues can reveal the relationship between the text and the tragic action. Gertrude's cue,
'the drink, the drink' (5.2.264), repeated four times (twice in
line 265 as well), remains unheard in the commotion and the
shouts 'treason, treason' (5.2.276) by all the courtiers present.
She dies unaided. Palfrey and Stern insightfully comment on the
moment of Gertrude's death, helping us see how Shakespeare
manages tragedy down to such verbal detail:

> The Gertrude-actor might well have recognized a tanta-
> lizing, almost cruelly denied temptation to seize the stage
> and die like a true queen. And this fastidious refusal
> of repeated cues is an emphatic sign that we, like the
> Gertrude-actor's fellow players, are not ultimately to be
> allowed 'in' to her dying, as we weren't into her life. She
> dies alone, and remains as impenetrably opaque as ever.
> (2007: 222)

Forgotten, unheard, opaque at the moment of her death,
Gertrude is a reminder of the relationship between theatre
as a shaping force of tragedy, and tragedy as a collection of
aesthetic elements and playing parts. This is an example of a
subtle but no less important element in Shakespeare's composition of tragedy.

The sense of tragedy in *Hamlet* was as much created by such
internal elements of dramatic craft as by the physical space
of The Globe, where the play was first performed. The stage
at The Globe was 'three-dimensional', thrusting into the yard

(the space for standing that surrounded the stage on three sides) and admitting 'a radically different dynamic from two-dimensional [staging] in the intimacies it grant[ed] to some of its characters with the audience' (Gurr 2004: 47–8). The audience which surrounded the stage, standing in the yard and sitting in the three tiers of roofed galleries in The Globe, was attentive to oral features of plays, and to acoustic dimension of the play's language; the audience of public theatres was an audience for which listening was a faculty through which that audience received drama. We could therefore think of the 'trag-ical speeches' to which Nashe refers as being aspects of tragedy that particularly suited this characteristic of the audience at The Globe: speeches which make *Hamlet* show that Shake-speare shapes thoughts in such a way that language contrib-utes to the aural richness and ingenuity of these speeches. This aural quality can be illustrated by Hamlet's 'O that this too too solid flesh would melt,/Thaw and resolve itself into a dew': the verbal repetition of 'too' and the repetition of the idea of disappearing through melting, represented by the words 'thaw' and 'resolve', work on the listening audience by the force of the repetition of words and concepts, and through emphasis. Rhetorical figures are intimately concerned with the 'acousti-cal' qualities of utterance; Shakespeare's rhetorical art is more concealed than that of Marlowe and Kyd. When he contin-ues, 'O God! O God!/How weary, stale, flat, and unprofitable/Seem to me all the uses of this world' (1.2.132–4), repetition and emphasis continue to enhance the impression of suffering, amplifying the acoustic quality of utterance, as if to 'increase [the] appetite' (1.2.144) for listening to the sound of tragedy. Ophelia's speech about Hamlet's loss of sanity illustrates how images and ideas create an abundance of language structured to stimulate thinking and appeal to the audience's listening alertness. Ophelia says:

> O, what a noble mind is here o'erthrown!
> The courtier's, soldier's, scholar's, eye, tongue, sword;
> Th' expectancy and rose of the fair state,
> The glass of fashion and the mould of form,
> Th' observed of all observers – quite, quite down!

> And I, of ladies most deject and wretched,
> That sucked the honey of his music vows,
> Now see that noble and most sovereign reason
> Like sweet bells jangled out of tune and harsh;
> That unmatched form and feature of blown youth
> Blasted with ecstasy. O woe is me
> T'have seen what I have seen, see what I see.
>
> (3.1.151–62)

Metaphor after metaphor, noun after noun, and adjective after adjective, emphasise the impression of the loss of Hamlet's sanity that Ophelia wishes to convey. Yet Ophelia also reminds the audience of what she has lost by losing Hamlet to his own thoughts and actions. She configures her own tragedy in a language that appeals to the senses of hearing ('his music of woe', 'sweet bells jangled'), taste ('honey', 'sweet') and sight ('glass of fashion', 'T'have seen what I have seen'), all of which enhance Ophelia's sadness. The rhetorical, affective and sensuous variety of her language gives tragedy ornamental richness which Nashe found irritating but which the acoustic capabilities of early modern public theatres may have invited. Earlier we described *Hamlet* as a new play that offered new possibilities for drama. How fitting, then, that it was first performed at the newly created Globe, 'whose identity', as James Shapiro says, 'was yet unfixed', and which 'offered a way forward' (2005:17).

The 1603 quarto and the 1623 folio texts of *Hamlet* both contain the word 'tragedie' on the title page (quarto) or in the list of plays (folio). These texts invite us to think about what tragedy meant to Shakespeare's audiences. This helps us to understand the place and even popularity of *Hamlet* in its own time and its influence on other revenge tragedies such as *Antonio's Revenge* and *The Revenger's Tragedy*.

REVENGE TRAGEDY AND SOCIETY: JOHN MARSTON, *ANTONIO'S REVENGE*

Hamlet had not yet been published when Shakespeare's contemporary John Marston wrote *Antonio's Revenge* (performed

1600; published 1602), probably using Shakespeare's tragedy as a model. The title page states that the play 'has been sundry times acted, by the Children of Paul's' (Chambers 1951: III, 429), a boy company which performed in Paul's playhouse. *Hamlet* evidently haunted Marston. A year after the publication of *Antonio's Revenge*, Marston wrote *The Malcontent*, another play inspired by *Hamlet*. In 1603 London theatres were dominated not only by *Hamlet* but also by the *Hamlet* effect in tragedies that came out of the popularity of *Hamlet*. Marston's plays, however, are not mere imitations of *Hamlet*. Their relationship with Shakespeare's plays is neither straightforward nor simple. For example, W. Reavley Gair, an editor of *Antonio's Revenge*, suggests that Shakespeare and Marston used the same source for their respective plays rather than Marston's play being a rewrite of *Hamlet*. Gair points out that Marston's and Shakespeare's plays 'have many similarities of plot, incident and character, but no exact verbal parallels, though both include precise verbal echoes from *The Spanish Tragedy*' (1978: 16). Although neither Shakespeare nor Marston was likely to have had access to each other's texts, Gair suggests, 'the collaboration in 1601' of Paul's and The Globe and the fact that the Children of the Chapel were their 'common enemies' makes it possible, Gair speculates, 'that each dramatist was aware of what the other was doing. The two theatres may have agreed to co-operate on a play of a similar kind . . . This co-operation without collaboration might help to explain the very close likeness of plot in the two plays but the absence of identical phrasing' (1978: 16). Shakespeare shows an awareness of this war of the theatres in *Hamlet*, when Rosencrantz refers to the boy actors as 'aerie of children, little eyases, that cry out on the top of question, and are most tyrannically clapped for't. These are now the fashion, and so berattle the common stages' (2.2.335–8). The relationship between these two playhouses different in size and audience capacity, between the small Paul's playhouse, 'located in the north-west quadrant of the Chapter House precinct' (1978: 27) in the old St Paul's Cathedral, and The Globe, a much bigger public playhouse across the Thames in Southwark, suggests that their respective physical features created conditions for tragedy to thrive as a dramatic genre on very different stages in

London. Different stages called for a different kind of tragedy. The relationship between Kyd, Shakespeare and Marston also shows that revenge tragedy was not only entrenched in the London theatre scene by the end of the Elizabethan era, but that it had become such a vibrant and innovative genre because it was able to overcome what Nashe singled out as the unfortunate saturation of the English stage with Senecanism. Tragedy's resilience as a genre continued to be evident in the way in which Kyd's sustained influence on new drama was enriched with fresh solutions to different elements in revenge drama.

The most evident influence of Kyd, which can be observed in both *Hamlet* and *Antonio's Revenge*, lies in the mixture of Christian and Senecan elements, and the issues that arise from this mixture in revenge tragedies. This clash stems from the pagan call for revenge coming into conflict with the Christian doctrine of forgiveness. The Ghost in *Antonio's Revenge* sums up this mixture by exclaiming: 'Heaven's just; for I shall see/ The scourge of murder and impiety' (5.1.24–5). The ghost also invokes 'providence' (5.1.10), and Antonio mixes his passion for revenge with Christian sentiment: 'May I be more cursed than heaven/Can make me if I am not more wretched/Than man can conceive me' (2.3.1–3).

Antonio's Revenge shows that Marston is aware of the theatre's role in producing the effect of tragedy just as he was sensitive to inviting the audience of Paul's Theatre to respond to his tragedy, and tragedy in general, as stagecraft. In the Prologue to *Antonio's Revenge*, Marston portrays tragedy as a show adapted to circumstances both outside and inside the theatre. Marston's tragedy is first advertised as entertainment that provides a break from the bleak and cold winter weather: 'methinks, a sullen tragic scene/Would suit the time with pleasing congruence' (6–7). Marston then promotes this particular tragedy, not as a story of blood and horror, but as a well-composed piece of theatre. This emphasis on the theatrical aspect of tragedy suggests that Marston was one of the playwrights for whom the meaning of tragedy lay in its performative quality. The Prologue goes beyond this advertising motif and describes the relationship between theatre as a physical space suited to tragedy and tragedy as a dramatic performance that draws on theatre for its meaning. Before the audience starts hearing and watching the tragic action of this, or indeed any, tragedy, that audience will have already seen tragedy as the 'black-visaged show' (20). This is a reference to the custom of draping black curtains or hangings upon the stage to identify the play to be seen as tragedy, whose effect is to 'affraight their eyes' (21). The Prologue explains the purpose and effect of tragedy:

> if a breast
> Nailed to the earth with grief, if any heart
> Pierced through with anguish, pant within this ring,
> If there be any blood whose heat is chocked
> And stifled with true sense of misery,
> If ought of these strains fill this consort up,
> Th'arrive most welcome. O that our power
> Could lackey or keep wing with our desires,
> That with unusèd peise of style and sense
> We might weigh massy in judicious scale.
>
> (21–30)

Tragedy, Marston tells his spectators, ought to be experienced not merely for blood and suffering displayed on the stage. Rather, it should be judged for the style and sense which went into producing such horrific scenes. The Prologue tells us that the late Elizabethan idea of tragedy emphasises drama as stage spectacle and its self-consciousness as stage performance, something not found in its early Elizabethan precursors, such as Kyd's *Spanish Tragedy*. The children's playhouses were known to present plays with classical themes, as well as more academic plays, and Marston responded to that demand. As a tragic playwright, Marston was a classicist in the sense that he stayed close to the unities of time, space and action characteristic of classical tragedy. The action of *Antonio's Revenge* is coherent and takes place at the court of Venice over two days. Marston makes the most of the available stage effects to augment the impact of tragedy. Stage entries involve the use of torches and candles, drawing attention to the fact that his plays were performed

indoors; the play contains horrific acts, like the tearing out of
Piero's tongue; other stage directions feature a coffin, hearse and
a procession of mourners. The stage directions and the opening
of Act 2 illustrate how Marston maximised the possibility of the
stage to enhance the meaning of tragedy:

> *Enter mourners with torches, two with streamers,*
> CASTILIO *and* FOROBOSCO *with torches, a Herald*
> *bearing Andrugio's helm and sword, the coffin; . . . the*
> *coffin set down, helm, sword, and streamers hung up . . .*
> ANTONIO *and* MARIA *wet their handerkchiefs with*
> *their tears, kiss them, and lay then on the hearse, kneeling.*

The small space at Paul's playhouse, lit by candlelight only, adds
intimacy and haunting immediacy to this stage image of death
and fallen glory. From this candlelit stage, Piero's lines must
have made this small indoor theatre seem like a tomb, inviting
the audience to participate in the burying ritual:

> Rot here, thou cerecloth that enfolds the flesh
> Of my loathed foe; moulder to crumbling dust;
> Oblivion choke the passage of thy fame!
> Trophies of honoured birth drop quickly down;
> Let naught of him, but what was vicious, live.
> Though thou art dead, think not my hate is dead;
> I have but newly twone my arm in the curled locks
> Of snaky Vengeance.
>
> $$(2.1.1-8)$$

Marston's explicit language and the stage image of death extend
the idea of tragedy as both a visual and verbal act. When the
avenger, Piero, speaks about his ability to execute a series
of murders in the language of horrific realism – 'I have been
nursed in blood, and still have sucked/The steam of reeking
fore' (2.1.19–20) – Marston shows that he is conscious that in
a barely lit small indoor theatre the language of realism has a
particular visual and acoustic impact on extending the sense of
danger posed by the avenger.

   The Prologue advertises tragedy by inviting the audience to
judge the action they are about to see on the basis of people's

actual, not imagined acts; to see 'what men were, and are/Who would not know what men must be' (18–19). For Marston, tragedy displays naturalistic emotions; grief and hot blood splattered on stage are to be taken as stagecraft. The Prologue's invitation to view tragedy as staging actions of people from the present moment, and not the idealized actions of a heroic person from the past, shows the extent to which tragedy had moved away from being a staged chronicle of an illustrious past to becoming a drama that scrutinised the ills of contemporary politics and the misfortunes of citizens. In the play, the character Pandulfo Feliche, a gentleman of the Venetian court, draws a close link between tragedy as a set of motifs and its subject, the decline of civic morality:

> They say that men of hope are crushed,
> Good are suppressed by base desertless clods,
> That stifle gasping virtue. Look, sweet youth,
> How provident our quick Venetians are
> Lest hooves of jades should trample on my boy;
> Look how they lift him up to eminence,
> Heave him 'bove reach of flesh.
> . . .
> Listen, young blood, 'tis not true valour's pride
> To swagger, quarrel, swear, stamp, rave and chide,
> To stab in fume of blood, to keep loud coil,
> To bandy factions in domestic broils,
> To dare the act of sins whose filth excels
> The blackest customs of blind infidels.
>
> (1.5.68–72; 87–92)

This description of tragedy shows Marston's sensitivity to the form and demonstrates his awareness of the possibilities, and limitations, of tragedy to compete with the excesses of affect and actions that threaten to turn tragedy into a spectacle of murder and intrigue full of exaggerated effects. In *The Revenger's Tragedy*, Thomas Middleton will more fully explore such exaggerated effects.

Modern criticism has regarded Marston's tragedies as significant socio-political and existential drama. The process of alienation of an individual from society, which in *Hamlet* is represented by both the court and the world outside it, continues in *Antonio's Revenge*. Antonio's vengeance is directed at the world he thinks has failed him. An individual's alienation and exclusion from the world, which serves as a basis for revenge in all Marston's tragedies (and not just in *Antonio's Revenge*), is a theme that Jonathan Dollimore associates with the radicalism of late Elizabethan revenge tragedy. Dollimore captures this sense of individual alienation against social hegemony in Marston's drama clearly and convincingly:

> Running through Marston's dramatisation of this process are attitudes to human identity, to revenge and to providence which are radical: thus his protagonists are not defined by some spiritual or quasi-metaphysical essence, nor, even, a resilient human essence; rather, their identities are shown to be precariously dependent upon the social reality which confronts them. Correspondingly, revenge action is not a working out of divine vengeance, but a strategy of survival resorted to by the alienated and disposed. Moreover, in that action is a rejection of the providential scheme which divine vengeance conventionally presupposed. (1989: 28)

Dollimore maps the critical approach to the themes in Marston's tragedies as political and ideological drama about society and subjectivity, and about an individual's resistance to an understanding of the world through religion. *Antonio's Revenge* captures the world of political corruption and social malaise that Dollimore identifies as key themes in Marston's tragedy, in which the avenger speaks in the language of Christian self-identification: 'I am all air and feel no weight/Of human dirt clog' (3.5.20–1). Among the many moral problems that Marston's tragedies raise, the relationship between revenge and humanity, personal morality and social justice, are the ones that continued to be tragedy's main concerns, which we will see again in tragedies of John Webster and John Ford.

CLOSET DRAMA AND SENECAN TRAGEDY:
MARY SIDNEY HERBERT'S *ANTONIE*

Senecan tragedy in the 1590s did not only include plays written for performance in public theatres like The Rose or The Globe but also so-called 'closet dramas', which were more academic, rhetorical and literary than theatrical in nature. Closet dramas were inspired by classical themes and figures, and occasionally by biblical themes as well; they were sometimes staged at the universities or in aristocratic homes. Closet dramas were performed without set or costumes, and they emphasised rhetoric, moralising poetry and narrative account over plot and action. Mary Sidney Herbert, Countess of Pembroke translated *The Tragedy of Antonie* (1578) from French at a time when closet drama had become popular and when tragedy proliferated, owing to the fact that weekday performances were permitted in London. Herbert's play was published in English in 1592. Her translation of a French tragedy about the heroic life of Mark Antony indicates that her model for tragedy was Continental drama, which preferred classical stories to domestic history as a way of speaking about contemporary events (Hannay 1998: 39) than domestic tradition. The relationship between closet drama written by women and theatre is problematic because we have no records of their performance history. Although Elizabeth Cary's *The Tragedy of Mariam* opens by drawing attention to the impact of a 'public voice' (Act 1, line 1), the public never had a chance to actually see her play. Marta Straznicky has argued that 'in appearance' closet plays 'resemble stage plays but were never professionally performed' and that 'they are the products of aristocratic leisure but are permeated with the traditions of commercial drama', ending her description of closet dramas by saying that 'they are charged with political purpose but their reception has no apparent bearing on the exercise of power' (2004: 1). Closet drama is a genre of tragedy which falls somewhere between drama written for reading and drama intended for performance, so that, on page at least, closet drama can look like stage drama that is too rhetorical. Other critics have offered a differing opinion about the theatre history of closet drama. For example, Natasha Korda has summarised competing arguments about the lack of records regarding productions in the commercial theatres and has argued that 'an absence of evidence does not necessarily indicate evidence of absence' (2011: 460). Yet more important is the fact that, although closet drama was not meant to be performed in commercial theatres, it can nevertheless bridge its purpose for private reading with meanings that concern the public sphere. Closet drama does that through print, not performance. In that sense, closet dramas are both private and public play texts.

Antonie is a blank-verse drama with act breaks but without scene breaks. Speeches and dialogues are expressed in elaborate rhetoric weighted by heavy didacticism, appropriating the dramatic convention of verse derived from Greek drama known as stichomythia. The play narrates events familiar from the classical story of one of the Roman triumvirs, Mark Antony, and his love affair with the Queen of Egypt, Cleopatra. Mary Herbert's translation is both an appropriation of a frequently recycled classical love story and a revival of the classical form of soliloquy which became the most expressive verse form in late Elizabethan tragedy intended for performance. The editors of the Oxford edition of *Antonie* state that 'The revival of these classical models helped to move the English stage from an emphasis on action toward an emphasis on character; Shakespeare notably combined the renewed interest in soliloquy so evident in *Antonie*' (Hannay et al. 1998: 141). In Act 2, Cleopatra invokes Antony in rhetorically elaborate terms:

> That I have thee betraid, deare *Antonie*,
> My life, my soule, my Sunne? I had such thoughts?
> That I have thee betraide my Lord, my King?
> That I would breake my vowed faith to thee?
> Leave thee? Deceive thee? Yeelde thee to the rage
> Of mightie for? I ever had that hart?
> Rather sharpe lightning lighten on my head:
> Rather may I to deepest mischief fall:
> Rather the opened earth devower me:
> Rather fierce *Tigers* feed them on my flesh:

Rather, ô rather let our *Nilus* send,
To swallow me quicke, some weeping *Crocodile.*

(2, 394–404)

These lines would have been spoken by a university student playing Cleopatra; they display a mastery of the art of rhetoric and use repetition to emphasise the argument. The rhetorical or literary quality of these lines tells us that the play was meant to be enjoyed during private reading, not performance. If lines like these sound like a step back from the theatrical immediacy of Kyd's tragedy, their place in the theatre history of tragedy in England should not be underestimated, for they had just as much of an impact on tragedy as Kyd. As the Oxford editors of the play state,

> The revival of these classical models helped to move the English stage from an emphasis on character; Shakespeare notably combined the renewed interest in soliloquy, so evident in *Antonie*, with action. In neo-Senecan drama, psychological probing is done in a highly stylied manner, focusing on universal passions (usually love and/or ambition) with heavy reliance on mythological references. (Hannay et al. 1998: 141)

If we turn to Shakespeare's version of the love story of Antony and Cleopatra, we can see that Shakespeare, in fact, worked within the very similar 'highly stylized manner' of dramatising this relationship, but that even in his highly rhetorical play the rhetoric of Cleopatra's short monologue fits with the self-aggrandisement that best describes her character. However, in a short passage from *The Tragedy of Anthony and Cleopatra* – a speech by the queen – we can see the difference between the ceremonial rhetoric of closet drama, illustrated in the lines above, lines which sound like they are spoken at a distance from the character, and rhetoric intended for stage delivery, structured around a similar combination of repetition and rhetorical questions:

O, Charmian,
Where think'st thou he is now? Stands he, or sits he?
Or does he walk? Or is he on his horse?

O happy horse, to bear the weight of Anthony!
Do bravely horse, for wot'st thou whom thou mov'st? –
The demi-Atlas of this earth, the arm
And burgonet of men. He's speaking now,
Or murmuring, 'Where's my serpent of old Nile? –
For so he calls me. Now I feed myself
With most delicious poison. Think on me,
That am with Phoebus' amorous pinches black,
And wrinkled deep in time.

(1.5.18–29)

Shakespeare's 'gorgeous rhetoric', as Michael Neill calls it (1994: 45), is dynamic largely because Shakespeare makes Cleopatra both a person and a persuasive performer at once. Cleopatra speaks in two voices; she asks and answers her own questions. In terms of cultural importance for the development of tragedy, both women's and men's closet drama represent important phenomena in the rich tradition of English Renaissance tragedy.

TRAGEDY, TYRANNY AND GOVERNMENT: FULKE GREVILLE'S *MUSTAPHA* AND *ALAHAM*

Closet drama written by men shared the same fate as that written by women when it came to such plays' relationship with commercial theatre; they were meant for reading, not staging. Yet these two worlds are not as removed as it may appear, for Fulke Greville's closet drama leaves us with some of the most important records about late Elizabethan conceptions of tragedy. As such, Greville's closet plays have an important place in the English theatre history and history of tragedy, and are essential to any discussion of late Elizabethan tragedy. Like stage plays, for example *The Spanish Tragedy* and *Hamlet*, closet drama is, if not meta-theatrical, then at least self-aware of tragedy. At times, Greville digresses from the main argument in his plays to explain the kind of play he is writing and how his play differs from its classical precursor while also questioning what tragedy emphasises.

Greville's tragedy *Alaham*, written around the same time as *Hamlet*, between 1600 and 1603, is one of the closet plays that reflects this self-aware approach to tragedy. The first chorus, which precedes Act 2, scene 1, declares that:

> our griefe and joy is in this Tragedy,
> To see the ill, amongst her owne, act vnprosperity;
> . . .
> Yet among stories, as the Authors winne no praise,
> Which *truly* write; but they who time with flatteries doe please:
> So in many muddy soule, the meane doth not content,
> Nor equally the two extremes; but that which fits his bent.
> This makes some soare, and burne; some stoope, and wet their wings;
> *For who maintains one vise to multiple another,*
> *Incestuously begets more heyres vpon his owne first mother.*
>   (Chorvs primvs, 75–6; 89–96; emphasis in the original)

The chorus warns against the path domestic tragedy has taken: multiplying scenes of horror and murder to the point of excess runs the risk of cutting domestic tragedy off from its original form ('first mother'). This is in keeping with Philip Sidney's lament, in *An Apology for Poetry*, that the tragedy of his time 'observ[ed] rules neither of honest civility nor of skilful Poetry' and was 'faulty both in place and time, the two necessary companions of all corporal actions' (1973: 133–4). Greville's critique of playwrights who overdo their presentation of vices with which they aim to fulfil their audience's expectations is self-promoting. He offers his own tragedy as a model in contrast to other tragedies.

Similarly, in *Mustapha*, a tragedy which Greville wrote around 1596, he offers his approach to tragedy by looking back at one familiar story:

> Nourisht at Court, *where no Thoughts peace is nourish*,
> Vs'd to behold the Tragedies of ruine,
> Brought vp with fears that follow Princes fortunes;
> Or neuer heard one story of Misfortune.

My heart doth fall away: feare falls vpon me.
Tame Rumors, that haue beene mine old acquaintance
Are to me now (like Monsters) feare, or wonder.

(5.1.1–8)

Greville's view contrasts tragedies based on the stories of misfortune, sin and the fall of princes with fictions like the Italian
novellas from which many of the stories found in Senecan plays
written in England derived. Instead of fictions, he promotes his
own version of tragedy, derived from a story of an actual heroic
figure from the past.

Greville's wish to distinguish his own tragedy from the classical Greek and Roman drama, and from modern Italian drama,
is further expanded in his ideas about tragedy, which he puts
forward in his prose work *A Dedication to Sir Philip Sidney*,
first published in 1652. In chapter 14, Greville introduces tragedy as a kind of text which helps him to address concerns about
the government and the nature of government in his time, and
says that, in contrast to the highly inflated rhetorical style in
which emotions and actions of popular Senecan tragedies were
expressed, the tragedies that he writes 'would prove more
acceptable to every good reader's ends than any bare murmur
of discontented spirits against the present government, or horrible periods of exorbitant passions among equals' (1986: 90).
Greville advises that tragedies be written in accessible language.
He also insists that tragedies should critique actual governments
and engage with the political attitudes concerning government
and those who govern. Such plays can be politically dangerous
and cause misunderstanding. This is why, Greville says, he burnt
his play about the love of Antony and Cleopatra, and adds:

concerning the Tragedies themselves; they were in their
first creation three; Whereof *Antonie and Cleopatra*,
according to their irregular passions, in forsaking Empire
to follow sensuality, were sacrificed to the fire. The executioner, the author himselfe. Not that he conceived it to be
a contemptible younger brother to the rest: but lest while
he seemed to looke over much upward, hee might stumble

into the Astronomers pit. Many members in that creature (by the option of those few eyes, which saw it) having some childish wantonness in them apt enough to be construed or strained to a personating of vices in the present governors and government. (1986: 93)

For Greville, the fall that follows pride is not simply a fall, but a fall into the void, described here as the 'Astronomers pit'. Greville's tragedy of *Antony and Cleopatra* is considered lost. Greville says that he burnt it so that it could not be misunderstood in a similar way, and he tells his readers that his contemporaries misunderstood the accounts surrounding the fall of the Earl of Essex, who was executed following his failed rebellion in 1601.

In chapter 18, Greville proceeds to summarise his short treatise on tragedy, continuing the point about the difference between his version of tragedy and classical tragedy. In writing tragedies, he says, his

purpose in them was not (with the ancient) to exemplify the disastrous miseries of man's life, where order, laws, doctrine and authority are unable to protect innocency from the exorbitant wickedness of power, and so, out of that melancholy vision, stir horror or murmur against divine providence, nor yet (with the modern) to point out God's revenging aspect upon every particular sin, to the despair or confusion of mortality; but rather to trace out the highways of ambitious governors, and to show in the practice of life that the more audacity, advantage and good success such sovereignties have, the more they hasten to their own desolation and ruin. (1986: 133)

At this point in his treatise, Greville picks up on his earlier idea about the difference between classical tragedies and his political tragedies. He says that Greek and Latin tragedies stage the fall and suffering of man as the universal fate. He also distinguishes his tragedies from those written by his contemporaries, because theirs imagine tragedy as God's unforgiving acts against human sins. Unlike classical and modern tragedies, Greville's tragedies describe discords that tear political careers apart and dramatise disharmonies in government. Greville maintains that ambition and cruelty are among the most destructive sins which political tyrants display. However much Greville presses the point that his tragedies draw on the historical age and explore tragic flaws of political persons, the terms with which they probe into the causes and core of such tragic flaws take into account a much larger tragic predicament of humanity. Thus, one critic has summarised Greville's closet dramas by saying that 'The overriding impression one receives from the plays is a sense of man as a helpless, bewildered creature, at the mercy of competing forces within' (Wilkes 1965: 6). When we come across lines like the ones from *Alaham* in which the title hero generalises about fear – 'Impossible is but the faith of feare;/To make hope easie fetch beliefe elsewhere' (1.1.256–7) – or when Mahomet lists the ills that may cause his fall – 'Visions I feele of better hopes arise./ Malice, and rage, whose hearts had barrennesse,/Are, with ambition of reuenge, made wise./Birth, chance, occasion, right, good fortunes be/To some; and wrong can all these be to me?' (1.1.185–9) – we can see that politics is not the only interest of Greville's in his political tragedies. His interest is also the emotions and the psychic state of people searching for ideas about subjectivity at a time when, as was the case in late Elizabethan England, when major social, religious and political changes caused concepts of subjectivity to be constantly re-evaluated. As Jonathan Dollimore has suggested, '[i]n the Renaissance . . . the individual was seen as constituted by and in relation to – even the effect of – a preexisting order', by which he means language, ideology and 'the material conditions of human existence', which depended on one's social status (1986: 54).

At the end of his mini-treatise on tragedy dispersed throughout his biography of his friend Philip Sidney, Greville says about his own closet dramas that

> the Arguments in these Tragedies they be no naked and casual like the Greek and Latin, nor (I confess) contrived with the variety and unexpected encounters of the Italians, but nearer levelled to those humours, councels, and practices wherein I thought fitter to hold the attention of the

reader, then in the strangeness or perplexedness of witty fictions, in which the affections or imagination may perchance find exercise and entertainment, but the memory and judgment no enriching at all. (1986: 133–4)

Greville's view is that his tragedies are based on a balanced relationship between actions and emotions; that they dispense with convoluted twists and turns of plot, something that is characteristic more of an Italian novella than of the kind of tragedy he promotes; and that his tragedies are not as light and frivolous as romance fictions ('witty fictions'), by which he presumably means those of his own time. His two tragedies of cruelty and his theoretical views on the form attest to the fact that Elizabethan Senecan tragedy was not a single phenomenon but a varied one. The Muslim figure, which he chooses as an example for his theory about the didactic role of tragedy, serves his purpose because this figure is already denigrated in culture by the virtue of that figure's non-Christian religion and because of Muslims' association with the stories of evildoing in the sources from which Greville took the material for his tragedies. This context is also crucial to Shakespeare's *Othello*.

Greville's thoughts on tragedy are directed at the playwrights of Senecan tragedies who outdid one another in writing elaborate plots in which vices are punished and violence is an extravagant stage spectacle of horror. *Mustapha* and *Alaham*, however, are both examples of a different kind of tragedy. *Mustapha* describes a strong tyrant who corrupts government; *Alaham* shows how a weak tyrant encourages evil to tear a state apart. In both plays, Greville turns not to Italian models of Senecan drama, which emphasised passions and complicated murder plots, but to the French translations of Seneca which turned to a real story of the past in order to build a plot on moral and didactic foundations. Geoffrey Bullough, an editor and critic of Greville's two plays, has summarised the relative authenticity of Greville's two tragedies in the following words:

we cannot read *Mustapha* and *Alaham* as we should read most Elizabethan dramas; their value must consist

in weight and aptness of thought, in the working out of
moral principles through the story, on the light they throw
on political habits and perils. Readers of Greville, usually
impatient with the Senecan manner, have often been sur-
prised by these features in his tragedies, by the frequent
felicity of his aphorisms, the occasional magnificence of
his dark rhetoric.

These are no mere tricks of style; ... they are the
result of what one may call Greville's 'cosmic obsession',
his determination to relate all earthly errors to flaws in
human nature which must themselves be placed against
the background of eternity. In this respect even more
than in the modernity of his themes ... Greville differs
from his fellow-Senecans. He substitutes for the fuzzy and
melodramatic mythology of the Latin Seneca the moral
puritanism of his own day coupled now and then with
a metaphorical symbolism inherited from the Morality
Plays. (1939: 4–5)

Bullough's idea is that the Senecanism of Greville's plays is different in quality and origin from other Senecan plays written
and performed in the 1590s. As Greville explains, his tragedies
combine a focus on specific political figures of the century in
which he lived with a colloquial style that makes it easier for the
political message and didacticism to reveal meanings about the
causes for the fall of ambitious rulers. In that sense, his tragedies
show clearly their adherence to the tradition of closet drama.

Both *Mustapha* and *Alaham* were written at the time when
England was heavily involved in a political, diplomatic and
commercial relationship with the Ottoman Empire in the eastern Mediterranean. This relationship was ambivalent because
Ottoman power held sway in the eastern Mediterranean where
the English went to trade, so the English had to counter that
power in strategic and diplomatic ways in order to assure the
flow of commerce between West and East. The English also
needed Muslims in order to fight Catholicism. Despite this relationship, the English responded to Muslim dominance in the
eastern Mediterranean and northern Africa with fear, believing

that Muslims might overrun Christianity across Europe because they had already subjected what had been ancient Christian lands in the eastern Mediterranean, northern Africa and parts of the Middle East to Ottoman rule. For example, in 1542 the Protestant preacher Thomas Becon worried that 'most spiteful and Nero-like tyrant the great Turk, that mortal enemy of Christ's religion, that destroyer of Christian faith, that perverter of all good order, that adversary of all godliness and pure innocency' (Brotton 2016: 9) was a threat to England as well. As Jerry Brotton has recently written, 'For many Christians, Islam was the antithesis of Christianity and an implacable foe' (2016: 9). When Greville set out to write his plays featuring 'the Great Turk' (Vitkus 2003: 211), he not only had at his disposal the familiar story of Mustapha, the menacing Turkish conqueror and warrior on the European continent, and the historical writing about the Sultan of Ormuz and his cruel family, but also a significant body of writing full of anti-Turkish sentiments that had accumulated between Becon's and Greville's time. In both tragedies, Greville supports justice and vehemently criticises the ruthlessness and shiftiness of monarchs. He also does not shy away from showing that 'the present state of things', meaning the power of the oppressor and the fate of the oppressed, 'was the inevitable result of man's fall from grace' (Bullough 1939: 37).

In *Mustapha*, Greville uses an example of a society governed by a tyrant to promote justice and humanity as social goals. These social ideals sound like preaching, as the Priest says:

> This Empires constitution Martiall is,
> Where hopes, and feares, must neuer be vnbent:
> *Anarchie* is call'd for here by discontent.
> To *Mustapha* I know the worlds affection;
> To *Solyman* feare only drawes regard,
> *And men stiree easily where the reyne is hard.*
> Then let them stirre, and teare away this veyle
> Of pride from Power; that our great Lord may see
> Vnmiracled, his owne Humanity.
> People! Looke vp aboue this *Diuans* name;

This vent of Error; snare of Libertie;
Where punishment is Tyrants taxe, and fame.

(4.4.199–210)

The Priest promotes anarchy as an instrument that can reform
society in which military force and tyranny maintain peace, and
insists that the stability of an autocratic government will be in
danger from the people who will rebel against it. Greville uses
Mustapha as an example of a ruthless ruler because Greville's
contemporaries have already thought of an Eastern ruler as a
tyrant. The association of tyranny with the East means that
Greville does not have to spend much dramatic space to build
the case against Mustapha. Rather, he can devote that space
to crafting declarative, moralistic tags to pass his humanising
message across: 'The faults of man are finite, like his merits/
His Mercies infinitie that iudgeth spirits' (4.4.73–4). These lines
capture the essence of a fall as punishment for unbridled political ambition, which is the theme at the heart of this tragedy
based on historical events that took place in 1553 'when Soly-
man II, the great Turkish rules whose career of conquest struck
fear throughout Western Europe, murdered Mustapha, his son
and heir' (Rees 1971: 142).

Alaham is constructed of long political speeches about virtue,
rule and government, which sometimes follow one another in
long blocks of text. Greville is not the same kind of a tragedian
as either Kyd or Shakespeare, but he is also not the same kind
of closet drama writer as Mary Herbert or Elizabeth Cary. His
plays are not meant for staging in the theatre, yet they appear to
draw on the structure of drama intended for performance. At the
same time, the literariness of his rhetorical closet drama is characterised by thick moralising and dense philosophical speculation about the nature of rule and rulers who govern tyrannically.
Greville sounds more like a political theorist of the early modern
state turned dramatist. For example, Alaham says:

Iudge not things with common eyes;
The Church it is one linke to Gouernment,
Of noblest Kings the noblest instrument.

> For while Kings sacred keepe her mysteries,
> She keeps the world to Kings obedient;
> Giuing the body to obey the spirit,
> So carrying power vp to infinitie.
>
> (1.1.236–42)

Alaham is a thinking man, like Hamlet, but his thoughts are not turned inward towards exploring the relationship between subjectivity and interiority in relation to the change of politics at court. Rather, he ponders over politics as a factor of an external world of rule and an abstract concept. The paradox here is that *Hamlet*, written for a large public theatre, explores interiority, while *Alaham*, written to be read, perhaps even alone, puts its emphasis on the exterior of politics. Greville refers to the 'common eyes' but there are no people to see his play. Alaham is good at recollecting in detail, and at delivering, long sections of historical narratives, as he does when he retells the story of Mahomet and his succession (1.1.52–91; 95–139), in speeches that grapple with one of the main themes of Greville's plays: the effect of infinite and finite power on the stability and prosperity of government. Alaham summarises this theme in the following lines:

> Preach you with firie tongue, distinguish might,
> Tyrants from Kings; duties in question bring
> Twixt God, and man; where power infinite
> Compar'd, makes finite power a scornfull thing.
> Safely so craft may with the truth giue light,
> To iudge of Crownes without enammelling;
> And bring contempt vpon the Monarchs State;
> Where straight unhallowed power hath peoples hate.
>
> (1.1.261–8)

This is a Senecan rhetoric and theme with which Greville's readers would have been familiar from hearing them in the plays of Kyd, Marlowe, Shakespeare, Tourneur and Webster. Even though he separates himself from the burgeoning tradition of Senecan revenge drama which swept the Elizabethan stage in the 1590s and the following decades, Greville also reminds his readers that he, too, belongs to the tradition of Senecan tragedy. However, he reconfigures that tradition in a different way than Shakespeare does. He does so in language that is more ceremonial, more declarative than Shakespeare's, and in plays that, like the tragedies of Shakespeare, show Greville's conviction that it is necessary for tragedy to expose the dark side of ambition, political power and tyranny.

Greville may still be 'one of the more remote of the Elizabethans' (Wilkes 1965: 1) because he remains in the shadow of his much more prominent contemporaries like Marlowe, Shakespeare, Marston and Kyd, both as a playwright but also as a subject of later criticism. Yet both his plays and his dedication to writing about the theory of tragedy represent a unique contribution to the history of tragedy in the Elizabethan age, solidifying the place of closet tragedy, not as a literary extension of tragedy as stage drama, but as a separate kind of late Elizabethan tragedy in its own right.

TRAGEDY, GENDER AND HISTORY: ELIZABETH CARY'S *THE TRAGEDY OF MARIAM, THE FAIR QUEEN OF JEWRY*

Greville's, Kyd's and Mary Sidney's tragedies influenced the tragic writing of Elizabeth Cary, Lady Falkland (1584–1639), who, although born in the late Elizabethan period, wrote most of her works after the death of Elizabeth I. Greville's closet drama has attracted less critical attention than Elizabeth Cary's plays, which have begun to receive a great deal of attention during the past two decades. Cary wrote *The Tragedy of Mariam*, a closet drama, sometime between 1602 and 1604. The play was first published in 1612. Like Greville, Cary set *Mariam* in the East. The recent popularity of *Mariam* especially among feminist critics can be related to the place of this closet drama in theatre history. Marta Straznicky has written about the form of Cary's tragedy:

> The conjunction of theatrical and literary effects produced by the typographic arrangement of *Mariam* suggests that the play is 'private' in a unique sense: its format resembles

the most classical of the closet dramas, but its accommodation of stage business links it equally with some of the
elite dramatic publications emanating from the 'private'
theatre. (2004: 59)

The emphasis on the textual form of Cary's play and the sug-
gestion that that form draws on the practice of the 'private'
theatre only underscores the fact that closet dramas were literary compositions; that any sense of tragedy they intended to
transmit among their readers would come from experiencing
this kind of play in an act of reading. In fact, when read aloud,
as they sometimes are today in drama reading groups, tragedies
like *Mariam* come alive. The performativity of closet drama
may not lie in stage action, but, in the case of Cary's play, in
the performativity of its rhetoric and meter. *Mariam*, written in
pentameter, contains most of the elements of a typical revenge
tragedy written in the Senecan vogue, including murder, suicide, bloodshed, violence, faked death, threat to woman's chas-
tity and some stichomythia.

Like Greville's tragedies, Cary's play is a historical drama,
but the politics of the play is strongly affected by a gender
dynamic involving both men and women. The main narrative source for the play is Thomas Lodge's 1602 translation of
Antiquities of the Jews (c. 94 AD), a work written by the early
Jewish historian Josephus (37–c. 1200 AD). In addition to the
Bible as both a narrative and verbal source, specifically verbal
sources also include Marlowe's *Doctor Faustus*, Ovid's *Metamorphoses*, Michel de Montaigne's *Essays*, and Shakespeare's
comedy *As You Like It* (Wiggins 2015: 236). Although Mary
Sidney's tragedy *Antonie* and Samuel Daniel's *The Tragedie of
Cleopatra* (1594) influenced Cary's tragedy, the themes and
language in *Mariam* 'suggest intertextual connections' with
Shakespeare's tragedies set in the East, *Antony and Cleopatra*
and *Othello* (Weller and Ferguson 1994: 41). Recent editors of
Cary's tragedy Barry Weller and Margaret W. Ferguson have
summarised some of the main instances of these thematic and
verbal connections with Shakespeare's tragedies (Weller and
Ferguson 1994: 41–3), arguing that 'the dramatic energy' of
Cary's play makes it more a stage than a closet drama, and

speculating that 'Shakespearean dramaturgy' may have influenced Cary's 'complex and flexible treatment of soliloquies' (Weller and Ferguson 1994: 43).

Considered independently of Shakespeare's plays, *Mariam* is an important play not only because it is a closet drama written by a woman but also because, like Mary Sidney's *Antonie* and like Greville's *Mustapha* and *Alaham*, it confirms the place closet drama had in the development of tragedy, especially in respect of political rhetoric and soliloquies. Her play also contributes to the rise of the female tragic hero as a dramatic figure in the tragedies of the English Renaissance. Cary's play is as much a play about ancient Jewish history as it is about gender. 'My sex pleads pardon, pardon then afford,/Mistaking is with us but too common' (1.1.7–8), says Mariam at the opening of the play. Cary's intervention in tragedy as a genre is most obvious in the way she uses a woman to reconfigure the traditional figure of Vice from medieval drama, a figure on which Elizabethan playwrights based the evildoers in their drama. Salome, Mariam's opponent in the play, is a female Vice figure. 'Subvertively witty' and 'a figure of manipulative sensuality' (Weller and Ferguson 1994: 40), Salome, like Iago, Richard III, Vindice and other villains who grew out of the Vice tradition, also carries the play by the power of her language and transgressive sexuality, which in the tragedy is sharply contrasted with Constabarus's misogyny. The most powerful moments in Cary's play are those in which she turns the language of the sexes into the subject of her drama as a tragedy rooted in gender.

As the villain of Cary's tragedy, Salome exhibits an extraordinary imaginative power to excite evil:

> First, jealousy – if that avail not, fear –
> Shall be my minister to work her end:
> A common error moves not Herod's ear,
> Which doth so firmly to his Mariam bend.
> She shall be charged with so horrid crime,
> As Herod's fear shall turn his love to hate:
> I'll make some swear that she desires to climb,
> And seeks to poison him for his estate.
> I scorn that she should live my birth t'upbraid,

To call me base and hungry Edomite:
With patient show her choler I betray'd,
And watch'd the time to be reveng'd by sleight.

(3.3.84–96)

Villains in English tragedies are almost without exception good speakers. Salome is no exception. Her linguistic ability links her to the tradition of rhetorically impressive villains, like Vindice, who are as eloquent as they are dangerous. But that ability also distinguishes her from them because her rhetoric, like Cleopatra's, is ceremonial, arising less out of her interiority as from her polished skill in performing in words. Mariam's reaction to Salome's lines,

Else Salome in vain might spend her wind,
In vain might Herod's mother whet her tongue:
In vain had they complotted and combin'd,
For I could overthrow them all ere long.

(3.3.167–70)

shows that Cary's tragedy is structured around verbal combat and threats between Salome and Mariam. This technique places a woman both in the role of villain and tragic hero/victim. When men like Herod speak about women like Mariam, Cary's play reveals the chill and horror of tragedy characteristic of the Senecan theatre of cruelty.

Herod: Think you [Salome] that swords are miracles
        like you?
        Her skin will ev'ry curtl' ax edge refell,
        And then your enterprise you well may rue.
        What if the fierce Arabian notice take
        Of this your wretched weaponless estate:
        They answer, when we bid resistance make,
        That Mariam's skin their falchions did rebate.
        Beware of this, you make a goodly hand,
        If you of weapons do deprive our land.
Salome: Why, drown her then.
Herod: Indeed, a sweet device.

(4.6.362–72)

Unlike Greville, Cary did not leave us any theoretical writings about tragedy. But moments like this in her drama show that her tragedy, too, is built on plain language and direct address; and on a grotesque humour which she uses to write about a cold-hearted murder. For Cary, history represents a way of dramatising conflict between genders as well as alliances across gender boundaries, alliances which are neither easily created nor sustained.

These examples of late Elizabethan tragedy show how complex and sophisticated the genre had already become. The complications, religious, political or otherwise, of revenge in *The Spanish Tragedy* are further developed in *Hamlet* and even parodied in *Antonio's Revenge*. Revenge tragedy remained a popular type of drama during the English Renaissance, as we will later see in Webster and Ford. Just as revenge tragedy was grounded in the Senecan dramatic tradition, Seneca also found an outlet in the closet dramas of Mary Sidney and Fulke Greville. Likewise, their interest in classical and, in the case of Greville, French neo-classical tragedies will later find its way on to the popular stage in tragedies such as Philip Massinger's *The Roman Actor*. Tragedies of the English Renaissance did not develop in a straight line; instead, they diversified in terms of their form, themes, locations, and in their treatment of the notion of the tragic.

CHAPTER 3

Early Jacobean Tragedy

With the death of Queen Elizabeth I in 1603, a new dynasty came to power and a new political regime was instituted. King James I became the first monarch to officially act as a patron of a playing company. This resulted in Shakespeare's company, the Lord Chamberlain's Men, becoming the King's Men. Despite this patronage, and despite James's enthusiastic support of drama, the corruption of his court resulted in some of the most damning critiques of court life ever to have been represented in tragedy. The Jacobean period also saw the growing popularity of private indoor theatres that would change the way tragedies were written and performed. Innovations in lighting, sound design and stage effects inspired English playwrights to become ever more daring and experimental.

TRAGEDY FOR THE NEW STAGE: *OTHELLO*

On Hallowmas Day, 1 November 1604, the King's Men performed a play called *The Moore of Venice* in the Banqueting House at Whitehall Palace, King James I's official residence in London. When the play was entered in the Stationers' Register, on 6 October 1621, the bookseller Thomas Walkley also had it recorded that the play had been performed numerous times at both The Globe and Blackfriars. In 1622 *The Tragedy of*

Othello, the Moor of Venice, was published in a small, quarto format. Only a year later, the play was published again, but this time in the larger, folio format. This was the so-called First Folio, a collection of Shakespeare's plays put together by his fellow actors and friends, John Heminge and Henry Condell, published in 1623. The folio text is 160 lines longer than the quarto one. Among the additions are Othello's short but moving and visually powerful speech referring to the Pontic Sea (3.3.454–62) and Desdemona's willow song (4.3.36–44):

DESDEMONA (sings):

> The poor soul sat sighing by a sycamore tree,
>   Sing all a green willow.
> Her hand on her bosom, her head on her knee;
>   Sing willow, willow, willow.
> The fresh streams ran by her and murmured her moans;
>   Sing willow, willow, willow.
> Her salt tears fell from her, and softened the stones.
>   Sing willow—
>
> (4.3.36–44)

Reasons for this revision remain unclear to modern theatre historians. It could be that this revision reflects a need to revise because of a change in the company. Namely, Desdemona's willow song in the quarto edition may have been there for a boy who was then either unable to sing or was replaced by a non-singer, whereas the folio text reinstates the singer. Yet the omission of the song in the folio text may indicate that the otherwise long play had to be cut for performance, as Ernst Honigmann suggests (1996: 13). Some passages which connect Othello and magic are also absent from the folio text (Stern 2004: 55). As the result of these changes, Tiffany Stern argues, '[t]he characters that surround Othello in folio are ... more implicitly racist than their counterparts in the quarto; the folio hero is more isolated' (Stern 2004: 55). The supernatural appears in all of Shakespeare's tragedies, but it occupies a unique place in *Othello* because it is related to Othello's religious origins in Islam and his race. This connection between tragedy and magic is not a Shakespearean invention but goes back to classical tragedy. Some critics maintain that the quarto version was a 'theatre-derived text' (Neill 2009: 421) intended for a shortened performance. Others endorse the idea that the folio text incorporates the author's 'second thoughts' (Neill 2009: 430). These are all conjectures based on the interpretation of evidence that we have.

What bearing do this and other evidence related to the two texts and the two theatres have on our interpretation of the tragedy? Both versions of the text may have been performed at Blackfriars and The Globe. The title page of the quarto text is the only Shakespeare title page to name both venues, Blackfriars and The Globe, seemingly suggesting that the text was performed in both venues: 'As it hath beene diuerse times acted at the Globe, and at the Black-Friers, by his Maiesties Seruants.' This, of course, may also be a promotional ploy on the title page without much credibility, but it makes us think about what possibilities each of these venues might have had on the differences in the production of these texts. We are mindful, however, that neither the textual history of the two versions nor the differences in the two venues give sufficient evidence for any conclusive views on this matter.

The first performance of *Othello* may have been timed to reflect King James I's interest in a great victory of a Christian fleet over the Ottomans, which the king 'proclaimed' in his long poem *The Lepanto*, published in 1591. In this poem, King James celebrates the naval victory of a joint Christian fleet, or the Holy League, over the Ottoman navy (Neill 2009: 399) at Lepanto, in Greece, in 1571. This major naval victory occurred 'just at the time when Islam seemed poised to overwhelm Christianity' (Brotton 2016: 9). Despite this victory, however, the Ottomans, as Tom McAlindon points out, 'retained Cyprus [and] multiplied their conquests' (McAlindon 1996: 127). By the time *Othello* was written, the Ottomans were considered a major threat to European Christendom, even though their conquests and power were contained within the eastern Mediterranean, North Africa and the Balkans. Shakespeare wrote *Othello* against the background of these political events and historical and cultural anxieties over the Ottomans. The play fictionalises the sense of anxiety over the Islamic threat to Europe, particularly the victory of the Venetian army, albeit one resulting from a pre-battle storm that shipwrecks the Turkish fleet.

History provided one context for *Othello*. Theatre provided another. Well before the first court performance of *Othello*, there were other plays that staged a Moor as a main character and that dramatised the contact between East and West in the Mediterranean. In 1588 or 1589 *The Battle of Alcazar*, a tragedy by Shakespeare's contemporary George Peele, was performed successfully in London. *Titus Andronicus*, a tragedy that the editors of the New Oxford Shakespeare date to late 1589 and consider a collaboration between Shakespeare and George Peele, with an 'added scene [possibly] by Thomas Middleton' (Taylor and Loughnane 2017: 490), was performed in London, featuring a Moor, Aaron. The combination of the complex and complicated history which England had with the Ottoman Empire, and the rise of interest of English theatre culture in staging plays featuring a Moor at the centre of the drama, connected late sixteenth-century English drama to the world beyond England; it made English drama more cross-national and cross-ethnic, and in that sense both more international and global, than it had been until then. The Moor appeared as a symbol of such a connected world, so much so that Emily Bartels has argued, '[f]rom *Alcazar* to *Othello*, the Moor stands pivotally at the intersection of the European and non-European cultures' (Bartels 2008: 28).

To early modern audiences, race, as skin colour, was important in so far as it was enmeshed with religion. *Othello* turns the religious connection with race into the subject of sexual slurs that diminish Othello's character. Brabantio cannot believe that his daughter would ran away to 'the sooty bosom/Of such a thing as thou [Othello](1.2.10–11), and considers Desdemona's love for Othello unnatural: 'A maiden never bold,/. . . in spite of nature,/ To fall in love with what she feared to look on/' (1.1.95, 97, 99); Roderigo renders Othello in a metonymy and calls him 'the thick-lips' (1.1.66) and calls him a 'lascivious Moor' (1.1.125), and Iago tells Brabantio that 'an old black ram/Is tupping your white ewe' (1.1.88–9), insulting Othello's race and revealing his own perverted view of sexuality as animal copulation.

Race, however, does not feature prominently in the story from which Shakespeare takes the story – the word 'Moor' appears only once in Shakespeare's main source – but Shakespeare complicates it. The main source for Shakespeare's play is in the collection of novellas *Hecatommithi* (1565) by the Italian writer Giovanni Battista Giraldi (1504–73), known as Cinthio. Yet Shakespeare exploits the 'dual meaning' of the term 'Moor', referring to 'Mahometan' or Muslim man, and 'Maurus', which refers to blackness in racial terms (Brotton 2016: 284). Before the play opens, the audience who came to see a tragedy of *Othello, the Moor of Venice*, would have been made aware of Othello as a 'doomed' character just by seeing his black face on the stage. Richard Burbage, the same actor who played Tamburlaine and Romeo, and who also performed as Hamlet at around the same time as Othello, would probably have had his face blackened for the role of Othello. That was done either by masking 'his face with a black vizard or "pitched" it by artificially colouring it with a burnt cork' (Stern 2004: 9), which was the same process as presenting devil, always as a black face. Tragedy is in Othello's race, and it is intensified by the theatre's practice of connecting blackness with devilishness.

Othello's complex racial identity is compounded by an equally complex religious identity as a double convert. He is a convert from the Islamic to Christian religion when the play opens. At the end of the play, he metaphorically converts back to Islam. These conversions are presented as unsettling forces that affect Othello's actions. Daniel Vitkus has argued that, 'The transformations of Othello, the "Moor of Venice", from a virtuous lover and Christian soldier to an enraged murderer may be read in the context of early modern conversion, or "turning", with particular attention to the sense of conversion as a sensual, sexual transgression' (Vitkus 2003: 84). *Othello* exploits the belief in Shakespeare's, and broader early modern, culture that Islam was a lewd religion.

In contrast to Brabantio's belief that it was magic, not love, which has made Desdemona fall for Othello, Othello's narrative of that love story reveals another dimension of this tragedy. The play continues to undermine Othello's heroic stature by couching his 'travailous history' (1.3.139), full of 'disastrous chances/ Of moving accidents by flood and field' (1.3.134–5), in the language of romance, a genre whose narrative was dependent on a high level of fantasy. Shakespeare imagines Othello as a 'roving warrior' (McAlindon 1996: 134) in battles across the Mediterranean and beyond. It is in this sense that Othello's famous lines, in which he explains that Desdemona indeed fell in love with him – 'She loved me for the dangers I had passed,/And I loved her that she did pity them' (1.3.167–8) – could be interpreted as the impact a romance-like story of Othello's life on Desdemona. Iago sums up the entire course of tragic action in the play by admitting, in yet another direct address to the audience, that his strategy works because he presents uncertainty as a sure thing. This removes any doubt and suspicion that what he says may not be so (Altman 2010: 38). 'I know not if't be true', Iago says, 'But I, for mere suspicion in that kind,/Will do as if for surety' (1.3.377–9). Tragedy in *Othello* is not based on validating evidence and proving the veracity of claims that are made. Rather, it tumbles towards the catastrophe on the basis of rumour and hearsay, because that makes it easier for Iago's 'purpose' (1.3.380) to work on Othello.

The Blackfriars was not strictly a Jacobean theatre. The first theatre constructed within a former Dominican priory, the Blackfriars was bought for performance by James Burbage in 1596, though no plays were put on there (because of local opposition) until 1600. A boy company then operated in the space until 1608. In 1609 the King's Men took charge of the venue, enlarging it, transforming and extending the stage and putting in galleries (Bowsher 2012: 118–22). As the theatre historian Oliver Jones observes, however, The Blackfriars' 'role in the development of Jacobean drama is undeniable, hosting plays . . . by Shakespeare' and other playwrights (Jones 2014: 66). *Othello* has been around for five years before it transferred to the second Blackfriars playhouse, and we may wish to consider how this venue affected Shakespeare's tragedy. In the smaller, private Blackfriars, the audience would not have been affected by light or weather changes as in the larger public Globe Theatre, where the audience was exposed to the open air, because the candlelight and indoor setting allowed for longer performances. The Blackfriars would have enhanced the sense of intimacy and even augmented the effect of 'close-up' moments. For instance, in Act 5, scene 2 Othello's reference to Desdemona's 'balmy breath' (5.2.16) and Desdemona's observation 'why gnaw you so your nether lip?' (5.2.44) may be regarded as close-ups where the text makes use of the venue to increase suspense at the point of tragedy. The intensity of the dialogue (5.2.23–42) between Othello and Desdemona in this intimate scene in which these close-up moments occur is further heightened by this intimate venue.

The Blackfriars had been around for some time before *Othello*, and Shakespeare had a different kind of relationship with this theatre at different stages in his career, and this ought to be acknowledged when considering how Blackfriars may have affected what, and how, Shakespeare wrote in plays like *Othello*. Bart van Es's observation that '[w]e need to think of Shakespeare as having had a protracted and changing relationship with the Blackfriars, stretching from early hostility, throughout accommodation, to absorption' (Van Es 2014: 251) is a cue to consider how Blackfriars Theatre might have been 'absorbed' in this tragedy and how this absorption may affect our interpretation of the play in relation to the conditions of staging and playing at the Blackfriars.

Andrew Gurr describes the Blackfriars as 'measuring' approximately 20 metres by 14 metres 'with a stone floor and a high roof' (Gurr 2004: 5). This made it smaller than the small Rose, a public theatre. Such a small indoor playing space 'resituated', Paul Menzer writes, 'the theatrical experience'. In that changed theatrical experience, Menzer continues, '[q]uite apart from the music and sound effects, the shift from outside to indoor had a significant impact on the human voice, not just in volume but also in quality' (Menzer 2014: 173). Voice and volume were not the only properties of the performance style that were 'resituated' in the Blackfriars; the visual effect of the staged scene should also be added, beyond the consideration of costumes and make-up, which theatre historians like Sarah Durstagheer and Farah Karim-Cooper (2014: 137–151) have documented. What effect, then, does this theatre space have on the way we interpret the scene in which Othello enters Desdemona's bedchamber? 'Enter Othello, and Desdemona is in her bed', reads the stage direction in the First Folio. Othello says:

> It is the cause, it is the cause, my soul –
> Let me not name it to you, you chaste stars:
> It is the cause. Yet I'll not shed her blood,
> Nor scar that whiter skin of hers than snow
> And smooth as monumental alabaster –
> Yet she must die, else she'll betray more men.
> Put out the light, and then put out the light –
> If I quench thee, though flaming minister,
> I can again thy former light restore,
> Should I repent me; but once put out thine,
> Thou cunning'st patter of excelling nature,
> I know not where is that Promethean heat
> That can thy light relume.
>
> (5.2.1–10)

The meaning and impact these lines would have had on the audience will depend how we imagine them being performed at Blackfriars as opposed to The Globe.

The fact that the meaning of these lines is built around the image of a lit candle, and around changes between light and darkness depending on whether the candle is lit or extinguished, makes the candlelight not just a metaphor for Desdemona's life, but suggests that any signification attached to light and dark should take into account how such changes might have been enhanced by the venue itself.

Some critics have pushed the argument about how a theatre venue could impact performance. Bruce Smith has offered one such alternative view. At Blackfriars, which could seat 512 people (Smith 1999: 215), these lines would have been experienced more intimately than in the much larger Globe. Desdemona's chamber is a small, enclosed space placed inside the small and enclosed space of Blackfriars itself, which was 'a playhouse with its curved galleries constructed inside a hall' (Gurr 2004: 5). This makes Blackfriars 'an altogether different acoustic environment' and a 'very "live" space', because sound was 'more highly reflective' (Smith 1999: 214), as it bounced against the stone walls and the floor of the hall within which Blackfriars was built. And these properties were tempered by the softness of the wood of which the galleries were made. Othello delivers the speech while also casting a light on Desdemona lying in bed, an effect enhanced by the intimacy of the small playing space found at Blackfriars. Othello's lines would have resonated differently in Blackfriars because of its different acoustic environment. Bruce Smith has further observed that 'With or without a vaulted ceiling, the rectilinear surfaces of the Blackfriars theater would have produced a "round" sound quite different from the "broad" sound of the Globe – just the reverse of the effect suggested by the physical shapes of the two structures' (Smith 1999: 217). This is an interesting speculation, which in its broader contours at least encourages us to think of different possibilities for staging this scene, one of the very few scenes in this tragedy in which Othello and Desdemona are alone on the stage, without at least one other person present as well. The light coming from the burning taper in a smaller, indoor theatre would have lit Desdemona's face more strongly, so that the verbal play based on the images of light and dark, references to candlelight and darkness, Othello's blackness and Desdemona's whiteness, and death and life, would all have been enhanced in this intimate playing venue. Yet this intimacy does not necessarily mean diminution, but rather a broadening of the effect, as it might have been in the case of the resonance of Othello's voice, or as it would have been in the case of the lighting.

REVENGE AND TRAGEDY: THOMAS MIDDLETON'S *THE REVENGER'S TRAGEDY*

Three years after the first performance of *Othello* in 1607, the King's Men performed *The Revenger's Tragedy*, one of the half-dozen non-Shakespearean early modern tragedies that are still regularly performed in modern times. It has even been turned into a film (dir. Alex Cox, 2002), While *Othello* dramatised contemporary politics and history, *The Revenger's Tragedy* captured some of the spirit of the Jacobean court. *The Revenger's Tragedy* represents an important moment in the history of English tragic theatre, and indeed European theatre. John Kerrigan, for example, has argued that, with this tragedy, 'Western theatre turns inside-out: technologies of artifice, and especially devices of concealment (curtained discovery spaces, masque costumes), are visibly put to use, themselves revealed' (Kerrigan, 1996: 203). What makes *The Revenger's Tragedy* a captivating play is a combination of opulent language and stage devices, effects and tricks that enhance the sense of eerie danger and fear that lurk at every turn of the plot.

The Revenger's Tragedy is a dynamic and verbally sophisticated play on a topic – revenge by a lover who feels thwarted by the establishment – that was starting to become very popular in Jacobean theatre. Revenge was not just the subject of drama but of philosophical meditation as well, described most famously in Francis Bacon's (1561–1626) essay 'Of Revenge', published in *The Essays or Counsels Civil and Moral* (1625), where a Jacobean reader would have read that 'Revenge is a kind of wild justice; which the more man's nature runs to, the more ought the law to weed it out. . . . The most tolerable sort of revenge is for those wrongs which there is no law and remedy' (Bacon 1999: 10). Bacon's view raises and interesting question about whether Vindice's revenge is or is not 'tolerable', that is, acceptable. Middleton complicates the moral as well as theatrical basis of this revenge. He presents Vindice, a young man and the revenger of the title, avenging the death of his beloved who has been poisoned by the Duke because she refused to have sex with him. There is no law in the autocratic dukedom to punish him for this crime, so Vindice takes the law of revenge in his hands, and the tragedy unfolds.

Thomas Middleton is now accepted as the author of this play. He wrote it at the time when he 'was seeking fresh employment after his early patrons the boy companies failed' (Gurr 1992: 163). By 1590 the boy companies had disappeared, which meant that the 'theatrical industry' of the London theatres was thriving (Sillitoe 2013: 18), and Middleton's play is a product of this moment of theatrical exuberance. Public theatre and tragedy went hand in hand because the public theatre, by its design, facilitated a more direct relationship between the playgoer and the actor, and because public theatres were situated outside the jurisdiction of the City authorities, which gave actors and theatre companies more freedom to tackle ideologically and politically tricky issues in a more direct manner. In *The Revenger's Tragedy*, Middleton freely exploits these new possibilities afforded by the public theatre, to craft the meaning of the play and to mount social critique in frequent direct addresses to the audience, treating the audience as a collective confidant of the protagonist's private thoughts.

Early Jacobean tragedies performed in public theatres like Middleton's used the physical space itself as an aid to facilitate the impact of revenge tragedy on the audience. Until 1608 public theatres were situated in the so-called 'Liberties', which lay outside the jurisdiction of the City's laws concerning playing, although the King's Men, who performed the play, had been under royal patronage since their foundation in 1603. In *The Revenger's Tragedy* Middleton makes use of the design and properties of the public theatre to close the distance between the audience and the tragic protagonist. This is evident mostly in the direct addresses to the audience and the frequent meta-theatrical and parodic elements in the speeches of Vindice, the main protagonist of the play and one of the most dazzling playing parts in a Jacobean revenge tragedy. This self-conscious engagement of Vindice with the audience reveals Middleton's knowingness of the ways in which the play works on the spectators to make them aware of the theatricality of the text performed before them, and on the text's power to steer the audience's response to the world of the tragedy itself. In doing so, Vindice provokes the audience to question the world around them. That world includes the genre of tragedy itself.

In the opening speech of the play, Vindice indirectly refers to himself as a 'tenant to Tragedy' (1.1.40), inviting the audience to interpret him, a playing part, as a literary type who is a subject to the rules of a dramatic genre. When Vindice tells the audience that 'When the bad bleeds, then is the tragedy good' (3.5.199), he turns tragedy into the subject of his own meta-theatre. He parodies tragedy by subverting the moral nature of its playing parts, making the evil ones its heroes while mocking the good ones as its victims. Vindice's facetious comment also exposes the hypocrisy of moral justice at the heart of *The Revenger's Tragedy*. This 'insistent theatricality' of *The Revenger's Tragedy* and the continuous questioning of both the characters and themes of love, hate, evil, and politics are the key strategy around which Middleton builds his tragedy (Streete 2011: 218). *The Revenger's Tragedy* is an early Jacobean tragedy, written for and performed by an adult company of players in a public theatre, whose frequent parodies of revenge drama suggests that the tragic theatre had already achieved a comfortable critical distance between the creator and the medium in which the tragedy was performed.

The Revenger's Tragedy evokes and perhaps parodies *Hamlet*, especially in its use of a ghost, disguise, role-playing and intrigue, and therefore could be said to be a self-conscious dramatic commentary on the development and status of revenge drama in London theatres (Clare 2006: 65). The absence of the inflated language of horror characteristic of Senecan tragic drama, like *The Spanish Tragedy*, points to Middleton's attempt to distance his work from an influential precursor and to write a new kind of tragedy whose power lies in its meta-theatrical effects. Revenge is as much a subject of theatrical performance as it is a moral act; it is as much a linguistic skill which shows that verbal style is also a way of speaking revenge, as it is an actual act, and plot, itself. Like the parts of Richard III and Iago, the part of Vindice draws on the figure of Vice from the tradition of medieval miracle theatre. Like his two Shakespearean precursors, Vindice shows that Vice-revenger succeeds largely because language is its best weapon.

Middleton was gifted with a 'hyperactive and very individual sensibility', which reflects his appetite for 'perverse sexuality, cruelty, self-abandon and decay' (Lever 1987: 28). The duplicity, hypocrisy, corruption and debauchery of the court, the state and the church are also the central features of the new Jacobean tragedy of revenge. With those features, early Jacobean revenge drama responded to the demand for novelty among an audience that was in the 'habit of seeing a fresh play every day' as theatres grew in numbers and performances increased in frequency (Gurr 1996: 28). *The Revenger's Tragedy* shows that the early Jacobean tragedy of revenge was a hybrid genre. It shows that Middleton 'draws on his experience working across a range of dramatic genres, from satiric city comedies to civic pageants, and disturbing tragicomedies to masques and entertainments' (O'Callaghan 2009: 104).

In *The Revenger's Tragedy*, perverted love becomes an index of a state in decline because lechery and murderous misogyny have undermined virtuous government. A state ruled by an adulterous 'royal lecher' (1.1.1), a sterile perverted lover – 'a dry duke,/A parched and juiceless luxur' (1.1.9–10) – indulging in luxury while in power in the 'marowless age' (1.1.5) of the play, is a dying state. This idea is presented in the image of Vindice's dead beloved, poisoned by the lecherous duke.

> Thou sallow picture of my poisoned love,
> My study's ornament, thou shell of Death,
> Once the bright face of my betrothed lady,
> When life and beauty naturally filled out
> These ragged imperfections;
> When two heaven-pointed diamonds were set
> In those unsightly rings – then 'twas a face
> So far beyond the artificial shine
> Of any woman's bought complexion
> That the uprightest man – if such there be,
> That sin but seven times a day – broke custom
> And made up eight with looking after her.
> Oh she was able to ha' made a usurer's son
> Melt all his patrimony in a kiss,
> And what his father fifty years told
> To have consumed, and yet his suit been cold.
> (1.1.14–29)

A clever and gifted rhetorician, a wounded man, Vindice revives the image of the dead young woman in gruesome detail. The picture of Vindice's dead beloved, once a young woman of bedazzling beauty (''twas a face/So far beyond the artificial shine') and of an erotic appeal powerful enough for a young man to squander wealth for a kiss ('Oh she was able to ha' made a usurer's son/Melt all his patrimony in a kiss'), Vindice's beloved is not only an emblem of romantic love corrupted by politics, but her image is also a reminder to the audience's that this play starts as a tragedy of young lovers. Vindice's motivation for revenge arises from the fact that the lecherous duke's pleasure robbed the young Vindice of his own experience of pleasure.

The Revenger's Tragedy self-consciously plays with the tradition of popular tragic drama that had already reached a high point with *Hamlet*. The skull is a clue to this connection. But, in the case of *The Revenger's Tragedy*, the skull belongs to the poisoned dead beloved ('This very skull,/Whose mistress the duke poisoned with this drug' [3.5.101–2]), even if it is kissed and caressed just as the skull of Yorick is by Hamlet. If in *Hamlet* the skull is a symbol of *memento mori*, a reminder that man's life is short and undercut by death, in *The Revenger's Tragedy* the skull is turned into a stronger image that is directly linked to the structure of revenge: it is not a reminder of the brevity and mortality of life, but an emblem of imminent revenge.

Vindice's revenge is driven by his desire to enter into the Duke's household and to ruin it from within. His brother, Hippolito, helps him in this attempt, acting as his accomplice. To help Vindice in his goal, Hippolito introduces him to Lussurioso, the morally corrupt son of the lecherous Duke and a courtier 'on the make' (Clare 2006: 66) with an appetite for deflowering virgins: 'I am past my depth in lust'/. . . All my desires/Are leveled at a virgin not far from Court' (1.3.91). His very name, Lussurioso, means lechery. The relationship between these two men is purely based on interest and it leads to a farcical and grotesque scene in which the revenger Vindice, in the guise of Piato, is encouraged by Lussurioso to kill his alter ego. More grotesquely, Middleton reveals the rottenness of the state at its most intimate core, in the family, by turning the theme of incest into a perverse stage spectacle. As Vindice says: 'Oh hour of incest!/Any kin now next to the rim o' the sister/Is man's meat in these days' (1.3.65–6).

The Revenger's Tragedy shows that sophisticated language full of stylistic artifice is a key ingredient of Jacobean tragedy.

Shortly before Vindice and Hippolito kill the Duke, Vindice treats the audience with lines whose stylistic artifice dazzles the hearer, as well as captures the disconnect between murder and any interior moral debate that the murder stirs up. He advises Hippolito: 'Let our two other hands tear up his lids/And make his eyes, like comets, shine through blood./When the bad bleeds, then is the tragedy good' (3.5.197–9). Middleton makes it obvious that the art of revenge tragedy consists of rhetorical eloquence, and of the humour such eloquence engenders, as much as of the moral predicament of a society in need of social healing.

Vindice and Lussurioso are the kind of dramatic parts upon which the revenge tragedy depends for much of its meaning. Other men that inhabit the ruthless world of revenge tragedy are also incited by destructive aspirations, and they are motivated by greed and evil. Vindice is a revenger, one who vindicates; Lussurioso stands for excess; Ambitioso is the ambitious and ruthless eldest son of the Duchess; Supervacuo is the vacuous and vain son; and Dondolo is the foolish and gullible servant. The meaning of this dukedom is reflected in its denizens' names. These are also dramatic types that will, like the bastard son or the foolish citizen, appear as instruments in the hands of evildoers in other revenge tragedies. The sub-humanity of these dramatic types indicates that they are not mere abstractions of vices that pollute the state and the court, even though they are more personified notions than imagined humans. Rather, by displaying desire and intelligence, but not self-awareness, some of them, like Vindice and Lussurioso, also show that their obsessions and destructiveness are a product of a dislocated moment in which these parts cannot 'discover a unified, autonomous self' (Dollimore 1989: 147). And these ruthless types – one might include Gratiana, Vindice's mother, in this group – do not discover an autonomous self within themselves because they are driven by schemes and plots that confuse their acts with their interiority. Their 'outward shape' and 'inward heart' (3.5.9), to quote Vindice, are always at odds with each other. What they say and how they act never matches the affect that underpins their words. The Duchess can both plead for her youngest son and plot to have her husband killed by his bastard son, with whom she will have an illicit affair (Dollimore 1987: 147). The contrast between appearance and reality, which drives the tragic plot in *Othello*, is acknowledged to be a key to understanding Middleton's tragedy when Vindice reflects on the very plot that he has created: 'Surely we're all mad people and they,/Whom we think are, are not: we mistake those./'Tis we are mad in sense, they but in clothes' (3.5.79–81).

With the syphilis-ridden Duke dead, Vindice does not bring his vengeance to an end but takes part in the 'masque of revengers' (5.3.38) during which he stabs Lussurioso. Supervacuo is stabbed by Ambitioso so that he may become Duke, but is immediately stabbed in turn by Spurio for the same reason, who is in turn immediately stabbed by another nobleman (5.3.53–5). This blood-soaked dumb show is a spectacular dramaturgical move on Middleton's part. When the dumb show's participants realise that the murder is not a choreographed dance piece but an actual murder, they step out of their roles in the dumb show and become stage characters whose shouts reveal treason and murder. But the dumb show is an example of Middleton's brilliant use of the inherited tradition of revenge tragedy, like the dumb show showing the murder of Gonzago in *Hamlet*, a tradition that he now alters. The dumb show in Middleton provides both the occasion for, and the unravelling of, the complex revenge plot, inviting characters to reveal themselves for the first time. At the end of this tragedy, Hippolito and Vindice are taken off stage, presumably for justice to take place away from the audience's eyes. But when Antonio comments, 'How subtly was that murder closed!' (5.3.129), his words are the last of many meta-theatrical comments that reminds the audience that what they have been watching was above all stage spectacle and an entertainment, as well as being a morally edifying story.

Middleton's play is a drama of pessimism, the sickness of society, exhaustion and discouragement. It captures the sins of the state and its rulers, and the immoral behaviour of men and women, both libidinal and economic, in such a state. In staging all this, Middleton's tragedy put on the stage a vision of Jacobean England that exposed the substance of the critique against that state that already existed in society. It did this in parodic and meta-theatrical vein, representing its critique in a grossly distorted and darkly comic way.

LOVE TRAGEDY AND ITS PARODY: SHAKESPEARE'S *ANTONY AND CLEOPATRA*

In 1608 Shakespeare's playing company, the King's Men, performed *Antony and Cleopatra* (written c. 1606–7), a tragedy based on one of the most complex classical accounts of the love affair between a Roman triumvir, Mark Antony (Marcus Antonius), and the Queen of Egypt, Cleopatra. Plutarch's rendering of this famous love story, in *Lives of the Noble Greeks and Romans* (also known as *Parallel Lives*, written in the early second century AD), was one of the most popular as well as most challenging. Similar to how the tragic action in *Othello* moves from west to east, from Venice to Cyprus, the action in *Antony and Cleopatra* jumps back and forth, oscillating between the Rome of military prowess and emotional restraint and the North Africa of emotional excess and unbridled desire. Love and desire blossom in Cleopatra's Egypt, where in comparison with other tragedies of love discussed in this book, love represents 'a marvelous enrichment and expansiveness of human language and experience' (Bates 2002: 197). This tragedy contains an abundance of language and an even equal if not greater abundance of emotions, as seen in Antony's first memorable expression of love for Cleopatra:

> Let Rome in Tiber melt, and the wide arch
> Of the ranged empire fall! Here is my space.
> Kingdoms are clay. Our dungy earth alike
> Feeds beast as men. The nobleness of life
> Is to do thus, [*embracing Cleopatra*]
>   when such a mutual pair
> And such a twain can do't – in which I bind,
> On pain of punishment, the world to weet
> We stand up peerless.
>   (1.1.35–42)

The hyperbolic grandeur appears to trap Cleopatra in the web of Antony's amorous lines. However, Cleopatra's rebuttal, 'Excellent falsehood!' (1.1.43), sharply turns Antony's words on their head, showing that, if anyone is going to be doing the trapping, it is going to be her. This speech also introduces the theme of empire as one of the dominant ideas of this tragedy, and already signals Antony's failure to fulfil his duty as a Roman warrior to forge the empire. The Antony of *Antony and Cleopatra* is no longer, as he admits at the end of the play, the Antony of Roman imperial might. He says, 'I, that with my sword/Quartered the world, and o'er green Neptune's back/With ships made cities, condemn myself to lack/The courage of a woman' (4.15 57–60). Made unheroic because he has pursued Cleopatra, Antony is presented as an emasculated parody of a triumvir of imperial and militant Rome. The 'nobleness of life' for a noble Roman would be to expand the empire on behalf of Rome. But his mission is undercut because, instead, he has been seduced by Cleopatra's 'dangerous glamour' (Neil 1994: 11) and has at the start of the play abandoned his militant and imperial duty. The ironic undercutting of the themes of heroic duty and of the love theme shows the extent to which tragedy of the English Renaissance evolved as a genre in the early period of James's reign, because by staging a satirical view of a tragic love the play also scrutinises the genre of love tragedy as such by putting on display personal contradictions within the lovers torn between, and confused by, love and duty; desire to preserve the empire and the threat that comes to an empire when a Roman falls in love with a woman of another race. This makes *Antony and Cleopatra* also a play about a race which brings out anxieties among the Romans over racial difference at their door. 'Cleopatra's darkness', writes Kim Hall, 'makes her the embodiment of an absolute correspondence between fears of racial and gender difference and the threat they pose to imperialism' (Hall 1995: 153–4). The very opening lines of the tragedy, in fact, register these fears and anxieties. When one of Antony's fellow Romans, Philo, reflects on the infatuation of his friend with the Egyptian:

> Nay, but this dotage of our General's
> O'erflows the measure: those his goodly eyes,

That o'er the files and musters of the war
Have glowed like plated Mars, now bend, now turn
The office and devolution of their view
Upon a tawny front; his captain's heart,
Which in the scuffles of great fights hath burst
The buckles on his breast, reneges all temper,
And is become the bellows and the fan
To cool a gypsy's lust.
     Look where they come:
Take but good note, and you shall see in him
The triple pillar of the world transformed
Into a strumpet's fool. Behold and see.

                         (1.1.1–14)

we hear the extent to which the love that overflows the language with which the physical presence of Antony and Cleopatra is captured on the stage ends up being, for those who observe it, be it Romans or spectators, a parody of such an affair, because it distorts the militant values of Rome. The buckles which had once secured Antony's breastplate to the other parts of his armour had 'burst' in the past, 'in the scuffles of great fights', because his heart was beating so fiercely. The beating heart, now emasculated, has become 'the bellows and the fan/ to cool a gypsy's lust'. Philo's speech shows that a Roman's love of a woman with dark skin ('tawny front') is a kind of deviation for a Roman. Antony's unrestrained character informs his desire, because his bosom both cools and rekindles, like bellows, such love. In the last few words of his speech, 'Behold and see', which come after the entry on the stage of Antony and Cleopatra, followed by her retinue of ladies and eunuchs, Philo invites spectators to watch the spectacle of this entry, as Rome is showing those spectators an exotic pageant; as if Egypt itself is an oriental show of sound, colour and desire on display. Just as Desdemona's father believed that the only way Othello could have seduced his daughter was through magic, which was often associated with those coming from the East, so Romans are also always ready to associate Cleopatra with witchcraft. As Pompey says, speaking of Cleopatra: 'Let witchcraft join with beauty, lust with both,/Tie up the libertine in a field of feasts,/Keep his brain fuming! (2.1.22–4). The denigration of Cleopatra on both racial and gender lines is one of the persistent preoccupations of the Romans in this tragedy.

The contradiction between what is performed and what might be meant by performance also extends to language, whose stylistic and ornamental richness and grandeur invite us to both admire its captivating effect that engages all the senses, while also asking us to think about how the use of such language constitutes a trick. In the theatre, and particularly in this play, love cannot be trusted as a feeling for it is a performed spectacle of words and images. Perhaps it is no accident, then, that hyperbole, the rhetorical figure of exaggeration in which a lie is presented as truth, is Cleopatra's most loved trope. For example, Cleopatra's way of telling one of the ladies attending on her, Charmian, the effect Antony has on her is to say: 'He shall have every day a several greeting,/Or I'll unpeople Egypt' (1.5.777–8). The tragedy of Antony and Cleopatra lies not only in the fact that their love affair ends in death, but also because their language of love and desire mismatches their situation: they speak about the abundance of love they have for one another, yet they are hardly ever alone on the stage together. They ecstasy of their love is all in language and performance. Not only do they always have an audience on stage to witness their exchanges, but they also rely as much on intermediaries as on each other to convey their feelings.

One of the signature speeches in the play, Enobarbus's story of his experience of watching Cleopatra's barge sailing down the River Cydnus serves as an example of the play's indulgence in language that evokes the exoticism of the East. Couched in visually elaborate language that also shows the extent of the play's indebtedness to the Baroque, Enobarbus's extraordinary language also serves as a verbal–visual stage image. So Enobarbus says:

> The barge she sat in, like a burnished throne
> Burned on the water; the poop was beaten gold,
> Purple the sails, and so perfumèd that
> The winds were lovesick with them; the oars were silver,
> Which to the tune of flutes kept stroke, and made

The water which they beat to follow faster,
As amorous of their strokes. For her own person,
It beggared all description: she did lie
In her pavilion – cloth-of-gold of tissue –
O'er picturing that Venus where we see
The fancy out-work nature; on each side her
Stood pretty, dimpled boys, like smiling Cupids,
With divers-coloured fans, whose wind did seem
To glow the delicate cheeks which they did cool,
And what they undid did.

                                                    (2.2.198–212)

The bombast with which the exoticism of Cleopatra's procession is described shows how Shakespeare has taken liberty with his source in Plutarch, elevating Enobarbus from a minor to major character in the story, who narrates one of the most visually striking scenes in all of the tragedies of the English Renaissance. The speech is an example of what Renaissance rhetoricians called amplification (*amplificatio*), or an elaborate expansion of the topic. Shakespeare not only displays his rhetorical skill here but, by creating this image in which the Renaissance aesthetics of love is used to compare Cleopatra's attendants to 'smiling Cupids', conjures a memorable image of a woman of love as if at second hand. The immediacy with which the Shakespeare of *Romeo and Juliet* captures the immediacy of Juliet's love and the flesh of her body is gone in this aestheticised image of Cleopatra as an idea of glamorous love. The inflated image of Cleopatra who 'made a gap in Nature' (2.2.224) is the culmination of Enobarbus's satirical commentary on Cleopatra's greatness, just as his comment about Cleopatra's 'infinite variety' (2.2.243) reveals his infatuation with the idea of desire that defies the Roman preference for balance and control.

Moments like the one when Enobarbus ambiguously represents Cleopatra as an object of sarcasm and admiration show that, although Jacobean Shakespeare approaches love from an ironic distance, this tragedy at least captures some key tragic elements, like the death scene. Even a spectacular event like Antony's botched suicide, which parodies classical tragedy, nevertheless serves as a resolution to the action and the cleansing of emotions. 'How? Not dead? Not dead?' (4.1.103), asks Antony as he falls on his sword, after which tragedy turns into melo-drama, when he reflects on the death scene gone wrong: 'I have done my work ill, friends./O make an end of what I have begun' (4.15.105). The tragedy thus manages to strike a strange bal-ance between the ironic and the tragic.

In contrast to this, the most unheroic death of a heroic man found in early Jacobean tragedy, Cleopatra's dying is, as Michael Neill puts it, 'the most self-consciously *performed*, the most elaborately gestural dying in all of Shakespearean tragedy' (1994: 78). Before the scene of dying, however, the play pre-pares the spectators for this scene by showing Cleopatra reflect-ing on the theme of death. She asks: 'is it sin/To rush into the secret house of death/Ere death dare come to us?' (4.16.81–3). The fabulous arrogance in that 'dare' is emphasised by allitera-tion, created by 'death . . . death . . . dare'. Death, like Roman messengers, takes his life into his own hands in daring to approach the regal Cleopatra. Once again, Shakespeare exposes to the ironic scrutiny of the audience's eyes and ears one of Cleopatra's exaggerated, even delusional, self-projections, while also treating them to sophisticated, highly lyrical and moving poetry. At the moment of dying, Cleopatra does not lose the sense of the cosmic dimensions with which she has already been associated. Dressed in her most resplendent regalia, her crown in her hand, and a poisonous asp in a wicker basket next to her, before she dies from the snake's bite Cleopatra denies death ('I have immortal longing in me' [5.2.279–80) and defines her-self in cosmic terms: 'I am fire and air – my other elements/I give to baser life' (5.2.288–9). When Charmian reflects on her dead queen, personifying Death – 'Now boast thee, Death, in thy possession lies/A lass unparalleled' (5.2.313–4) – Shakespeare makes Cleopatra at once part of the world of England and of the world far beyond it. For example, 'lass' is a word of Anglo-Saxon origin, a word that makes distant Egyptian Cleopatra comprehensible and closer to the English audience of The Globe. *Antony and Cleopatra* can be treated as a counterpart, and even a satirical obverse, of the love tragedy as presented in *Romeo and Juliet*. It shows what the tragedy of adult lovers can look like in contrast to the tragedy of young lovers. The abundance of imaginative poetry which Shakespeare emphasises in *Antony and Cleopatra* shows that, in this tragedy, he privileges lyricism over dramatic plot and the pace of dramatic action.

If late Elizabethan tragedies developed in terms of form, themes, locations in which their plots are set, and the idea of the tragic, early Jacobean tragedy offered a new direction of development with the emergence of smaller, private indoor theatres. As we have seen in the case of *Othello*, these new theatres provided not only an advance in stage spectacle, but also created the physical conditions for a new way of dramatising the tragic. Although *Othello* shows signs of having been performed in both public and private theatre venues, the later tragedies that we explore, such as Webster's *The Duchess of Malfi* and Massinger's *The Roman Actor*, will suggest the many ways in which playwrights took full advantage of new performance venues in London.

CHAPTER 4

Late Jacobean Tragedy

As we saw in Chapter 3, shifts in theatrical venues began to affect both audience demands and playwrights' attempts to satisfy those demands. For example, the changes between the 1608 quarto edition of *King Lear* and the 1623 folio edition of this play were perhaps influenced as much by a difference in the kind of venue, private or public theatre, as much as by authorial revision (Warren and Taylor 1983) or even the actions of printers (Vickers 2016). All of these shifts in theatrical taste, practice and composition become clear the more one considers the tragedies of John Webster, particularly *The Duchess of Malfi*. What does seem clear is that, following the failure of *The White Devil* in 1611/1612, a failure due in part to his lacking 'a full and understanding auditory', Webster's *The Duchess of Malfi* 'hoped to cater specifically for the more learned hearers at the Blackfriars' (Gurr 2004a: 99). However, it was not only the hearing that would change as Webster moved to Blackfriars for, as we will see, the new theatre offered just as many visual advantages as audible ones.

'I AM DUCHESS OF MALFI STILL': JOHN WEBSTER'S *THE DUCHESS OF MALFI* AND THE REVENGE TRAGEDY

Before moving on to these advantages, it must be stressed that *The Duchess of Malfi* was not simply a Blackfriars play. On the title page of the 1623 quarto edition of the play, printed by

Nicholas Okes and published by John Waterson, appears the declaration that the play had been 'presented priuately, at the Black-Friers, and publiquely at the Globe, By the Kings Maiesties Seruants'. This in fact was a key point later to be seized upon in an important article on the tragedy's stage effects, especially its lighting: R. B. Graves's '*The Duchess of Malfi* at the Globe and Blackfriars'. Nevertheless, as noted in Chapter 3, there is evidence that such 'chameleon-like' plays (Thompson 2016: 67), plays performed at both public and private theatres, began, by around 1610, to show more and more signs that performances at the latter were having the larger impact on both the writing and the stage practice. As we will see, scene divisions, music and a whole host of other elements generally associated with the indoor theatre began to find their way into plays performed at both venues (Turner 2006: 180; Taylor 1993: 3–7; Snuggs 1960: 37–45; Chambers 1930: I, 200).

What were some of these elements? How did they begin to affect the tragedies, not only of Webster but of other later Jacobean playwrights? To begin with perhaps one of the more striking of instances, it is unlikely that Webster could have ever conceived of the infamous 'dead man's hand' scene (4.1), during which the Duchess is told by Bosola that her brother Ferdinand will come to her but will not see her. In order to achieve this, 'neither torch nor taper' is allowed to 'shine', and so the Duchess orders Bosola to 'take hence the lights' (4.1.25–6, 29), an order that would have plunged the Blackfriars stage in darkness. As Ferdinand enters, he remarks to his sister that 'this darkness suits you well' (4.1.30), leaving one to wonder how the scene would have, or indeed could have, been played at the outdoor Globe. Of course, there are many instances of playwrights using descriptive words and actions to suggest light, darkness and a whole host of other conditions on the early modern stage, so the lack of light may not necessarily have been impossible to recreate in an outdoor theatre. Nevertheless, one is puzzled by how Ferdinand's reveal would have been handled elsewhere. Ferdinand has given his sister a dead man's hand, which she believes to be Antonio's and which she proceeds to 'affectionately kiss'; this macabre moment of affection, as so often in Webster, is made all the more grotesque by the Duchess's concern that

Antonio must not be well after his travels, for his hand is 'very cold' (4.1.51). When she calls for lights, she can see how 'horrible' Ferdinand's game with her has been (4.1.52); in fact, it is so horrible that even Bosola begins to want no part in Ferdinand's schemes. On the surface, such a scene only seems possible in an indoor theatre, and in an indoor theatre alone, for where else could one control the lights and make such use of them for dramatic effect? Nevertheless, when one considers the example of the 'cliff scene' in *King Lear*, a scene in which Edgar, disguised as Poor Tom, creates with words cliffs so believable that audiences may have been as convinced of their existence as Edgar's blind father Gloucester is:

> Come on, sir; here's the place: stand still. How fearful
> And dizzy 'tis, to cast one's eyes so low!
> The crows and choughs that wing the midway air
> Show scarce so gross as beetles: half way down
> Hangs one that gathers samphire, dreadful trade!
> Methinks he seems no bigger than his head:
> The fishermen, that walk upon the beach,
> Appear like mice; and yond tall anchoring bark,
> Diminish'd to her cock; her cock, a buoy
> Almost too small for sight: the murmuring surge,
> That on the unnumber'd idle pebbles chafes,
> Cannot be heard so high. I'll look no more;
> Lest my brain turn, and the deficient sight
> Topple down headlong.
>
> (4.6.11–24)

In other words, such effects could still have been achievable in the outdoor theatres, only there actors would have had to have done much more of the work. Perhaps the pantomime scene that immediately follows the 'dead man's hand' scene may give us some indication of this, for it is possible that the actor performing the role of the Duchess could have feigned the darkness on The Globe stage without the need for actual darkness on the stage itself. As William Rowley, who would go on to collaborate with Webster on *A Cure for a Cuckold* (c. 1624), would note

of the performance of the Duchess's role: 'I never saw thy duchess till the day/That she was lively body'd in thy play;/Howe'er
she answer'd her low-rated love,/Her brothers' anger did so fatal
prove, /Yet my opinion is, she might speak more, /But never, in
her life, so well before' (qtd in Morrison 2016: 67). Clearly, the
performer was able to embody the role quite effectively, and such
embodying may have involved suggesting effects on The Globe
stage that it could not have achieved otherwise; in keeping with
the subject of performance, the 1623 quarto of *The Duchess of
Malfi* is unique not only because it is one of the few instances of
a cast list being provided, but because it actually includes two
cast lists, for 1614 and for sometime around 1621, that tell us
much about the make-up of the King's Men at this time (Bentley
1984: 210–11). Again, The Blackfriars offered new advantages
and new techniques, but the outdoor theatres were still capable
of holding their own; in keeping with this, perhaps this is why,
as a selling point, 'the Blackfriars did not prevail over the Globe
with publishers till the 1630s', for the latter remained popular
with audiences long after the addition of the former to the King's
Men's holdings in 1608 (Gurr 2010: 20). This popularity may
have been due to the greater prominence given to commanding
performances on The Globe stage, a prominence perhaps best
suggested by the anonymous funeral elegy written in honour of
Richard Burbage in 1619: 'Thyself a world the Globe thy fit-
test place!/Thy stature small, but every thought and mood/
Might throughly from thy face be understood' (qtd in Stopes
1970: 121; Wickham 2000: 181–3). Perhaps, as with Burbage,
the actor performing the role of the Duchess was also able to
make himself understood. Although Burbage had also been performing at Blackfriars for over a decade, it was clearly felt that
The Globe allowed for his performative brilliance to express
itself most strongly.

There are other features of *The Duchess of Malfi* worth considering in relation to the use of both theatres. To begin, the
tragedy, as David Coleman argues, 'displays a much clearer
use of the five-act structure than does *The White Devil* (which
was perhaps composed for continuous performance – that is,
with no intervals, in an outdoor theatre)' (2010: 80). In indoor

theatres, such pauses allowed for the lighting of candles and scenery changes that was beginning to be used more prominently. Webster also provides for dramatic punctuation through the use of *sententiae,* or aphoristic couplets that help to bring a sequence to an end and prepare the audience for the scene to come. The tragedy abounds with these, and so a small few will have to serve as examples. In the above-mentioned 'dead man's hand' scene (4.1), Ferdinand asks for a fire to be made, one that is as great as his revenge, 'which never will slack, till it have spent his fuel:/Intemperate agues make physicians cruel' (4.1.141–2). Later, when Bosola resolves to protect Antonio from his enemies, he declares that he wishes to drink from the vessel of forgiveness: 'O penitence, let me truly taste thy cup,/ That throws men down, only to raise them up' (5.2.343–4). In keeping with the aphoristic mode, these couplets tend to offer a kind of judgement on the characters or the scene, often, especially with Webster, of a disapproving kind. At times, they can seem like the famous aphorisms of the French writer François de La Rochefoucauld (1613–80), for they too can carry a strong sense of morality tinged with bitterness.

As mentioned in Chapter 3, indoor theatres had much better acoustics than their outdoor counterparts, and so music, particularly as performed by professionals, began to feature in many Blackfriars productions. Although, or perhaps because, the performers at Blackfriars were famous for their fine playing (Gurr 1980: 170), Webster actually includes the stage direction during the 'mad' scene (4.2) that the song should be 'sung to a dismal kind of music'. The dismalness of the song is apparent in its lyrics, which call it a howl rather than a melody:

> O, let us howl some heavy note,
>> Some deadly dogged howl,
> Sounding as from the threatening throat
>> Of beasts and fatal fowl!
> As ravens, screech-owls, bulls, and bears,
>> We'll bell, and bawl our parts,
> Till irksome noise have cloy'd your ears
>> And corrosiv'd your hearts.

At last, when as our choir wants breath,
   Our bodies being blest,
We'll sing, like swans, to welcome death,
   And die in love and rest.

(4.2.61–73)

Perhaps this was Webster's joke, like his comparison between hell and the glassworks near Blackfriars Theatre (4.2.78–80), and perhaps he was having a little fun with what the audience could now hear in Blackfriars Theatre as opposed to the 'open and black' Red Bull (Weis 1996: 3). However, it was not simply music that Webster expected his audience to hear, for he provides far more learned references and echoes in *The Duchess of Malfi* than had been present in *The White Devil*. For example, Bosola appears to reference Michel de Montaigne's essay 'An Apology for Raymond Sebond' when he talks of rewards for hawks and dogs (1.1.55–6), and he paraphrases that same essay later when he asks: 'if simplicity direct us to have no evil, it directs us to a happy being; for the subtlest folly proceeds from the subtlest wisdom' (2.1.75–7). Likewise, in the same scene the Duchess and Antonio later refer to the French practice, a practice mentioned by Montaigne, of 'French courtiers/Wear[ing] their hats on 'fore the King' (2.1.110–11). There are also numerous references to Sir Philip Sidney's *Arcadia*, as when the Duchess tells Antonio that he 'ent'red you into my heart/Before you would vouchsafe to call for the keys' (3.2.61–2), an echo of a similar description of love and keys in Book 1, ch. 11, line 69, or when Bosola places virtue above pedigree (3.2.261–2), an echo of Book 1, ch. 2, line 15. In addition to these, there are also numerous allusions to the closet dramas of William Alexander, 1st Earl of Stirling (c. 1567–1640), known for his collection of closet dramas, *The Monarchic Tragedies* (1607), which included the *Alexandrian Tragedy* and *Julius Caesar*. As Leah Marcus notes, the references to Sidney and Alexander seem to have derived in part from Webster's connection with the 'Sidney circle' (2009: 52), but they also suggest Webster's desire to pack his tragedy with learnedness more suited to the Blackfriars audience; in fact, Andrew Gurr has even argued that the allusions are such that Webster 'could have expected few of the quotations from these sources to be identified by even the most alert and well-read hearer' at Blackfriars (2004: 84). Likewise, there is a nod to Horace's *Odes* in the final couplet, '*Integer vitae scelerisque purus*' (1.22), or, as Delio puts it: 'Integrity of life is fame's best friend,/Which nobly, beyond death, shall crown the end' (5.5.119–20). However, this is an epigram that can be read on a variety of levels. As Gurr suggests, 'what Webster seems to have been doing was to aim at a split-level audience, offering one thing, the routine epigrammatic moral, for the main audience, and an oblique *lusus*, whether a complex final irony or not, to the learned' (2004: 85). Gurr sees this split within Blackfriars Theatre itself, which is possible, although Webster may have conceived of the split-level audience as the contrast between Blackfriars and The Globe. This contrast was deepened by the King's Men's decision to stage the play at both theatres (Gurr 1992: 235).

The Duchess of Malfi is a tragedy well suited to both its time and its venue, and it is not surprising that John Ford would later call it a masterpiece in the poem that he included in the 1623 quarto. The social and patriarchal constraints of the society that Webster depicts, constraints that punish the Duchess for try-ing to love and marry according to the dictates of her heart as opposed to those of her class and position, also carry wide rele-vance for modern audiences. As with so many revenge tragedies set in Italy, this play clearly evoked the Jacobean court as much as it did any Italian one. As Bosola wryly notes, people often look far afield for evil instead of in their own backyard, and they look at others when they should be looking in a mirror:

> Man stands amaz'd to see his deformity
> In any other creature but himself.
> But in our own flesh though we bear diseases
> Which have their true names only ta'en from beasts, –
> As the most ulcerous wolf and swinish measle, –
> Though we are eaten up of lice and worms,
> And though continually we bear about us
> A rotten and dead body, we delight
> To hide it in rich tissue
>
> (2.1.46–54)

As if to underscore this, Bosola then describes an Italian fashion that is actually an English one; his 'there's somewhat in't!' may reflect this nod to similarities rather than differences between the Italians on the stage and the English in the audience (2.1.62–4). The source for *The Duchess of Malfi* can be found in the twenty-sixth tale of Matteo Bandello's (c. 1480–1562) *Novelle* (1554), a tale that was later adapted and included in William Painter's (1540?–95) *The Palace of Pleasure* (1567). The story itself deals with a historical Duchess of Amalfi who, after being widowed at nineteen, secretly married and had a child with the major-domo of her family's household. When her brothers discovered the truth, she was forced to flee, after which her story ends ambiguously. Webster takes this story and creates a masterful work of revenge and corruption, focusing on the cruelty of the Duchess's brother Ferdinand, who vows from the opening that he 'would not have her marry again' (1.1.258). The Duchess is a commanding figure in her society, for she is in charge of a great title and great wealth without being under the direction or control of a father, a husband or another male guardian. This position causes resentment in those around her, particularly her brother Ferdinand, who will do whatever he can, no matter how heinous, to make sure that his ends are achieved. Such resentment and fear were addressed in many seventeenth-century pamphlets and tracts, such as Jeremy Taylor's *Rule and Exercise of Holy Living* (1650), which admonished widows and warned them not to take advantage of the status that widowhood had conferred upon them; however, it should also be noted that some religious thinkers, such as Thomas Becon, argued that widows should not be seen in such a negative light (Mikesell 1983: 265–7). In any case, while there does seem to be political and financial reasons for attempting to impose their will on the Duchess – Ferdinand does make reference to an 'infinite mass of treasure' (4.2.284) at one point – it does seem as though the opposition that the Duchess faces is far more patriarchal than anything else. It is also, at least for Ferdinand, sexual, and his imaginings of her having sex or giving birth both arouse and disgust him (2.5.43–6, 64–7). This ambivalence will play a role in Ferdinand's plot against his sister, as it will also in his later madness. It will also help to underline the tragedy's concern with taboos that we will see again in Chapter 5, in the tragedies of John Ford.

Despite the frequent threats against her and the numerous plots to make her question her own sanity, such as her torments at the hands of madmen, Ferdinand's trick involving the dead man's hand, the use of wax figurines to confuse her and make her despair, and the simple and constant threat of death, the Duchess manages to maintain her authority and sense of self. As she tells the disguised Bosola, 'I am Duchess of Malfi still' (4.2.131); likewise, when the executioners enter the stage with 'a coffin, cords, and a bell', she says that such a sight 'affrights not' her (4.2.164). The tragedy has several strong characters as well as villainous ones, but their ends are rarely improved by their moral goodness. A good example of this is Antonio, who is shown to be a capable and reliable member of the Duchess's household; equally important, he does not seek the Duchess for her money or prestige, as this truly is a love match. In fact, it is the Duchess who seeks out Antonio as a partner, and her reminder that she still has wants, needs and desires (Bartels 1996: 417) suggests both Antonio's lack of mercenary qualities and her quite modern sense of independence: 'This is flesh and blood, sir;/'Tis not the figure cut in alabaster . . . Awake, awake, man!' (1.1.454–6). However, the horrors and the losses that Antonio will suffer suggest that, even without the more mercenary forms of ambition, those who attempt to rise up beyond their given place will be punished by the society they are in (Whigham 1985: 167). The Duchess may be willing be 'put off all vain ceremony' (1.1.457), but there are many others who clearly are not. In many ways, Antonio's foil is Bosola, who comes from the same class and who also must find a way to survive in society. However, whereas Antonio is shown to not harbour ambitions for the Duchess's wealth, Bosola is far more cynical and far more willing to serve whoever will get him higher up the rung. He enters the stage having already murdered for the Cardinal and having already been severely punished as a result:

I fell into the galleys in your service: where, for two years together, I wore two towels instead of a shirt, with a knot on the shoulder, after the fashion of a Roman mantle. Slighted thus? I will thrive some way. Black-birds fatten best in hard weather; why not I in these dog-days? (1.1.34–8)

If everyone else at the court – as Antonio calls them, the 'flatterers, panders, intelligencers, atheists, and a thousand such political monsters' (1.1.153–5) – all succeed by guile and cunning, then why not Bosola? When Ferdinand offers him gold, his first reaction is to ask, 'whose throat must I cut?' (1.1.240). However, Ferdinand does not need a throat to be cut, at least not for the moment; instead, he wants Bosola to spy on his sister and Antonio to make sure that they will never marry. As with *Hamlet*, *The Duchess of Malfi* makes much use of spying and surveillance, a wider commentary perhaps on early modern English society. Bosola is just the type of Jacobean 'upstart' attacked as a threat to all society in pamphlets like 'The Just Downfall of Ambitious, Adultery, and Murder' (1616), which expresses high levels of mistrust for those who have come from obscurity and who seek advancement. Bosola is just such a man. He has nothing but contempt for his masters, from the Cardinal to Ferdinand, and he manages to see the worth in the Duchess as a potential master, tragically, only after she has been murdered:

> My estate is sunk
> Below the degree of fear: where were
> These penitent fountains while she was living?
> O, they were frozen up! Here is a sight
> As direful to my soul as is the sword
> Unto a wretch hath slain his father.
> Come, I'll bear thee hence,
> And execute thy last will.
>
> (4.2.355–62)

Now, and only now, can he serve her and try to save Antonio; unfortunately for Bosola, Antonio will eventually die, albeit by accident, at his hands (5.4.44). Webster's tragedy is laced with such ironic reversal and deflation, nowhere more so than when, after having killed both Ferdinand and the Cardinal, the mortally wounded Bosola exclaims with his dying breath that his mistaken killing of Antonio was like something out of a play:

> In a mist; I know not how:
> Such a mistake as I have often seen
> In a play. O, I am gone.
> We are only like dead walls or vaulted graves,
> That, ruin'd, yield no echo. Fare you well.
> It may be pain, but no harm, to me to die
> In so good a quarrel. O, this gloomy world!
> In what a shadow, or deep pit of darkness,
> Doth womanish and fearful mankind live!
>
> (5.5.93–101)

The ironies continue with the late arrival of Delio with Antonio's eldest son, but at least there is some hope that those who are still alive can 'make noble use/Of this great ruin' (5.5.109–10). However, whether the play ends with such clear-sightedness or in the shadow, moral and otherwise, referred to by Bosola above and elsewhere (4.2.181–4), remains open to debate.

'LOVE TRICKS': THE TRAGEDIES OF FRANCIS BEAUMONT AND JOHN FLETCHER

On 28 April 1619 a tragedy by Francis Beaumont and John Fletcher was entered into the Stationers' Register. By that point, Beaumont was dead and Fletcher had gone on to collaborate with Shakespeare on his final plays, although by 1619 Shakespeare was also dead and Fletcher was the chief playwright of the King's Men. Later that same year, Francis Constable published a quarto edition of the tragedy and noted that it 'hath beene divers times Acted at the Black-Friers by the Kings Maiesties Servants'. This tragedy was The Maid's Tragedy, and it would be published an additional six times before being included in the second folio edition of Beaumont and Fletcher's works (1679). When the play was first performed remains uncertain, but a tantalising clue comes from Sir George Buck, the Master of Revels. In the 1611 manuscript copy of *The Second Maiden's Tragedy*, a tragedy believed to have perhaps been penned by Thomas Middleton, Buck seems to have created the title in response to certain similarities between this tragedy and the one by Beaumont and Fletcher; as if to further the confusion, the London publisher Humphrey Moseley would actually call this play a sequel to *The Maid's Tragedy* (Wiggins 1998: xxx). This reference by Buck would date it before 1611, and some scholars have suggested 1610 as a possible performance date (Braunmuller and Hattaway 2003: 434). The play was widely popular, so much so that in 1678, in *The Tragedies of the Last Age*, Thomas Rymer gave it the compliment of being 'one of the choicest and most applauded English tragedies of this last age' before going on to attack it mercilessly for not following the classical unities (qtd in Clark 2013: 114); this would put the play in good company, for in 1693, in *A Short View of Tragedy*, Rymer would go on to criticise *Othello* and *Julius Caesar* on the same grounds. Part of this concern over the unities should not be surprising when it comes to Beaumont and Fletcher for, with *Philaster* (c. 1609) and other plays, these two playwrights are generally credited with helping to popularise tragicomedy on the English stage.

While *The Maid's Tragedy* may not be a tragicomedy, it does open itself up to some of the critiques often levelled at tragicomedies, a genre hated by some while considered by others to be 'the century's most popular dramatic form' (Bliss 2003: 235). The term 'tragical comedy' was first used in the prologue of Richard Edwards's *Damon and Pithias*, which was written in 1564 and published in 1571. In *The Defense of Poesie* Sir Philip Sidney expresses his detest for the genre for being neither properly tragical nor properly comical, and he even referred to it as a 'mongrel' form; ironically, Sidney's *Arcadia* (1590) would become a major source of inspiration for many playwrights of tragicomedies. However, on the Continent tragicomedy began to grow in both popularity and respectability. This was aided by Giovanni Battista Giraldi, otherwise known as Cinthio, who argued for tragedies with a comic ending, or *tragedia de lieto fin.* This was seconded and taken even further by Giovanni Battista Guarini (1538–1612), whose *Il Pastor Fido* (1590), or 'The Faithful Shepherd'. This tragicomedy was widely successful, appearing in Italian in London in 1591 and being translated into English by 1602. This 1602 translation included the *Compendio della poesia tragicomica*, which put forward Guarini's argument that much could be gained from blending genres and from moving past the rules of the Ancients; far from breaking decorum, Guarini argued that he had helped bring about a new genre with a new form. Guarini's tragicomedy and his arguments about the genre had a tremendous impact in England, although many English tragicomedians, from Beaumont and Fletcher to Shakespeare in his final plays, yet again rethought the form and expanded its range of possibilities.

The Maid's Tragedy is not strictly a tragicomedy, but it is important nevertheless to remember this context when considering the play, as its apparent artifice and self-aware reflexivity are in keeping with the tragicomic mode. The tragedy is full of such moments, many of which draw attention to meta-theatrical elements and to early modern stage practice. For example, Martin Wiggins notes how the seduction scene between Evadne and her husband teases the audience: 'with the prospective breakdown of the dramatic illusion . . . the disrobing, if completed, would . . . reveal an unequivocally male leading lady' (1998: viii). This is compounded all the more by Amintor's exclamation 'was ever such a marriage as this?' (2.1.242), a marriage doomed before it even began. It is a meta-theatrical nod to the audience while also serving as a possible allusion to Richard III's exclamation 'Was ever woman in this humour wooed?/Was ever woman in this humour won?' (1.2.213–14). Unlike Richard, Amintor has not won, and *The Maid's Tragedy* will dramatise a series of disappointments as experienced by all of the characters. There will be many such moments. As mentioned above, a key source for Beaumont and Fletcher was Sidney's *Arcadia*, which had also provided material for their earlier *Philaster* and *Cupid's Revenge* (c. 1615). At the same time, Bandello's *Novelle* – or Painter's *The Palace of Pleasure* – would also provide inspiration. When it comes to *Arcadia*, the fighting between Aspatia and Amintor, with the former in male clothing, clearly evokes the battle between Parthenia and Amphialus in Book III, while the death of Aspatia is, with some clear changes, modelled on Parthenia's death in Book III, chapters 12–16: both characters essentially seek their deaths in the form of a duel. Likewise, Evadne's killing of the King in Act 5 echoes Book I, chapter 42 in the *Novelle*.

As mentioned above, *The Maid's Tragedy* was a play performed at The Blackfriars. Likewise, as with *The Duchess of Malfi*, this play also had a masque, one that reveals corruption rather than extolling virtue or promoting royal authority. At first glance the masque in Beaumont and Fletcher's tragedy seems unnecessary, especially at such an early point in the play. However, its key function is to draw parallels between the seemingly timeless and removed setting of Rhodes and the actual court of James I, with all of its sycophancy and corruption on full display. This corruption is encapsulated in the plot, for it centres upon the consequences of the King ordering Amintor, one of his chief courtiers, to marry Evadne instead of his beloved Aspatia. The King's reason for promoting this marriage stems from his ongoing affair with Evadne; the King wants his lover to have an aristocratic marriage that can better cover their own clandestine affair. As David Bevington notes, all of the characters in this play 'find themselves in conflict at one time or other as to how, and to what extent, they ought to countenance the abuses of royal power' (2002: 1142).

Much of the action of the play thus hinges on the question of loyalty to the King, which is presented as something that can be tested and, excitingly, as something that can be lost. However, the play always walks a fine balance when it comes to criticising or promoting royal power. For example, when Lysippus exclaims that 'the breath of kings is like the breath of gods!' (1.1.16), one is reminded of King James I's desire for more and more control over Parliament and his kingdom; in keeping with this, James dissolved Parliament shortly after this play was probably first performed. Perhaps this is why there is at least some speculation that the play may have been censored (Clare 1990: 184). Again, Beaumont and Fletcher stress the lustful corruption of

the King while giving no hint of any other kinds of bad gover-
nance. There is a strange irony, one that neither Beaumont nor
Fletcher could have predicted, for they make their king a wan-
ton libertine in an effort to help better support what will happen
to him later. However, the historically libertine James survived
to die in his bed while his comparatively chaste son Charles
I met his end on the executioner's block. The King's liaisons
with Evadne, liaisons that must be concealed, become central
for the plot. Promiscuity is even celebrated in Dula's song:

> *I could never have the power*
> *To love one above an hour,*
> *But my heart would prompt mine eye*
> *On some other man to flie;*
> *Venus, fix mine eyes fast,*
> *Or if not, give me all that I shall see at last.*

> (2.1.83–8)

However, in a tragedy that deals so much with sexual desire and
that builds on the tensions aroused by lust, sex is more likely
to be affected by *coitus interruptus* than revealed *in flagrante*.
Both Aspatia and Amintor are thwarted in their sexual and
romantic desire, and the latter is likewise thwarted from using
violence as an outlet for his frustrations (2.1.304–5). Evadne
wants nothing to do with Amintor on their wedding night, and
when he asks her who has done her wrong so that he can seek
his revenge, she says that he should kill himself (2.1.170–2,
183–4). Dishonour and disappointment dog these characters,
be it Melantius shaming Evadne in Act 4, scene 1; the pitiful
death of the King at Evadne's hands, as he is stabbed while tied
to his own bed; Aspatia seeing her role in the duel more as an
act of suicide than as an act of honour; and the suicide awaiting
both Evadne and Amintor. Even suicide is thwarted in the case
of Melantius, who ends the play with the possibility of seeking
out his death conflicting with the possibility of relenting and
going on to serve the new king.

If the masque may suggest echoes of other plays, it is worth
noting that *Hamlet* has often been seen as a possible influence

on *The Maid's Tragedy*, with particular characters echoing those from Shakespeare's tragedy. For example, Melantius has some-times been compared to Fortinbras, not simply because he sur-vives but because of his pragmatism and ability to take advantage of the chaos created by others. The counsellor Calianax, too, seems to find a ready model in Polonius, both in terms of his argumentative nature and his daughter Aspatia's plight. Aspatia is truly heartbroken by her break from Amintor, although his feelings are harder to pin down. He clearly feels anguish for having done 'that lady wrong' (2.1.127), but whether this is because his own honour has been besmirched or because his heart has been broken is difficult to say. On a side note, the Polonius-like Calianax survived as a droll character during the Commonwealth, featuring in small sketches performed on very small stages. Such characters were popular during this period, for they allowed performances to continue, even in a limited form, in spite of the ban on theatres during the Commonwealth. Likewise, Hamlet's need to disguise his intentions by putting on an 'antic disposition' is echoed by Aspatia's disguise, only in her case she is disguised as a man. Perhaps, in keeping with their interest in tragicomedy, Beaumont and Fletcher could see the dramatic possibilities of mixing the scenarios featuring Viola in *Twelfth Night* and Rosalind in *As You Like It* with the revenge tragedy tradition. Clearly, such a hybrid approach to drama pro-duced some startling results. This hybridity also extends to the tragedy's handling of scenes mixing sex and death, most notably Evadne's killing of the King, which begins as a kind of game or 'pretty new device' (5.1.47), a game that even allows Evadne to describe the first stab wounds as 'love tricks' (5.1.103), an appellation so comic and yet macabre that it could have come out of *The Revenger's Tragedy* or *The Duchess of Malfi*. Like those plays, and like *Hamlet*, *The Maid's Tragedy* is a tragedy of despair and of thwarted ambitions and dreams:

> Thus, Amintor does not marry Aspatia. He does not sleep with Evadne. He does not kill the King. Evadne retreats from a selfish . . . individuality into becoming a receptor for her brother's ideas. Aspatia simply retreats, consummating

only her morbid desire not to live. Her father is chronically in retreat – like Lysippus, following the impulse of the coward not to be on the losing side. Melantius is a control freak, whether in directing the affairs of his sister and friend or in the little power game with Calianax and the King. And in the end he does not succeed in committing suicide. (Trussler 2006: 166)

In keeping with this note of disillusionment, this is one of the only revenge tragedies in which suicide is the prime means of dispatching the characters from the stage. Many of the characters fall victim to themselves rather than to some revenger like Vindice or Hamlet.

The Maid's Tragedy was once described by John Dryden as having a 'labyrinth of design', for 'you see some of your way before you, yet discern not the end till you arrive at it' (1971: 49). Dryden is certainly right in noting this, for the tragedy is less a tragedy of character of the kind one might find by Shakespeare and more a tragedy filled with plots, twists and surprises. At the same time, it does not have a subplot and it sticks quite strictly to its five-act structure. The play conforms to the classical unities of time and space, with the setting being confined to Rhodes and the action seemingly limited to a twenty-four-hour period. As mentioned above, this structure came into vogue during the rise of the indoor theatres, largely due to the stage practice of preparing and relighting candles between scenes and acts. At the same time, the use of the masque reflects the growing interest indoor theatres had for this form of drama, although the masque had been performed in numerous outdoor theatres as well. More specific to Blackfriars was both the use of the upper level in Act 4 to represent the walls of the fort, and with the use of the bed as a prominent prop, something that we will see again in John Ford's *'Tis Pity She's a Whore*. *The Maid's Tragedy* was clearly a success on this stage, which no doubt explains why is later 'received the accolade of a commission for a performance at court' (Bevington 2002: 1141). One wonders what James would have made of such a dramatisation of both the potential evils of monarchy and, equally problematic, the genuine conflicts of conscience that such evils could produce in a monarch's subjects.

''TIS TIME TO DIE, WHEN 'TIS A SHAME TO LIVE': MIDDLETON'S LATE TRAGEDIES

To do full justice to the range of Thomas Middleton's dramatic output would require a book; or, to be more precise, it would require several books. In 2007 Oxford University Press released a collection of Middleton's dramatic work, edited by Gary Taylor and John Lavagnino, that credited Middleton with eighteen solo plays, ten surviving plays written in collaboration, and two adaptations of plays by other authors. He thus certainly wrote more than the 'six or seven' suggested by T. S. Eliot (1951: 162). In some editions, the number of dramatic works is actually increased to thirty-two (O'Callaghan 2012: 165), bringing Middleton's output into direct competition, at least quantitatively, with Shakespeare's; in addition to this, Taylor and Lavagnino speculate that half of Middleton's works may be lost, which would thus make his potential dramatic output much higher (2007: 51–2). This element of competition was clearly on Taylor and Lavagnino's minds when they dubbed Middleton 'our other Shakespeare' (2007: 1, 57). As Taylor later noted, with much annoyance, many scholars, such as Jonathan Bate, Michael Neill and Lukas Erne, have questioned this designation, for they 'denied that Middleton wrote any masterpieces that belong to the genre of the history play' or that Middleton should be seen as 'our other Shakespeare' (2012: 47). Taylor goes on to offer a rather convoluted, and rather unconvincing, argument of how 'our other Shakespeare' was meant to be seen as a metaphor, one that seeks to 'dethrone' Shakespeare, 'invoke a definition and justification of (in)equality, and hence [serve as] an appeal to political theory, including the political theories embodied in the history plays . . . The metaphor itself is thus foundationally historical. Like history plays, it relates history to hierarchy, time to legitimacy, a local past to a local present' (2012: 48). It is an odd defence, particularly when one considers that Taylor could have more easily, and more effectively, simply pointed to the tremendous range of Middleton's oeuvre for, in a career that began with the poem *The Wisdom of Solomon Paraphrased* (1597) and ended almost thirty years later with the masque *The Triumphs of Health and Prosperity* (1626) (Erne 2010: 493), Middleton tackled – aside from history plays – almost every conceivable genre of the early modern English stage.

This range is quite immense, for Middleton penned, alone and in partnership with others, revenge tragedies like *The Revenger's Tragedy* (1606); domestic tragedies like *A Yorkshire Tragedy* (1608); city comedies like *The Roaring Girl* (c. 1610) and *A Chaste Maid in Cheapside* (1613); tragicomedies like *The Witch* (1616) and *A Fair Quarrel* (1616); baroque tragedies like *Women Beware Women* (c. 1621) and *The Changeling* (1622); and even satires like *A Game at Chess* (1624), a political allegory so controversial that it closed after just nine performances at The Globe (Howard-Hill 1993: 17). Part of the reason for such variety stems from the fact that Middleton did not settle with any particular playing company, or any particular theatrical venue, for long, which meant that he had to write plays to meet a variety of different theatrical tastes. As he notes in his Epistle for *The Roaring Girl*, he believes that his plays could be played by 'many of your companies', for performances of his work was very widespread throughout London (Taylor and Lavignino 2007: 727). Middleton also collaborated with several different playwrights, such as Thomas Dekker, John Webster and William Rowley, and these collaborations no doubt expanded Middleton's range all the more. The current scholarly opinion is that he also collaborated with Shakespeare on *Timon of Athens* (c. 1606) and had a hand in revising *Measure for Measure* (c. 1604) in 1621 and *Macbeth* (1606) in 1616 (O'Callaghan 2012: 165). This versatility gave Middleton an interesting view of his craft, for he seems to have seen his dramas as examples of great craftsmanship. As he notes in his Epistle to *The Roaring Girl*, playwriting should be

> to nothing so naturally as the alteration in apparel; for in the time of the great crop-doublet, your huge bombasted plays, quilted with mighty words to lean purpose, was only then in fashion: and as the doublet fell, neater inventions began to set up. Now, in the time of spruceness, our plays

follow the niceness of our garments; single plots, quaint conceits, lecherous jests, drest up in hanging sleeves: and those are fit for the times and the termers. (qtd in Taylor and Lavignino 2007: 726)

Middleton's 'neater inventions', his 'alteration[s]' to popular genres and plots, are on full display in his later tragedies, which borrow from the revenge tragedy tradition, domestic tragedies, and even, at times, the city comedy.

Middleton's ability to construct plots, 'single', double and otherwise, with the skill of a dramatic architect is quite remarkable, particularly in *The Changeling*, which he co-wrote with William Rowley, as it expertly balances the main plot involving the love-triangle between Beatrice-Joanna, Alsemero and Alonzo, and the subplot involving Alibius, his young wife Isabella and her many suitors. It is generally maintained by scholars that, both in this tragedy and in other collaborations between Middleton and Rowley, the tragic plot climaxing in Act 3, scene 4 was handled by Middleton while the comic plot and the ending of the play was handled by Rowley (Black 1966: 6); however, given Middleton's obvious gifts for comedy in other works, such a strict demarcation may not give us the whole picture. In any case, this gift for dramatic structure helped to provide Middleton and his collaborators with 'a highly sophisticated and symbolic approach to the architecture of the stage, frequently setting in motion a complex interplay between dramatic and metaphorical spaces, whose full resonance is revealed in the course of the plot' (O'Callaghan 2012: 165–6). On the other hand, it should be noted that other critics have disputed Middleton's assertion that his work is clear and unified and have opted instead to look at his messiness, his hybridity. Such critics, like Gordon McMullan, argue that Middleton's work, *The Changeling* in particular, 'denies its admirers the aesthetic comfort of authorial unity-of-purpose – the beauty of tragedy, as understood by generations of critics – and refuses the self-coherence, the clarity of trajectory, of the revenge genre to which it belongs' (2010: 222); for McMullan, this is 'exemplary both of the nature of playwriting and of the development of tragedy in Jacobean England – hybrid, multiple, grotesque' (2010: 222). Whether one sees Middleton as a consummate professional, neatly tailoring his neater inventions to better fit with the theatrical conditions of the moment, or as one given to serving up a smorgasbord of revenge and blood, parody and pastiche, there is no question that the effect of Middleton's late tragedies remains incredibly powerful.

This mix, of the architecturally planned with the instinctually pursued, can be seen quite clearly in *Women Beware Women*, which is believed to have been first performed around 1621, probably by the King's Men (Braunmuller and Hattaway 2003: 438), although it was not entered into the Stationers' Register until 1653 and not published, by Humphrey Moseley, until 1657. It is a tragedy artfully conceived and laid out, and yet it also contains one of the bloodiest endings in all of Jacobean drama. As with *The Duchess of Malfi*, *The Revenger's Tragedy* and *Hamlet*, the tragedy of this world stems from the corruption at the heart of those who rule it. As Margot Heinemann points out, this concern with corruption and power can be found in many early modern plays, such as history plays, revenge tragedies and

> classical history plays, based mainly on Tacitus (which were not subject to the general ban imposed on writing English history after the Essex revolt). Since the earlier, heroic Rome of Plutarch's Lives had been a republic, tyrannous emperors could not claim a divine right to rule sanctioned by the Christian God, but only the right of conquest and power. Hence the indictment of arbitrary rule arose naturally from the historical narrative and became symbolic. (2003: 184)

Symbolic is right, and something is rotten in the state, in this case, of Tuscany. The Duke of Florence has spread corruption throughout his dukedom, and this corruption, as the Cardinal warns, will continue to spread so long as the Duke pursues this path:

> what a misery 'tis then
> To be more certain of eternal death,
> Then of a next embrace? nay, shall I shew you

How more unfortunate you stand in sin,
Then the love private man; all his offences,
Like inclos'd grounds, keep but about himself,
And seldom stretch beyond his own soul's bounds;
And when a man grows miserable, 'tis some comfort
When he's no further charg'd, then with himself;
Tis a sweet ease to wretchedness.

(4.1.199–208)

The pain felt and caused by the small is small, but the pain felt and caused by the great is, in so many ways, great. This is particularly so because such pain can be felt by everyone, and so the sins of the powerful serve as examples to be followed by all who live under them. The Cardinal situates the Duke on a mountain that all can see, an image that Middleton perhaps plays on as a contrast to how the Duke originally saw Bianca, up in a window: 'Did not the Duke look up? Methought he saw us' (1.3.105). Then the focus was on the 'look' the Duke 'casts', which are 'at his own intentions, and his object/Only the public good' (1.3.109–11), but now the focus is on not who the Duke sees but on who sees the Duke. There are some who interpret the Cardinal and his words as indications of Middleton's own theological concerns (Heinemann 1980: 1), while others argue that his words and actions are more politic than theological (Levin 1998: 214). Regardless of his motivations for making such warnings, the dangers that the Cardinal warns of are real, and he evokes Shakespeare's Sonnet 129 as he outlines how corruption leads by example and thus leads directly to hell:

But great man,
Every sin thou commit'st, shows like a flame
Upon a Mountain, 'tis seen far about,
And with a big wind made of popular breath,
The sparkles flie through Cities: Here one takes,
Another catches there, and in short time
Waste all to cinders: But remember still
What burnt the Valleys first, came from the Hill;
Ev'ry offence draws his particular pain,

But 'tis example proves the great man's bane.
The sins of mean men, lie like scatter'd parcels
Of an unperfect bill; but when such fall,
Then comes example, and that sums up all:
And this your reason grants, if men of good lives,
Who by their virtuous actions stir up others
To noble and religious imitation,
Receive the greater glory after death,
As sin must needs confess; what may they feel
In height of torments, and in weight of veng'ance,
Not only they themselves, not doing well,
But sets a light up to show men to Hell?

(4.1.208–27)

Because he stands, at least metaphorically, on a mountain, the Duke's crimes can be seen 'far about', and their burning nature allows them to be seen from even further, helps to spread them, like cinders, through cities and towns, and ultimately leads one and all to the fiery pits of hell. This is a light, not towards enlightenment, but towards damnation.

As with Sonnet 129, *Women Beware Women* is also very much concerned with both sexual obsession and with the dangers and disgust that can arise from such an obsession. The plot itself could even be said to reflect, to an uncanny degree, 'lust in action', lust that

Is perjured, murderous, bloody, full of blame,
Savage, extreme, rude, cruel, not to trust,
Enjoy'd no sooner but despised straight,
Past reason hunted, and no sooner had
Past reason hated, as a swallow'd bait
On purpose laid to make the taker mad;
Mad in pursuit and in possession so;
Had, having, and in quest to have, extreme;
A bliss in proof, and proved, a very woe;
Before, a joy proposed; behind, a dream.

(Sonnet 129.2–12)

Several of the themes and motif that appear in Webster will later appear in Ford: the tragedy has suitors who are both foolish, elopements that are ill-conceived, marriages that are unwanted, incestuous desires that are dangerous, and passions that are exposed to disastrous results. There are hints of happiness but, as with Antonio and the Duchess in *The Duchess of Malfi*, these seem only to underscore the much more troubling forces that frequently threaten to boil over. What makes all of these dramatic forces even more remarkable is that they come not from the imagination of Middleton but, at least in part, from actual history. The plot of *Women Beware Women* was inspired by the events surrounding the second marriage of Francesco de' Medici, Grand Duke of Tuscany (1541–87). Why this marriage between a Tuscan duke and a Venetian noblewoman should be the subject of an English tragedy is a matter of much historical debate (Oakley-Brown 2011: 172). It was believed that Francesco de' Medici had murdered – or at least had ordered the murder of – his first wife, Joanna of Austria, Grand Duchess of Tuscany (1547–78), in order to marry Bianca Capello (1548–87). This belief was given credence by the definite murder of Bianca's husband, Pietro Bonaventuri, in the streets of Florence in 1572. While the cause of death was quite clear – murder – the question of who was responsible was much less so. Nevertheless, suspicion soon fell on Francesco and Bianca, who married shortly after the death of Joanna in 1578. The two had long been involved in an affair, and Bianca had already given birth to a son by Francesco in 1576, a son who would actually become heir to the dukedom of Tuscany following the death of Francesco's first son, although he never made it to the ducal throne. Both Francesco and Bianca died in 1587 while staying at the Medici villa in Poggio a Caiano, and many at the time believed that they had been poisoned by Francesco's brother Ferdinando de' Medici (1549–1609), who went on to become the next Grand Duke of Tuscany. The real story was probably far less sensational than the rumours surrounding it, as Joanna probably died in childbirth while Francesco and Bianca probably died from malaria. Nevertheless, in keeping with the Cardinal's point that the great are on a mountain for all to see, many quickly began to draw far more sensational conclusions about what had happened. Many lurid accounts were soon circulating, the most famous of which being found in Celio Malespini's

Ducento Novelle (1609), which some critics, such as Samuel Schoenbaum, have argued that Middleton probably had direct access to (1955: 10–11). In any case, it was a tale that almost demanded dramatic treatment.

However he became aware of it, the plot of *Women Beware Women* is clearly indebted to this historical couple. Leantio is a banker's clerk, and he has married a far richer woman from the upper classes, Bianca, who comes to live with him and his mother. Bianca is kept indoors while Leantio is away in an effort to keep her from falling in love with another, but she is soon seen by the Duke who passes by her window during a courtly procession. He gains access to Bianca with the help of Guardiano and Livia, a friend of Leantio's mother. In *A Game at Chess* Middleton would achieve great notoriety by making analogies between the game and international diplomacy; however, in this play the game is used as a source of distraction, and also as an analogy for the game of life, for Livia plays chess with Leantio's mother while the Duke seduces Bianca. The plot becomes even more complicated as Livia's niece Isabella is forced against her will to marry Guardiano's nephew; Livia's brother Hippolito confesses to a love for his niece Isabella; Isabella marries Guardiano's nephew as a cover for her relationship with Hippolito, as Livia has falsely told her that Hippolito is not actually her uncle; and Livia begins an affair with Leantio, who is horribly distraught over the loss of his wife to the Duke. The case of Livia and Leantio is a strange one but, as Livia acknowledges, she is 'cunning in all arts but [her] own love' (3.3.322). The second, incestuous plot derived from *The True History of the Tragic Loves of Hipolito and Isabella Neapolitans* (1628). The Duke has used his money and power to force Leantio to agree to give up Bianca, but he now runs into conflict with his brother the Cardinal, who disapproves of the match. As mentioned above, this disapproval has been read in a variety of ways: for those who, like Richard Levin (1998: 201–17) and Joost Daalder (2011: 79), argue that the Cardinal might not be as virtuous as he appears, it is worth noting that the man who eventually succeeded Francesco de' Medici, his brother Ferdinando, was made a Cardinal at the age of fourteen, though, as it was a political rather than a religious appointment, he was never actually ordained into the priesthood. In any case, the Duke desires to remove Leantio as a threat, and so he orders Hippolito to murder him. Distraught over the loss of her lover, Livia exposes the fact that the lovers Isabella and Hippolito are actually related, an exposure that also reveals Isabella's disloyalty to her husband, Guardiano's nephew. Everyone now has a desire for revenge, and they all plot to achieve it during a masque to be performed at the Duke's marriage to Bianca.

However, as with so many revenge tragedies, these plots for revenge backfire horrendously, resulting in the deaths of all of those involved, including the Duke and Bianca, and perhaps reminding us of Horatio's description at the close of *Hamlet* of

> carnal, bloody, and unnatural acts,
> Of accidental judgments, casual slaughters,
> Of deaths put on by cunning and forced cause,
> And, in this upshot, purposes mistook
> Fall'n on the inventors' heads.
>
> (5.2.386–90)

The ending of *Women Beware Women* is a bit more pious, at least on the surface, as the Cardinal, who is the only one to survive, says that lust and love cannot live as one, as 'two kings on one throne', for 'where lust reigns, the prince cannot reign long' (5.1.263–6). However, the true depth of the tragedy derives less from such moral lessons and more from the force of seeing these characters being confronted and destroyed by their inner drives. At the same time, in keeping with the division between the architecturally conceived and intricately planned on the one hand and the hybrid, overwhelming smorgasbord on the other, Middleton manages to expertly balance all of his many plots before, in essence, violently smashing them into one other during the final masque. In *The Changeling*, Middleton and Rowley will take this effect even further, creating, as McMullan argues, a

> tragic form . . . sufficiently hybrid as to confront its own validity as a genre . . . one in which the distinctions required to differentiate the good and the bad (and the ugly) seem

to have been mis- (or dis-)placed, along with stereotypical identities such as 'revenger' or 'malcontent'. This intense, savage, self-parodying play is both exemplary of Jacobean revenge tragedy and marks the point at which that genre or sub-genre can be said to have developed beyond itself. (2010: 232)

As also shown in the revenge tragedies of Ford (see Chapter 5), we have come a long way since Kyd's *The Spanish Tragedy*, Shakespeare's *Hamlet* and even Middleton's own *The Revenger's Tragedy*. Where we have come to is another question.

Licensed for performance in 1622 by Sir Henry Herbert, Master of the Revels, Middleton and Rowley's *The Changeling* was first performed by the Lady Elizabeth's Men, an acting company formed under the patronage of James I's daughter Elizabeth Stuart, Queen of Bohemia. The tragedy was performed at the indoor Cockpit Theatre, which was located in Drury Lane and was later renamed The Phoenix after Christopher Beeston took over ownership in 1616. The theatre was significantly redesigned in 1617 following damage during rioting, and it is believed that Inigo Jones was responsible for the surviving architectural plans of The Phoenix (Gurr 1987: 148–50). Although it was still sometimes associated with its earlier time as a place for cockfighting (Gurr 1987: 201–2), this indoor theatre was among the most fashionable in London, and it was one of the two theatres to be reopened following the Restoration in 1660. As we will see, it was an ideal setting for *The Changeling*, a tragedy that makes the most of closed, confined settings and the contrasts between darkness and light. The main plot is believed to have been based on the first book of Joshua Reynolds's *The Triumphs of God's Revenge Against Murther* (1611), a collection of didactic and sensational stories which also provided inspiration for James Shirley's *The Maid's Revenge* (1639), although the subplot involving madness appears to have been Rowley's, or Middleton and Rowley's, own. Middleton's *A Game at Chess* was infamous for infuriating the Spanish ambassador, and this tragedy plays on the anti-Spanish sentiment that was rife at the time (Randall 1986: 189–90). For example, Barbara Fuchs refers to Reynolds as an 'anti-Spanish pamphleteer', and she notes that 'Reynolds locates Alsemero precisely as a Spanish soldier, frustrated by the truce in the Netherlands, and bemoans the immorality of Alsemero and Beatrice-Joanna meeting in a "Popish" church' (2012: 411).

However, as with so many revenge tragedies, be they set in Spain, Italy or Denmark, the criticisms of corruption and the abuse of power are always aimed much closer to home. For example, the tragedy has 'manifold' 'echoes of the Howard case' (Fuchs 2012: 413), one of the greatest court scandals of the Jacobean era. This scandal began in 1606 when the Earl of Essex married Lady Frances Howard. Around 1611 Howard began an affair with Robert Carr, a favourite of James I who had recently been created the Earl of Somerset (Lindley 1993: 1). In order to keep this affair from being exposed, Howard began to look for ways to poison her husband, or at least divorce him. She frequently accused him of impotence, which may be referenced in *The Changeling* when De Flores cuts of Alonzo's ring finger after having killed him. Carr's friend and ally at court, Sir Thomas Overbury, opposed Howard and her desire to marry Carr, and he even refused a diplomatic post that had been offered to him to essentially buy his approval. This refusal cost Overbury dearly, for he was soon sent to the Tower of London, where he died in September 1613, probably having been poisoned. Such poisons are no doubt responsible for the pronounced emphasis on disease, malady and poison in the play (Neill 1991: 95). Howard was granted her divorce after her husband was declared impotent and a panel of midwives found her to still be a virgin, a finding that many questioned at the time. Despite these doubts, Howard and Carr were married in December 1613, and all seemed well. Unfortunately for the new couple, the truth came out in 1615 when evidence emerged of the poisoning of Overbury and

> all those involved were arraigned – in reverse order of their social standing. Frances was at last tried and found guilty, as finally was Carr, by a tribunal of fellow-peers, both being condemned to death. The first and lowliest conspirator had said, in entering his own plea, that he hoped he would not be helping to 'make a net to catch the little birds, and let the great ones go'. In the event the

'little birds' were all executed, and the 'great ones', after spending a few years in the Tower, were released into safe (though estranged) obscurity. (Trussler 2006: 227)

The plot involving Beatrice-Joanna is clearly connected with the Howard case. When she discovers that Alsemero has fallen in love with her, she does not tell him of her betrothal to the wealthy Alonzo. Beatrice is also pursued by De Flores, whom she despises but keeps in hope so that she can use him to rid herself of Alonzo. De Flores kills Alonzo on the fortifications of the castle of Alicante, and he cuts off Alonzo's finger as proof of the murder. Beatrice is initially elated that Alonzo is gone, but she is disgusted by the finger and terrified by De Flores's demand that she submit to him sexually in payment. Beatrice submits, but she now finds herself with a new problem, for she must be able to prove her virginity in order to marry Alsemero. Perhaps due to his involvement in revising *Measure for Measure* (Maguire and Smith 2012: 194–5), Middleton makes use of the 'bed trick' to allow Beatrice to cheat Alsemero by replacing herself with her servant Diaphanta on their wedding night. However, as with *Women Beware Women*, the plot soon unravels as people begin to suspect their accomplices and begin to kill in order to keep others silent. Beatrice herself is forced to confess to both the adultery and the murder before being stabbed to death by De Flores, who also kills himself. Alsemero is distraught at the crimes that have been committed and at the loss of so much life, and he comes to the realisation at the end that 'man and his sorrow at the grave must part' (5.3.230).

Vermandero's citadel, with its claustrophobia sense of confinement, is well suited to the indoor Phoenix. However, this closed world does not bring community; instead, it simply indicates just how isolated all of the characters are from one another. As Michelle O'Callaghan points out, Middleton and Rowley make

highly inventive use of stage machinery. The famous claustrophobia of the play owes much to the more intimate space of the indoor playhouse, which allowed lighting to be manipulated for dramatic effect. But *The Changeling* also makes extensive and unparalleled metaphorical, architectural, and dramatic use of the discovery space, the curtained-off area at the back of the stage that is in full view of the audience, yet hides action from view. The discovery space in *The Changeling* is a dark place of secrets and the domain of the illicit. (2012: 175)

This space is made use of with strong effect during the murder of Alonzo, as De Flores hides his body, and during the virginity test Beatrice is asked to take in Act 4. Of equal interest in this regard are the asides spoken by Beatrice and De Flores to the audience as they both reveal themselves to us and reveal how little they actually understand each other. Beatrice is genuinely shocked not only by the finger of the dead Alonzo – 'Bless me, what hast thou done?' (3.4.28) – but by the fact that De Flores does not want her money but her as his bride. Likewise, De Flores is genuinely pained for being so misconstrued in his intentions, for being seen as a simple killer instead of a potential lover:

> That were strange, lady; 'tis not possible
> My service should draw such a cause from you.
> Offended? Could you think so? That were much
> For one of my performance, and so warm
> Yet in my service.
>
> (3.4.53–6)

Although Beatrice sees this incongruity, this lack of understanding, in terms of social class – 'Think but upon the distance that creation/Set 'twixt thy blood and mine' (3.4.13–31) – Middleton and Rowley suggest that the rift is much deeper and more universal.

This sense of isolation between one person and another is palpable in the tragedy, and it is one of the factors that ensures that the plot unravels as it does, for in the end the characters cannot trust one another, and they cannot even trust themselves. Paradoxically, even perversely, Beatrice and De Flores actually do become kindred, for, after the second murder, of Diaphanta, they realise that they are now tied, linked, trapped together. As with Richard III, as with Macbeth, as with so many early modern villains, they realise that murder 'is followed by more sins' (3.4.164). Once this path has been chosen, they are forced to take it together. As Beatrice says, 'I'm forced to love thee now,/'Cause thou provid'st so carefully for my honour' (5.1.47–8), and after he kills Beatrice, De Flores compares himself and her to Adam and Eve, for now they are joined together in murder: 'Here we are. If you have any more/To say to us, speak quickly; I shall not/Give you the hearing else. I am so stout yet,/And so, I think, that broken rib of mankind' (5.3.152–5). They are a match made in hell; Beatrice dies in shame and dishonour – ''Tis time to die when 'tis a shame to live' (5.3.191) – while De Flores dies proclaiming that he loved Beatrice 'in spite of her heart' (5.3.174). This tragedy may explore a 'rhetoric of love' (Eaton 1984: 371), but it also examines how that love is inextricably linked with hate. This link will emerge again as we move on to the tragedies of the Caroline period, most notably in the tragedies of John Ford.

CHAPTER 5

Caroline Tragedy

'THIS BESOTTED AGE': PHILIP MASSINGER, *THE ROMAN ACTOR* AND THE STATE OF CAROLINE TRAGEDY

When one thinks of Caroline tragedy, that word 'state' comes immediately to mind, both in its senses of condition or quality and the polity. This is because the tragedies of the era are invariably compared, often harshly, to the tragedies of the Elizabethan and Jacobean periods. At the same time, Caroline tragedy, perhaps even more than the tragedies of the past, is often inextricably bound up with the political state itself. In what ways do these tragedies reflect this sense of being bound? Does such binding result in their constriction, or do they find ways to break free from such constraints?

All of these forces, and all of these tensions, can be found in the tragedies of Philip Massinger, particularly *The Roman Actor*. This may be surprising, as Massinger was not then and is not now best known for his tragedies; in fact, it was as a writer of comedies that Massinger achieved the most fame, particularly with *A New Way to Pay Old Debts* (c. 1621), a comedy that, while loosely based on Middleton's *A Trick to Catch the Old One* (1605), went on to become one of the most popular plays of the 1620s and, after its revival by David Garrick in 1748 at Drury Lane, a stock piece for repertory companies until the end of the nineteenth century. Massinger is also famous for his collaborations with John Fletcher, who became the principal playwright for the King's Men following the death of Shakespeare in 1616, and then becoming the principal playwright himself following Fletcher's death in 1625 (Clark 2014: 1). As Andrew Gurr notes, the transition to being principal playwright was smooth at time, rocky at others, particularly when it came to the issue of royal patronage and how one was expected to respond to it:

> The most intricate twist in the long trail of the company's public repertory and its innovations is what went on under the royal shadow. Like any courtier, the company's privilege of proximity to the royal presence meant fawning, but it also allowed the occasional explicit statement of concern . . . In general Massinger continued Fletcher's programme, giving priority to gentlemanly questions of love and honour, though he got into much more trouble than Fletcher with his political comments. It was Massinger who picked up the royalist term of abuse 'the many-headed multitude' applied to democrats and parliamentarians, but he put it into the mouth of Domitian Caesar, a tyrant who is justly murdered. (2004: 160)

As we will see with the turbulent friendship between Domitian and Paris, Massinger was well aware of just how rocky relationships between patron and artist could be (Howard 2008: 117–18). There are a few recorded instances of Massinger writing for the Lady Elizabeth's Men and the Queen Henrietta's Men in the mid-1620s, but the vast majority of his output was written to be performed by the King's Men at Blackfriars. This is certainly the case of *The Roman Actor*, which was licensed by the Master of Revels, Sir Henry Herbert, in October 1626 and performed later that same year. Joseph Taylor, who succeeded Richard Burbage as the lead actor of the King's Men in much the same way that Massinger had succeeded as principal playwright, and who would go on to be one of the most famous actors of the Caroline era, played the starring role of Paris. As an indication of the star power surrounding the role, Thomas Betterton played the same role during the one recorded instance of the tragedy being performed after the Restoration, in 1692. The tragedy is set during the times of the Emperor Domitian (51–96), an emperor reviled by Tacitus and others as a tyrant and who, after being assassinated by court officials and possibly by members of the Praetorian Guard, was condemned to what the Romans called *damnatio memoriae*, which involved concerted attempts to erase his memory from history. Such attempts were, it should go without saying, unsuccessful. For sources Massinger relied less on Tacitus than on Suetonius' *De vita Caesarum*, known as *The Twelve Caesars*, Book 66 of Cassius Dio's *Historia Romana*, or *Roman History*, the Second *Satire* of Horace, which inspired the first inset play performed within the action of *The Roman Actor*, and Book 14 of Ovid's *Metamorphoses*, which inspired the second inset play; the source for the third inset play, *The False Servant*, has been connected to the biblical story of Joseph and Potiphar's wife. Thomas May, who translated Lucan, Martial and the *Georgics* of Virgil in addition to his damning anti-Stuart history *History of the Parliament* (1647), added a commendatory verse to the tragedy that argues that, because of Massinger, Paris, probably 'the best of Actors in his age/Acts yet, and speaks upon our Roman Stage/Such lines by thee, as do not derogate/From *Romes* proud heights, and Her then learned State' (1–4). Coming from such a distinguished scholar of Latin, this was high praise indeed. Massinger certainly shared these high views, for he called the tragedy his finest work and favourably remarked on its reception by 'some learned, and some judicious Gentlemen' (qtd in Gibson 1978: 97). However, while Massinger clearly impressed with his use of sources, how does his tragedy stand up as drama?

The Roman Actor was published in a quarto edition in 1629 for Robert Allot, the principal publisher of Shakespeare's Second Folio in 1632. The quarto edition of *The Roman Actor* notes that the tragedy 'hath divers times beene, with good allowance Acted, at the private Play-house in the Black-friers, by the Kings Majesties Servants'. In keeping with rising concerns over political pressures and censorship, a commendatory poem by Taylor wonders if the actor's poem can 'alter but a looke/Of some sowre Censurer, who's apt to say/No one in these Times can produce a Play/Worthy his reading' (3–6). While the tone is jovial, there is no question that there were 'sowre' censors looking for political analogies in the drama being performed, be it set in Renaissance Italy or ancient Greece. This was a time when the 'Tribe of Ben', including writers such as Richard Brome, Thomas Killigrew and William Davenant, were beginning to pick up steam, and their master, Ben Jonson, had certainly tried to inject political commentary into his Roman tragedies *Sejanus His Fall* (1603) and *Catiline His Conspiracy* (1611). Such injections were often duly noted by the powers that be, and Jonson and others frequently ran afoul of them when they did. In fact, 'after *Sejanus* was performed at court during the 1603–4 holiday season, Jonson was called before the Privy Council and accused of treason, presumably because of the play's highly negative portrayal of imperial power in the persons of Nero and Tiberius' (Marcus 2000: 34–5). *The Roman Actor* makes several nods to *Sejanus*, in terms both of structure and language, particularly in the trial scene of Paris in Act 1, scene 3, which seems closely modelled on the trial of Cordus in the third act of Jonson's tragedy. And so, both during the reign of James I and during the reign of his son Charles I, there were real consequences to writing something that was so open to varying interpretations (Butler 2008: 139). The times were also marked by a growing sense that the dramatic culture was not what it had been, and so Taylor's commendatory verse can speak of the theatrical conditions being such that 'of late, 'tis true/The old [plays] accepted are more than the new' (6–7). Likewise, although John Ford's commendatory verse for the same tragedy acknowledges that Massinger 'hast out-done the Roman story' (9), he concurs with Taylor that writing 'is growne so common in our Time/That every one, who can but frame a Rime/However monstrous, gives Himselfe that praise' (2–4). Again, such were the times that, political and culturally, people began to feel as though things were getting increasingly, to paraphrase the Danish prince, stale, flat and unprofitable.

This is certainly the case as we enter the world of *The Roman Actor*, a play with many nods to *Hamlet*, for it too presents 'the world ... as pervasively corrupt and corrupting, where all motives are expedient and evil brings about the downfall of everyone' (Gurr 1987: 15), although Massinger manages to upstage Shakespeare's greatest tragedy by having not one but three plays-within-the-play. *The Roman Actor* is a tragedy, but like Hamlet it is a play about playing, about acting and performing, and it is about how we are affected by such pervasive performances. As Joanne Rochester points out, this is 'Massinger's most metatheatrical play' (2010: 15). Massinger draws our attention to this by making his tragic hero a tragedian of the Roman stage and by opening the tragedy with Paris discussing the theatre with his fellow actors Latinus and Aesopus. The consensus view is that times are tough for actors, a grim view indeed for actors experiencing similar hardships in the seventeenth, or indeed in the twenty-first, century. As Ellen MacKay points out, the tragedy's concerns are perpetually '*nouvant*', or new (2011: 76). The one advantage that the acting troupe enjoys is that it has the patronage of Emperor Domitian, a situation that no doubt evokes both the benefits and perils of noble patronage during Massinger's own time. As Aesopus points out, while Paris holds his 'grace and power with Caesar,/We from your bounty find a large supply,/Nor can one thought of want ever approach us' (1.1.27–30). However, although such patronage may have brought protection, it also allied actors with particular factions at court, a dangerous game in ancient Rome or in early modern England. Rui Carvalho Homem has even linked this concern with faction to the state of Massinger's literary reputation over the years, for 'the vagaries of his reputation reflect trends in intellectual and cultural history, but also elements of accident – the contentiousness of the literary-theatrical scene and the effects of fashion as much as faction' (2012: 213). Such a description could almost serve as a synopsis for the tragedy. When it comes to faction, Aesopus reminds Paris of an enemy and spy, Aretinus, who 'said at his table, ere a month expir'd/For being gall'd in our last comedy,/He would silence us for ever' (1.1.35–8). Whether it be an English noble or a Spanish ambassador, such as Diego Sarmiento de Acuña, 1st Count of Gondomar, who managed to end the performance of Middleton's *A Game at Chess* in 1624 for what he seemed to feel was an unfair portrayal (Taylor and Lavignino 2007: 1825–6), the threat of such audience members was genuine. Paris may declare that their 'aim is glory, and to leave our names/To aftertimes' (1.1.31–2), but they, like everyone, still have to worry about their own times, right this moment.

Paris is duly reminded of this reality by the appearance of two officers, or civil servants, who enter and inform him that he must come to the Senate immediately to answer various charges. As the three actors exit the stage, three senators, Aelius Lamia, Junius Rusticus and Palphurius Sura, watch from the side and note, cautiously and quietly, that no one is safe. Just like Rome under the rule of Tiberius, life under Domitian is dangerous for friend and foe alike, and 'traditional notions of social and political legitimacy' are under attack (Homem 2012: 215). As Rusticus, who was, historically, a great Stoic in addition to being a Roman senator, notes, the grander years of Vespasian and Titus have given way to times of greed, corruption and tyranny:

> So dangerous the age is, and such bad acts
> Are practis'd everywhere, we hardly sleep
> Nay cannot dream with safety. All our actions
> Are cal'd in question, to be nobly borne
> Is now a crime; and to deserve too well
> Held Capital treason. Sons accuse their Fathers,
> Fathers their sons; and but to win a smile
> From one in grace in Court, our chastest Matrons
> Make shipwreck of their honours. To be virtuous
> Is to be guilty. They are only safe
> That know to sooth the Prince's appetite,
> And serve his lusts.
>
> (1.1.70–81)

Such a world seems right out of the revenge tragedies of Webster and Middleton, although even they, for all their powers with language, did not come up with such a devastating line as Massinger does here: 'to be virtuous is to be guilty'. The senators also complain that Domitian has forgotten his duties to the aristocracy and has given too much power to the plebeians and his freedmen, who now 'scorn the nobility' (1.1.95–6). An example of such scorn is quickly seen in the next scene, as one of Domitian's freedmen, Parthenius, seduces Domitia, the wife of Aelius Lamia, on his master's behalf. When Aelius Lamia objects, he is forced at the point of a centurion's sword to give his wife a divorce so that she can be with the Emperor. This sense of corruption becomes even more rife during the interrogation of Paris, who is forced to defend himself to the Senate. Aretinus, an informer straight out of Tacitus' *Annals*, accuses actors and playwrights of using their plays as vehicles for satire and political polemic, a charge, and a threat to artistic expression, that had much currency during the time of Charles I and during times subsequent as well. According to Aretinus, the actors

> are they
> That search into the secrets of the time,
> And under fain'd names on the Stage present
> Actions not to be touched at; and traduce
> Persons of rank, and quality of both sexes,
> And with satirical and bitter jests
> Make even the Senators ridiculous
> To the Plebeians.
>
> (1.3.36–43)

This argument, that there are 'actions not to be touched at', must have had strong resonance for playwrights such as Massinger, particularly in the wake of the Gondomar affair, for *A Game at Chess* had been performed by Massinger's own King's Men (Barish 1986: 196).

The arrival of Domitian serves as respite for Paris against the Senate, but the Emperor proves to be just as horrible as the audience has been prepared to expect him to be, and he even orders Aelius Lamia to be executed when he continues to speak out against the loss of his wife Domitia. Domitia herself does not seem too displeased either by the loss of her first husband or by the attentions of Domitian, and those in the imperial circle are genuinely shocked by this horrible turn of events. In an apparent subplot that blends itself into the main plot, Paris and the actors stage a short play with Parthenius, a play that will hopefully convince the old man to give up his miserly ways. Paris evokes Hamlet's play-within-a-play as he remembers that theatre has the ability to move and change minds:

> I'll offer my advice! I once observ'd
> In a Tragedy of ours, in which a murder
> Was acted to the life, a guilty hearer
> Forc'd by the terror of a wounded conscience,
> To make discovery of that, which torture
> Could not wring from him . . .
>   command
> Your Father to be a spectator of it,
> He shall be so Anatomiz'd in the Scene,
> And see himself so personated; the baseness
> Of a self-torturing miserable wretch
> Truly describ'd that I much hope the object
> Will work compunction in him.
>
> (2.1.90–108)

Unfortunately, theatre does not always win, nor does it always 'work compunction' in those that one would like to move; as James Bulman notes, Massinger 'betrays some ambivalence about the theatre's claim to be morally instructive' (2003: 355). This play, which features an old man just as miserly as Parthenius's father, is actually enjoyed by the old man, who sees no reason to change his ways after so pleasing a performance. Theatre often fails in achieving the desired effect, a fact made abundantly clear by Paris's relationship with Domitian, who shows no signs that the great tragedian has ever managed to 'work compunction' in him either. To make matters worse, Domitian orders the old man's execution for being so foolish, and to make matters even more worse, at least for Paris, Domitia begins to fall in love with the actor as a result of seeing him play an Ovidian lover. Things are beginning to become very dangerous in Domitian's court, and this becomes all the clearer when Stephanos offers to kill Domitian himself, an offer that becomes quite tempting after Domitian has the senators Junius Rusticus and Palphurius

Sura, friends of Aelius Lamia, tortured, an act that Massinger opts for showing onstage. Why he does this is not entirely clear at first, but as the Stoics are able to endure their torture with equanimity, Massinger's audience, along with Domitian, cannot help but be moved. Amazingly, this play also does not have the desired effect. It should be called a play, for Domitian clearly sets the torture up as an example for all to see; however, he wants to not only control the show but control his audience's reaction as well:

> let me see
> One man so lost, as but to pity 'em
> And though there lay a million of souls
> Imprison'd in his flesh, my Hangmen's hooks
> Should rend it off and give 'em liberty.
> Caesar hath said it.
>
> (3.2.41–6)

The guards are even charged, as in a true totalitarian nightmare, to watch closely for the audience's reaction:

> 'Tis great Caesar's pleasure
> That with fix'd eyes you carefully observe
> The peoples looks. Charge upon any man
> That with a sigh, or murmur does express
> A seeming sorrow for these traitors deaths.
>
> (3.2.46–50)

Not even a sorrow, but 'a seeming sorrow' is all that is needed to condemn, a phrase that evokes Hamlet's connection of seeming and acting, as well as of seeming and mourning, while also evoking Tacitus' description of Rome under Tiberius, the period also depicted in Jonson's *Sejanus*, a time when hypocrisy was widespread and eagerly pursued, and when looks were carefully studied to see who one cheered and who one damned (*Annals* 1.7). This emphasis on acting and performance, an emphasis underscored with the use of inset plays and meta-theatrical references, 'force' Massinger's 'audience into an awareness of their own status as spectators', thus prompting a 'consideration of the function and purpose of the theatre, the question that the play overtly raises throughout' (Rochester 2010: 50). Such theatre can entertain, but it can also, as Domitian intends, serve a very clear political purpose. Unfortunately for Domitian, these senators are no longer willing to bend to such times or to such pressures from him, and their suffering, which he had hoped to dramatise for all to see, is now being replaced by their strength, which all can also see; as Rusticus says, 'To guilty men/It may bring terror; not to us, that know/What 'tis to die' (3.2.59–61). Domitian may conceive 'of the court as a private theatre where he can act any role and . . . impose his absolute will' (Bulman 2003: 356), but neither he nor Paris nor anyone else can ever fully control the reaction of his audience.

Theatre also reveals itself as a strong metaphor in the love match between Paris and Domitia. Not only is Domitia drawn to Paris because of his stage presence and rhetorical prowess, but Domitian is unable to see through the performance of Paris and Domitia who try to keep him from discovering their love. However, their performance is not as effective with other members of the court, and so, in another kind of performance, this time one that is unknown to the actors performing in it, Domitia and Paris are tricked by Aretinus into revealing their feelings for each other in front of Domitian. Domitian has Domitia arrested, but he also orders Aretinus to be killed and for the other conspirators to be arrested, for the drama that they showed him revealed something that he did not want to know. Again, performances are staged by characters in the effort to achieve an effect that frequently seems to backfire.

What is Massinger saying about this in relation to his tragedy? Domitian confronts Paris, who is almost about to talk, or act, his way out of the situation. Or so it seems. Domitian asks Paris and his performers to put on yet another play, *The False Servant*, a play that will reflect Paris's betrayal but that will also help to reconcile master and servant:

> I'll promise nothing,
> Yet clear thy cloudy fears and cherish hopes,
> What we must do, we shall do; we remember

> A tragedy, we oft have seen with pleasure,
> Call'd, the *False Servant*.
>
> (4.2.202–6)

Despite the fact that all such attempts to use performance as a means of persuasion have failed dismally, Paris agrees to take part in the performance of the play, a performance that will actually feature Domitian himself in the role of the injured husband. In yet another nod to *Hamlet*, and *The Spanish Tragedy*, and so many other revenge tragedies, the foil that Domitian is meant to use to stab Paris is replaced by the emperor with a real sword, a replacement that results in the actor being stabbed alive on stage. Domitian himself will finally be killed in the conspiracy that has been building against him throughout the tragedy, but this assassination merely serves as an anti-climax compared to the death of Paris. Massinger has tried to show his audience how theatre can move spectators, but he is also trying to show how often it can fail to move and, even more tragically, how it can sometimes move audiences in directions the performer might have never dreamed of. Many critics have argued that *The Roman Actor* offers a forceful defence of acting and of drama, and Gurr has even gone so far as to call it 'a playwright's manifesto', one bent on 'defending its author's own interests' while making a 'spirited case for players and playing', who are 'necessary members of the commonwealth' (1987: 27). This may be true, and certainly Paris does make the case that actors, with delight,

> join profit and endeavour
> To build their minds up fair, and on the stage
> Decipher to the life what honours wait
> On good, and glorious actions, and the shame
> That treads upon the heels of vice.
>
> (1.1.21–5)

Gurr ignores the fact that this declaration is sandwiched within a plea for at least six sestertii, but more importantly he ignores the countless different ways that drama, far from showing the honours that wait on good actions or the shame that treads upon the heels of vice, is often, as can be seen in the relationship between Paris and Domitian, complicit in much that is shameful and corrupt. This complicity comes with a price, as Domitian murders the playing company he has once patronised; while Charles I did not murder his playing company, there is no question that he placed the King's Men under a much heavier thumb than his father had done. What can drama do in such a situation? Depressingly, Massinger's greatest tragedy suggests that even drama that tries to fight against such forces may produce the exact opposite of the desired effect. Paris may argue on behalf of his company that "is not in us to help' how a play is perceived or responded to (1.3.136–40), but *The Roman Actor* suggests that such an answer, quite simply, is just not good enough.

'REVENGE PROVES ITS OWN EXECUTIONER': JOHN FORD'S *THE BROKEN HEART* AND *'TIS PITY SHE'S A WHORE*

James Bulman has argued that the Caroline era saw a crisis in drama, a 'defensive spirit' that 'provides evidence that the theatre was suffering a crisis of identity in which dramatists asserted their power to influence an audience while in fact fearing their own impotence' (2003: 356). Such fears were no doubt exacerbated by the growing encroachment on their liberty by the Caroline court and, even more troublingly, a clear drop in audience interest in new plays. As many critics have noted, the 1620s and 1630s saw a large increase in nostalgia for the earlier plays of the Elizabethan and Jacobean periods (Barton 1981: 706–7), a nostalgia that playwrights could not simply wish away or scorn into oblivion, as they often tried to do, especially in their prologues and epistles. Such attempts were clearly not effective, as the following anecdote from Edmund Gayton suggests. Describing his theatrical experiences during the 1630s, among other things, in *Pleasant Notes Upon Don Quixot* (1654), Gayton remembers audiences actually calling for performances of new plays to be stopped so that the old favourites could be put back on:

I have known upon one of these festivals, but especially at Shrovetide, where the players have been appointed, notwithstanding their bills to the contrary, to act what the major part of the company had a mind to; sometimes *Tamerlane*, sometimes *Jugurth*, sometimes *The Jew of Malta*, and, sometimes, parts of all these, and, at last, none of the three taking, they were forced to undress and put off their tragic habits, and conclude the day with *The Merry Milkmaids*. And unless this were done and popular humour satisfied, as sometimes it fortuned that the players were refractory, the benches, the tiles, the lathes, the stones, oranges, apples, nuts, flew about most liberally, and as there were mechanics of all professions, everyone fell to his own trade, and dissolved a house on the instant, and made a ruin of a stately fabric. It was not then the most mimical nor fighting man, Fowler, nor Andrew Crane, could pacify; prologues nor epilogues would prevail; the Devil and the Fool were quite out of favour; nothing but noise and tumult fills the house. (qtd in Braunmuller 2003: 58)

Although these early plays by Kyd, Marlowe and Shakespeare still remained strongly in the public memory, such nostalgia did raise a lot of alarming problems for new playwrights, all the more so since 'Cavalier drama did not figure significantly in the repertory of the theatres, which throughout the Caroline period survived on Elizabethan revivals' (Bulman 2003: 344). Such revivals occurred not only at the public theatres such as The Fortune or The Red Bull, but even at the more expensive indoor theatres such as Blackfriars and The Phoenix, and so younger dramatists faced a genuine artistic, and financial, dilemma during this period. Did one simply turn up one's nose and scoff at popular tastes, like William Davenant and so many others? Did one create elaborate pastiches of popular genres, recreating them while also parodying them at the same time? Or did one try to create a new drama, one that drew from the traditions of the past while also creating something wholly unique, wholly its own?

Luckily, John Ford, the last truly great English tragedian of the early modern stage, chose the latter, and as a result he produced two masterpieces of English Renaissance tragedy: *The Broken Heart* and *'Tis Pity She's a Whore*. As Bulman notes, Ford was

> not content to merely work within the parameters of tragedy defined by Elizabethan and Jacobean dramatists, [for] Ford set out to discover new heaven, new earth; and though he regularly mined the plays of his forebears . . . he did so with an understanding that only original moral premises – the shock of breaking already permissive social codes – could revitalize the genre. (2003: 352)

As we will see, original moral premises are certainly on display in Ford's tragedies. Ford wrote primarily for the indoor theatre, both for Blackfriars and The Phoenix, and this shows in the focus and structure of these tragic works, which are so 'skillfully controlled' despite their seemingly elaborate, and even outlandish, plots (Munro 2010: 90). Equally startling, Ford's two greatest tragedies seem to have been entirely his own invention, for while there are echoes of other English Renaissance tragedies, particularly those in the revenge tragedy tradition, the plots of the plays have not been traced, at least conclusively, to any definite sources. This is particularly strange given the setting of *The Broken Heart*, for a play set in ancient Greece could have made use of a vast range of materials, but Ford clearly chose not to do so. The 1633 edition of *The Broken Heart* says that it was performed at Blackfriars by the King's Men, but the precise date when this may have happened is uncertain; nevertheless, 1629 is the date given by some critics as a possible date (Braunmuller and Hattaway 2003: 441).

The plot is, despite its focus, rather confusing in its telling. The tragedy takes place in Sparta and centres around the character of Penthea, who has married the much older Bassanes as a result of pressure from her brother Ithocles. Penthea's former lover, much to her new husband's jealousy, is Orgilus, who decides to leave Sparta for Athens, but not before getting his sister Euphrania to promise the she will not marry without his consent. Ithocles and Prophilus win a tremendous victory over Messene, and the King of Sparta, Amyclas, along with his daughter, Calantha, celebrate the two soldiers and the battle. It is then revealed that Orgilus has not left Sparta but has stayed on in disguise as a disciple of a great philosopher. Penthea and Orgilus are reunited and declare their love for each other in the royal gardens, but Panthea refuses, despite her dislike of Bassanes, to be unfaithful to her husband. Ithocles apologises to his sister and declares his desire to marry Calantha, Princess of Sparta, although her father would prefer her to marry the King of Argos. Bassanes comes upon this discussion between brother and sister and suspects that the two are having an incestuous affair, a theme that will emerge again with much force in *'Tis Pity She's a Whore*. Penthea's despair has boiled over into madness, and she starves herself to death. Orgilus traps Ithocles and stabs him to death for being so cruel to his sister in the past, and Ithocles welcomes his death gladly. Princess Calantha is then brought news of her father's death and her lover's murder, and the despair that she feels as a result reaches breaking point during a very painful wedding dance. Orgilus opens his veins and bleeds to death, while Calantha, after settling Ithocles' estate and the fate of Sparta, places a ring on her dead lover's finger. She then kisses Ithocles before dying herself of a broken heart:

> One kiss on these cold lips, my last – crack, crack! –
> Argos now's Sparta's king. – Command the voices
> Which wait at th' altar, now to sing the song
> I fitted for my end.
>
> (5.3.77–80)

As Richard Madelaine points out, the breaking of Calantha's heart is nearly audible as a result of Ford's dramaturgy (1986: 38). Calantha dies as the music does, an effect that suggests Ford's growing dramatic sophistication (Anderson 1986: 171), and as the song ends Bassanes acknowledges that 'her heart is broke indeed' (5.3.95).

Although *The Broken Heart* is set in ancient Greece, the story itself, as mentioned, is entirely Ford's invention. Nevertheless, the qualities generally associated with the Spartans, such as stoicism and austerity, are on clear display in *The Broken Heart*, which suggests that Ford was trying to catch the mood of the place even if he was not trying to be completely historically accurate (Hawkins 1988: 129). There is a true sense of precision in this tragedy, one that handles its images, its characters and its action very carefully in order to achieve the desired dramatic effect. There is also a strong emphasis on issues such as love and honour, something that Tecnicus, who performs a kind of choric function in the tragedy, outlines rather well:

> But know then, Orgilus, what honour is.
> Honour consists not in a bare opinion
> By doing any act that feeds content,
> Brave in appearance, 'cause we think it brave;
> Such honour comes by accident, not nature,
> Proceeding from the vices of our passion,
> Which makes our reason drunk: but real honour
> Is the reward of virtue, and acquir'd
> By justice, or by valour which for basis
> Hath justice to uphold it. He then fails
> In honour, who for lucre [or] revenge
> Commits thefts, murders, treasons, and adulteries,
> With suchlike, by intrenching on just laws,
> Whose sovereignty is best preserv'd by justice.
> Thus, as you see how honour must be grounded
> On knowledge, not opinion, – for opinion
> Relies on probability and accident,
> But knowledge on necessity and truth.
>
> (3.1.31–48)

At the same time, there has even been some argument that the tragedy can be linked to the courtly love tradition of medieval literature. If so, one link may be the influence of Queen Henrietta Maria who, after coming to power with her husband Charles I, clearly sought to create a contrast, both in the court and in the arts, with the court left behind by her rather notorious father-in-law, James I. Perhaps this explains the epigram and anagram on the title page of the 1633 quarto of *The Broken*

Heart. 'Fide Honor' can be very nearly rearranged to read 'John Ford', especially since 'i' and 'j' were effectively the same letter in the Latin alphabet.

Ford's handling of his rather complex plot is effective, but it also raises a lot of questions about his dramatic motives. Why is Ithocles already ashamed of his actions before the audience can see him making that transition while Bassanes takes two acts to feel similar shame over his behaviour towards Penthea? Why is so much made of Orgilus's disguise when he then goes on to cast it off so suddenly in Act 2, scene 2? T. S. Eliot may have thought Ford to be careless in his craft, but it actually seems clear that Ford has some very definite dramatic concepts in mind as he lays out his play (1963 [1932]: 127). One strong example of this can be seen in the way that Ford handles the deaths of his characters. Generally, tragedies of the English Renaissance tended to have several characters dying one almost on top of the other, to such an extent that the stage could be felt to resemble a pile of corpses by the end. However, Ford clearly and cleverly separates his deaths in order to give each one its own special dramatic treatment. Far from being careless, he actually seems to be greatly expanding the potential for the tragic form. For example, his use of music clearly suggests his belief that music could be used to enhance the drama instead of merely accompanying it. One can see this in Act 5, scene 3 in particular, as his stage directions, which are quite detailed and carefully laid out, seek to utilise the music at the best possible moments. Also, Ford handles the declarations of his characters very differently from many of the tragedians discussed up to this point. Unlike, for example, Webster, Ford opts for short, elliptical statements that sometimes reflect, but just as frequently conceal, a character's motivation or state of mind. Nothing is quite what it seems in this play, and the means for communicating our inner self seems more likely to conceal than reveal. As Armostes tells Ithocles, ''Tis the tongue informs our ears./Our eyes can never pierce into the thoughts,/For they are lodged too inward' (4.1.16–18). This distrust of language may also be reflected in Calantha's showing her ring as a sign of her love instead of declaring it outright, or of her manic dance and placement of the ring on Ithocles's dead finger, which are likewise much more palpable and dramatically effective than a larger speech may have been. Such small gestures were probably ideally suited to the intimacy of the indoor theatres, whereas in a large, outdoor theatre such as The Globe they may not have been noticed at all (Sturgess 1985: 17–18). On a large stage, it is frequently necessary to declare one's intentions, but a smaller stage gives much greater precedence to the eye. At the same time, the emotional repression that may not have been as easy to effectively convey on the outdoor stage seems well tailored to the demands of the small stage that allows for such small, quiet moments to be better noticed. This sense of emotional repression can be found in the language of her exchange with Calantha in Act 3, scene 5 or with Orgilus's hiding of his true self, an act that he ends only at the end of the play. As Keith Sturgess notes, 'stoical fortitude, besides committing the tragic protagonists to inaction in a world governed by fate, demands from them an emotional restraint in which silence becomes the best eloquence' (1985: 17). While this silence is sometimes connected to suffering (Hopkins 2012: 197–8), there is no question that Ford also finds great strength in such moments.

Nevertheless, this is not to say the The Broken Heart is without moments of high drama and grand display, for Orgilus's method of killing himself before the whole court is clearly meant, both by Orgilus but also by Ford, to operate as a large spectacle. Thus, little attention is paid to Orgilus until the moment when all attention is paid to him; perhaps this is why Bassanes declares that Orgilus' end will be celebrated and will become 'the writer's glory and his subject's triumph' (5.2.134). Calantha's death has been equally grand and equally spectacular, as Bassanes likewise notes: 'O royal maid, would thou hadst miss'd this part;/ Yet 'twas a brave one' (5.3.96–7). Such deaths at the end of the play would seem to suggest a connection to revenge tragedy, and yet there is no clear revenger in this play, nor is there any clear character to be revenged upon. It is true that Orgilus has killed Ithocles as an act of revenge, but it is also true that Ithocles is no lecherous duke out of Webster or Middleton but a brother who made a mistake and who pays quite dearly for it. He welcomes his own death at Orgilus's hands, but it is still unclear why he should respond to his own murder in this way. Ithocles was wrong, but he was certainly not evil. As Sturgess notes, 'rarely are Ford's heroes committed with human evil in a tangible or simple-minded form; the Jacobean villain is unimportant in Ford's scheme of things' (1985: 17). While it may not be true to call the Jacobean villain simple-minded, it is certainly true that Ford is trying to explore something new in his tragedies, something that truly distinguishes him from both his predecessors and his contemporaries. As Dorothy M. Farr argues,

> The Broken Heart challenges the entire traditional notion of traditional Revenge Tragedy. Here no character acts alone; the logic of cause and effect is never forgotten, but the trials and ambitions of individuals are absorbed into the pattern of destiny and the moral sanctions are not only those which apply between one man and another, but rather those which ensure the safety and well-being of a whole community. . . . The conflict in which the main characters are engaged is not with a few power-seekers in a restricted circle, but with the ironies of the human condition . . . (1979: 79)

Perhaps this sense of irony and accident explains the apparent lack of judgement in the tragedy. The characters are engaged in actions that arise out of the consequences of their previous actions, and Ford does not judge his characters any more harshly than that. For example, Bassanes could have easily have been made a stock villain, or a stock fool, and yet Ford does not judge him – in fact, Bassanes actually becomes marshal of Sparta following the death of the King. Ford also does not judge love that others would regard as morally transgressive, and this open view will be on even fuller display in 'Tis Pity She's a Whore. Incestuous feelings, between Ithocles and Penthea on the one hand and Orgilus and Euphrania on the other, are never condemned by Ford; not only this, but the one character who does condemn it, Bassanes, is shown to be wrong for doing so, not only because he is incorrect but also because he is not in a position to judge in the first place. As Tecnicus notes, opinion 'relies on probability and accident,/But knowledge on necessity and truth' (3.4.46–7). Too often people judge on probability, in that they assume something without having possession of all the facts, or on accident, in that they come across a piece of information, usually partial or unclear, that they incorrectly assume gives them the whole picture. Ithocles incorrectly judges based on the probability that his sister will be happier with the security of marrying an older, wealthier man. On the other hand, Bassanes incorrectly judges based on the accident of his stumbling upon Ithocles and Penthea, an accident that makes his believe that he has stumbled upon the truth. Both judgements are wrong, for real knowledge is based on 'necessity and truth'. Ford does not judge his characters, and he does not invite us to do so either, and it is this lack of judgement that truly makes his work unique. To judge someone is often to judge falsely, but it is always to reduce someone to an interpretation or stance or single moment of behaviour – to judge someone in this way is to reduce their humanity. Ford begin to explore such reductive judgements, and their disastrous consequences, in *The Broke Heart*, but he will explore them even more fully in *'Tis Pity She's a Whore*.

In 1633 the English printer Nicholas Okes printed a quarto edition of a tragedy, one that seems to have first been performed the year before (Braunmuller and Hattaway 2003: 442). As the quarto states, this tragedy was 'Acted by the Queenes Majesties Servants, at the Phoenix in Drury-Lane'. This play, both for its subject matter and, in keeping with Ford's hesitancy to cast judgement, its handling of that subject matter, has become one of the most controversial tragedies of the English Renaissance: *'Tis Pity She's a Whore*. Despite, or perhaps because of, such controversy, it is also considered to be one of the greatest, the crowning achievement of Caroline drama. Why is it so controversial? Why has it come to be seen as one of the greatest of all English dramas?

As with *The Broken Heart*, there is no clear source for the plot, although the tragedy is filled with numerous echoes of Ford's predecessors, his contemporaries and even his own previous plays. While this can be seen in verbal echoes and allusions, it is really in the plot itself that one finds a complete reimagining of the revenge tragedy tradition that had begun with Kyd. The play opens with Friar Bonaventura, who has much in common with Friar Laurence in *Romeo and Juliet*, receiving a shocking confession from his young tutee, Giovanni (Smallwood 1981: 49). The young man is in love with his sister, Annabella. The rivalry between Grimaldi and Soranzo for Annabella is such that Grimaldi even finds himself in a street fight – echoing the opening fight between Montagues and Capulets in *Romeo and Juliet* – with Soranzo's servant, Vasques, and Annabella's father, Florio, has tried his best to quell things before they get out of control. 'However, Annabella feels nothing for either Grimaldi or Soranzo, and after she and Giovanni declare their love for each other, they swear an oath to remain faithful for ever; as Giovanni declares, "tis my destiny/That you must either love or I must die' (1.2.236–7). Grimaldi wants to remove Soranzo as a rival, and so Richardetto gives him a poisoned rapier, like the one used in *Hamlet*, to use against him.

Friar Bonaventura learns of the incestuous relationship between Annabella and Giovanni and condemns it in the highest possible terms; he also insists that Annabella must be married as soon as possible for the safety of her and Giovanni's souls. In keeping with this plan, Soranzo pays court to Annabella, but she refuses him outright, for she only loves Giovanni. At the same time, Giovanni has been spying on this courtship the whole time, for he too cannot give up Annabella. The nurse Putana tells Giovanni that Annabella is ill, for she is about to have a child, their child. At this point, Friar Bonaventura succeeds in scaring Annabella over the torments of hellfire and eternal damnation, and she agrees to marry Soranzo as a result. Meanwhile, Grimaldi mistakenly kills Bergetto, who had been preparing to elope with Philotis, and so he flees to the Cardinal for protection. At the wedding of Annabella and Soranzo, Hippolita tries to poison Soranzo with the help of Vasques, only to find herself tricked and poisoned by the wily servant. Soranzo discovers that Annabella is already pregnant, and his anger at this discovery causes him to threaten his new bridge with violence to try to find out the name of baby's father. Vasques believes that Putana will be easier to intimidate, and so he first uses trickery to get the information he wants, before ordering, in a possible echo of *King Lear*, that the nurse's eyes be put out. Annabella has written a letter in her own blood urging her brother Giovanni to repent of his sins, and she asks Friar Bonaventura to deliver it to him, which may allude to Friar Laurence's letter in *Romeo and Juliet*. Tragically, Giovanni stabs Annabella to death in her bedroom before showing himself to Soranzo and his guests, brandishing the heart of Annabella plunged through with his dagger, 'trimmed in reeking blood/That triumphs over death; proud in the spoil of love and vengeance' (5.6.9–11). Florio dies at the sight of it, and Giovanni manages to stab Soranzo to death before being killed himself. The Cardinal banishes Vasques and Soranzo's men before establishing order and, like Fortinbras, seizing everything for himself and offering a moral, of sorts, on the action that has just unfolded before them

> We shall have time
> To talk at large of all; but never yet
> Incest and murder have so strangely met.
> Of one so young, so rich in nature's store,
> Who could not say, ''Tis pity she's a whore?'
>
> (5.6.159–63)

As many critics have noted, *'Tis Pity She's a Whore* is both startlingly unique while also firmly embedded in the drama of the past; not only *Romeo and Juliet* but also *Antony and Cleopatra* and *Othello* provide models for such single-minded love, for those who love not wisely but too well, and for the utterly disastrous consequences that can arise from pursuing love in this way. As Emily Bartels points out, the tragedy

> draws attention to the inscrutability of drama and the tenuousness of its terms. More, perhaps, than any dramatist of his era, Ford exposes the deeply intertextual nature of dramatic fictions – the fact the no play is ever entirely original, that all plays incorporate elements (words, phrases, ideas, actions, costumes, actors, or

entire plots) from prior texts, if not also gestures, props, costumes, actors or interpretations from other performances. (2010: 250)

Nevertheless, just as Ford shows drama to be in constant interaction, even friction, his characters find themselves in a similar position. While Ford is careful not to judge the young lovers, he is fully aware of the catastrophe that awaits them. The tragedy also draws, particularly with Giovanni, on the Marlovian character of the overreacher, and it also makes much of its foreign setting in much the same ways that Kyd, Middleton and Webster do. Likewise, while the deaths in *The Broken Heart* had a controlled, even pace, the deaths in *'Tis Pity She's a Whore* come at the audience with a rapid and startling ferocity.

However, there are important differences as well, most notably, and perhaps shockingly, in regard to the treatment of incest. Incest appears in other revenge tragedies, from *Hamlet* to *The Revenger's Tragedy* to *Women Beware Women*, but it was always something engaged in by the villain, something that signified the corruption, degeneration and evil of the kingdom. As Bevington notes, 'many dramatists, even while they stage incest, hold it at a considerable moral and emotional distance. By contrast, Ford, in a play about consensual sexual intercourse between a sister and a brother, resolutely avoids any such palliating or marginalizing factors and forces his audience to give the matter of incest sustained, serious attention' (2002: 1905). Likewise, Giovanni and Annabella are presented as chaste rather than sexually rapacious or insatiable. If anything, their sexual urges seem somewhat dull and low key, particularly when it comes to anyone other than each other, which is no doubt why the Friar encourages Giovanni to become more sexually adventurous and sleep with other women (1.1.59–62).

Thus, the sheltered lives that both Giovanni and Annabella live make their ultimate love far more likely, for neither is shown to have any real experience of the world outside of their immediate family circle. Perhaps this is why Giovanni's expression suggests a wide knowledge of sonnets rather than a wide knowledge of women. In a startling twist on the Neoplatonic image of lovers as two parts of one whole, Giovanni points out that, as his sister, Annabella is already a part of him:

> Say that we had one father, say one womb
> (Curse to my joys!) have both of us life and birth;
> Are we not therefore each to other bound
> So much the more by nature? Nay, if you will have't,
> Even of religion, to be ever one,
> One soul, one flesh, one love, one heart, one all?
>
> (1.1.28–34)

Giovanni sees love as a passion, as something that breaks down walls and throws taboos: 'The more I strive, I love; the more I love,/The less I hope' (1.2.145–6). This all sounds very similar to the melancholic, lovelorn Romeo pining away for Rosaline and relying on cliché and convention rather than his true feelings. All of this changes or, at least, because of Juliet, it begins to change, when Romeo meets the fair daughter of the rich Capulet. The question is whether or not Annabella is that Juliet for Giovanni, or whether he may not have actually found his perfect love despite all of his claims that he has: 'Where in *Romeo and Juliet*, it is not the lovers' bond but the obstructing feud that is officially outlawed, in *'Tis Pity* the nature of the bond itself is taboo' (Bartels 2010: 250). This does not mean that Ford negatively judges Giovanni and Isabella, but he may be aware that they may not know as much about love or about each other as they think they do. Perhaps Ford has this undertone, which carries with it the heart of the tragedy, in mind as he makes use of the same stichomythic series of exchanges that Richard Gloucester used against Anne in *Richard III*; Giovanni even offers her his sword in much the same way that Richard does to Anne. Like Richard, Giovanni is also willing to lie to get what he wants, for he lies when he says that he has 'asked counsel of the Holy Church,/Who tells me I may love you, and 'tis just/That since I may, I should, and will, yes, will!' (1.1.249–52). This darker undertone is also reflected more humorously in the caustic jokes of the nurse Putana, who, like Juliet's nurse or like

Desdemona's maid Emilia, is wonderful when it comes to puncturing the rather idealistic images of love and sex Annabella and Giovanni are concocting. They are young and naive, but they are also so determined and headstrong that they, and Giovanni in particular, can become quite dangerous. Such consistency can become its own kind of lunacy, and Giovanni reflects this as he kills Annabella and declares that he holds 'fate/Clasped in my fist and could command the course/Of time's eternal motion, hadst thou been/One thought more steady than an ebbing sea' (5.5.11–14). Giovanni may love his sister, but he is the one who ends her life.

In *The Broken Heart*, Ford was interested in the rhetoric of silence, be it as a sign of suffering or as a sign of strength. However, in *'Tis Pity She's a Whore* Ford seems much more interested in what such silences hide. So much of importance happens either in private or behind closed doors, and so many of the characters are engaged in some kind of disguise; perhaps this is why the second to last person to speak in the tragedy is Richardetto, who has spent the play disguised as a doctor and who only now looks to reveal himself. The world of Parma that Ford depicts is one of immense cruelty and corruption. Everyone is either lying to someone or is being lied to by someone else, and everyone seems to be pursuing his or her own Machiavellian self-interests. Perhaps it is this that makes the love between Giovanni and Annabella, however problematic its nature and however unsettling its pursuit, the only ray of light in a very dark play. As Bulman notes,

> In a world of jaded self-interest such as Ford creates, where adultery flourishes, revenge is commonplace, and even the cardinal makes no pretence to morality, the love of Giovanni and Annabella stand as something finer, nobler, and more passionate than anything those around them are capable of. (2003: 353)

As time goes on, all of their secrets are revealed, and eventually everything gets taken out of the private and into the public sphere. Again, usually such exposure would be seen as a good thing; the evils are exposed, caught and punished. However, in Ford's tragedy it is Giovanni and Annabella who are exposed and caught. The illumination of sins does not promise enlightenment, but only more darkness, which may also underline the blinding of Annabella's nurse, Putana. Not only is this blinding horribly cruel, but it also suggests that such exposure will not result in truth but only in chaos and cruelty (Champion 1975: 78). Likewise, the language of the play becomes far more concrete and less vague as these discoveries begin to occur, but such concreteness does not bring clarity. Discovery and revelation occur at several points in the play, but Ford plays with our desire to regard such revelations as being revelatory. Someone may be revealed, or exposed, but in 'Tis Pity She's a Whore, nothing appears to be learned. Perhaps it is no accident then that the play ends on a question.

Or is that not the case? One of the questions tackled in all of these tragedies is that central issue of revelation, not simply of a particular scheme or machination, but of what that then reveals about the plot, about the characters, and about the themes and ideas that the tragedy has been exploring. This is why Aristotle placed such emphasis on anagnorisis, or recognition, in the *Poetics*. As George Whalley rightly notes: '*Knowing* is the root of both Greek *anagnorisis* and Latin *recognitio*. The element of knowing or not-knowing is crucial in Aristotle's analysis of tragedy' (1997: 86). Such revelations, which are 'central to tragic experience' (Hattaway 2013: 122), often occur on the stage, such as when Lear realises his mistake in banishing Cordelia or Gloucester his in banishing Edgar, recognitions linked to madness and understanding, blindness and sight; or they may occur off the stage, as those watching the play can be moved, not only to pity and fear but to thought and introspection. Gerald Else, who argues that anagnorisis 'is the hinge on which the whole structure of [tragedy] turns' (1957: 439), also points out that such recognitions occur with the characters and not with the spectators; however, the impact of anagnorisis need not be confined to either the onstage or the offstage world. Perhaps the revelation that seems denied to the characters onstage in 'Tis Pity She's a Whore suggests not an absence of recognition but a desire to bring about recognition on the part of the audience.

It is certainly the case that audience did respond strongly to the plays that we have discussed, for tragedy was the foremost dramatic genre of the English Renaissance stage. Tragedies of the English Renaissance span the period from the 1560s, which saw Sackville and Norton's *Gorboduc*, to the 1580s and 1590s, which saw the explosion of tragedies by Kyd, Marlowe and Shakespeare on the popular stage, to the Jacobean period, which witnessed the emergence of private, indoor theatre and innovative ways to dramatise the tragic, and finally to the court-centred dramas of the Caroline period. We end our discussion of English Renaissance tragedies with Ford, as he represents the pinnacle of tragedy during the Caroline period. Nevertheless, he certainly has his challengers, as Massinger, for example, produced many tragedies in addition to *The Roman Actor*, such as *The Duke of Milan* (1621) and *Believe as You List* (1631). These tragedies, clearly inspired by Shakespeare, Middleton and the history of early modern Italy, suggest how tragedy continued to be the most disruptive and subversive of the dramatic genres. Similarly, Ford's and Massinger's contemporary James Shirley, while best known for his comedies, also wrote many successful tragedies of which *The Traitor* (1631) and *The Cardinal* (1641) are widely seen as the most successful (Ravelhofer 2017: 87–8). James Bulman argues that Shirley, while aiming for 'intricacy rather than depth' and thus avoiding the 'ideological concerns' of his dramatic predecessors (2003: 350), nevertheless offers intriguing 'baroque variations' on the revenge tragedies of Shakespeare, Middleton, Webster and Ford (2003: 352). While not as profound or as unsettling as Ford's, Shirley's tragedies do represent a fascinating response, full of tantalising dramatic and textual echoes, to the tragedies of the English Renaissance. For example, the plot of *The Traitor* is clearly reminiscent of Middleton's *The Revenger's Tragedy*, while Duchess Rosaura's desire to marry for love in *The Cardinal* strongly suggests the dilemma faced by the Duchess of Malfi in Webster's tragedy. While certainly not as frequently performed as their Elizabethan and Jacobean counterparts, Massinger and Shirley have been kept alive on stage: Massinger's *Believe as You List* was revived by the Royal Shakespeare Company in 2005, while a very successful production of *The Cardinal* was performed at the Southwark Playhouse in London in 2017.

Of course, much of the drama from this period continues to be loved and revived, and so it must speak to something that, however much these tragedies are situated in a particular place and time, also manages to look beyond them. English Renaissance tragedy is a dramatic form that reaches kings, queens and everyday persons alike. Artistically, it represents the high-water mark in English drama, and it is no accident that so many contemporary commentators, from Francis Meres to Ben Jonson, were quick to not only put the drama on a par with that of the classical past but to place it above it. As Jonson puts it in his poem 'To the Memory of My Beloved the Author, Mr. William Shakespeare', in which he writes about the enormity of Shakespeare's achievement, he says that one should

> call forth thund'ring Aeschylus,
> Euripides and Sophocles to us;
> Pacuvius, Accius, him of Cordova dead,
> To life again, to hear thy buskin tread,
> And shake a stage; or when thy socks were on,
> Leave thee [Shakespeare] alone for the comparison
> Of all that insolent Greece or haughty Rome
> Sent forth, or since did from their ashes come.
> Tri'umph, my Britain, thou hast one to show
> To whom all scenes of Europe homage owe.
>
> (33–42)

While Jonson is referring specifically to Shakespeare, the poem's many references to other dramatic contemporaries, such as Thomas Kyd, Christopher Marlowe and Francis Beaumont, do suggest that Jonson has in mind the period as a whole. This immensely rich period during which tragedy flourished, which runs from 1561 to the closure of theatres by Parliament in 1642, saw tragedy become the most popular of Renaissance dramatic genres in the theatre. The period of this flourishing saw the emergence of many dramatic innovations, from the use of the blank verse for dramatic effect, to the rise of star performers, such as Edward Alleyn and Richard Burbage, and to the creation of professional playing companies, with playhouses specifically designed to meet both their needs and the demands of their audiences. These playhouses advanced rapidly during these years to become large public venues with tremendous acoustic capabilities that provided Alleyn, Burbage and many other fine actors with the potential to belt out some of the best blank verse in the language. The Jacobean period also saw the rising popularity of smaller, indoor theatres that allowed for different, perhaps subtler, acoustic capabilities, more room for experimentation with music, lighting and stage mechanics, and an increased ability for playwrights to involve audiences more directly in the action. As this book has shown, so many of these changes in London's theatres coincided with changes in London's political and cultural life, and this responsiveness and adaptability helped to make English Renaissance tragedy such a challenging and exhilarating dramatic form, a form that continues to inspire and move audiences to this day.

Bibliography

Adler, Doris (1987), *Philip Massinger*, Boston: Twayne Publishers.

Altman, Joel B. (2010), *The Impossibility of Othello: Rhetorical Anthropology and Shakespearean Selfhood*, Chicago: The University of Chicago Press.

Anderson, Donald (ed.) (1986), *Concord in Discord: The Plays of John Ford, 1586–1986*, New York: AMS Press.

Anonymous (1599), *A Warning for Faire Women, Containing the Most tragicall and lamentable murther of Master George Sanders of London merchant, nigh Shooters hill*, London: Valentine Sims for William Aspley.

Aristotle, *Aristotle's Poetics* (1997), George Whalley (trans.), John Baxter and J. P. Atherton (eds), Montreal and Kingston: McGill-Queen's University Press.

—, *Aristotle's Poetics: The Argument* (1957), Gerald F. Else (trans.), Leiden: E. J. Brill.

Armstrong, William A. (1959), 'The Audience of the Elizabethan Private Theatres', *The Review of English Studies* 10, 234–49.

Astington, John H. (1999), *English Court Theatre, 1558–1647*, Cambridge: Cambridge University Press.

— (2001), 'Playhouses, Players, and Playgoers in Shakespeare's Time', in *The Cambridge Companion to Shakespeare*, Margreta de Grazia and Stanley Wells (eds), Cambridge: Cambridge University Press, pp. 99–114.

— (2006), 'Playing the Man: Acting at the Red Bull and the Fortune', *Early Theatre* 9, 2, 130–43.

Atherton, Ian, and Julie Sanders (eds) (2006), *The 1630s: Interdisciplinary Essays on Culture and Politics in the Caroline Era*, Manchester: Manchester University Press.

Bacon, Francis (1999), 'Of Revenge,' in *The Essays*, Brian Vickers (ed.), Oxford: Oxford University Press, pp. 10–11.

Barber, C. L. (1988), *Creating Elizabethan Tragedy: The Theater of Marlowe and Kyd*, Richard P. Wheeler (ed.), Chicago and London: The University of Chicago Press.

Barish, Jonas (1986), 'Three Caroline "Defenses" of the Stage', in *Comedy from Shakespeare to Sheridan*, A. R. Braunmuller and J. C. Bulman (eds), Newark: University of Delaware Press, pp. 194–214.

Barker, Roberta, and David Nicol (2004), 'Does Beatrice Have a Subtext?: *The Changeling* on the London Stage', *Early Modern Literary Studies* 10, 1, 1–43.

Bartels, Emily C. (1996), 'Strategies of Submission: Desdemona, the Duchess, and the Assertion of Desire', *Studies in English Literature, 1300–1600* 36, 2, 417–33.

— (2008), *Speaking of the Moor: From* Alcazar *to* Othello, Philadelphia: University of Pennsylvania Press.

— (2010), ''Tis Pity She's a Whore: The Play of Intertextuality', in *The Cambridge Companion to English Renaissance Tragedy*, Emma Smith and Garrett A. Sullivan, Jr. (eds), Cambridge: Cambridge University Press, pp. 249–60.

Barton, Anne (1984), *Ben Jonson, Dramatist*. Cambridge: Cambridge University Press.

— (1981), 'Harking back to Elizabeth: Ben Jonson and Caroline Nostalgia', *ELH* 48, 706–31.

— (2001), 'The London Scene: City and Court', in *The Cambridge Companion to Shakespeare*, Margreta de Grazia and Stanley Wells (eds), Cambridge: Cambridge University Press, pp. 115–28.

— (2008), 'The Distinctive Voice of Philip Massinger', in Douglas Howard (ed.), *Philip Massinger: A Critical Reassessment*, Cambridge: Cambridge University Press, pp. 221–32.

Bate, Jonathan (2008), *Soul of the Age: The Life, Mind and World in William Shakespeare*, London: Viking.

— (1997), *The Genius of Shakespeare*, London: Picador.

Bates, Catherine (2002), 'Shakespeare's Tragedies of Love', in *The Cambridge Companion to Shakespearean Tragedy*, Claire McEachern (ed.), Cambridge: Cambridge University Press, pp. 195–217.

Bawcutt, N. W. (1999), *The Control and Censorship of Caroline Drama: The Records of Sir Henry Herbert, Master of the Revels, 1623–73*, Oxford: Clarendon Press.

— (2005), 'The Assassination of Alessandro de' Medici in Early Seventeenth-Century English Drama', *The Review of English Studies* 56, 225, 412–23.

Bayer, Mark (2009), 'The Red Bull Playhouse', in *The Oxford Handbook of Early Modern Theatre*, Richard Dutton (ed.), Oxford: Oxford University Press, pp. 225–39.

Beaumont, Francis, and John Fletcher (2002), *The Maid's Tragedy*, in *English Renaissance Drama*, David Bevington (ed.), New York and London: W. W. Norton.

Belsey, Catherine (1993), *The Subject of Tragedy: Identity & Difference in Renaissance Drama*, London and New York: Routledge.

Bentley, Gerald Eades (1948), 'Shakespeare and the Blackfriars Theatre', *Shakespeare Survey* 1, 38–50.

— (1984), *The Professions of Dramatist and Player in Shakespeare's Time, 1590–1642*, Princeton: Princeton University Press.

Berry, Herbert (2000), 'Playhouses, 1560–1660', in *English Professional Theatre 1530–1660*, Glynne Wickham, Herbert Berry and William Ingram (eds), Cambridge: Cambridge University Press, pp. 285–674.

Bevington, David (2000), 'The Major Comedies', in *The Cambridge Companion to Ben Jonson*, Richard Harp and Stanley Stewart (eds), Cambridge: Cambridge University Press, pp. 72–89.

Black, Matthew (ed.) (1966), *The Changeling*, Philadelphia: University of Pennsylvania Press.

Blatherwick, Simon (1997), 'The Archaeological Evaluation of the Globe Playhouse', in *Shakespeare's Globe Rebuilt*, J. R. Mulryne and Margaret Shewring (eds), Cambridge: Cambridge University Press, pp. 67–80.

Bliss, Lee (2003), 'Pastiche, Burlesque, Tragicomedy', in *The Cambridge Companion to English Renaissance Drama*, A. R. Braunmuller and Michael Hattaway (eds), 2nd edn, Cambridge: Cambridge University Press, pp. 228–53.

Blissett, William (1991), 'Roman Ben Jonson', in *Ben Jonson's 1616 Folio*, Jennifer Brady and W. H. Herendeen (eds), Newark: University of Delaware Press, pp. 90–110.

Boehrer, Bruce (1984), '"Nice Philosophy": *'Tis Pity She's a Whore* and the Two Books of God', *Studies in English Literature, 1500–1900* 24, 2, 355–71.

Bowsher, Julian (2012), *Shakespeare's London Theatreland: Archaeology, History, Drama*, London: Museum of Archaeology.

Bradbrook, M. C. (1980), *Themes and Conventions of Elizabeth Tragedy*, 2nd edn, Cambridge: Cambridge University Press.

Bradley, A. C. (1966), *Shakespearean Tragedy*, London: Macmillan and New York: St. Martin's.

Bradley, Jesse Franklin, and Joseph Quincy Adams (eds) (1922), *The Jonson Allusion-Book*, New Haven: Yale University Press.

Braudel, Fernard (1995), *The Mediterranean and the Mediterranean World in the Age of Philip II*, Vol. II, Siân Reynolds (trans.), Berkeley: University of California Press.

Braunmuller, A. R. (2003), 'The Arts of the Dramatist', in *The Cambridge Companion to English Renaissance Drama*, A. R. Braunmuller and Michael Hattaway (eds), 2nd edn, Cambridge: Cambridge University Press, pp. 53–92.

Bray, Alan (1990), 'Homosexuality and the Signs of Male Friendship in Elizabethan England', *History Workshop Journal* 29, 1–19.

Britland, Karen A. (2006), *Drama at the Courts of Queen Henrietta Maria*, Cambridge: Cambridge University Press.

Bromham, A. A., and Zara Bruzzi (1990), The Changeling *and the Years of Crisis, 1619–1624: A Hieroglyph of England*, London: Pinter Publishers.

Brooke, Nicholas (1968), *Shakespeare's Early Tragedies*, London: Methuen.

Brooks, Peter (2014), *The Quality of Mercy: Reflections on Shakespeare*, London: Nick Hearn Books.

Brotton, Jerry (2016), *This Orient Isle: Elizabethan England and the Islamic World*, New York: Random House.

Brown, John Russell (2001), *Shakespeare: The Tragedies*, Houndsmills and New York: Palgrave.

Bueler, Lois E. (1984), 'The Rhetoric of Change in *The Changeling*', *English Literary Renaissance* 14,1, 95–113.

Bulman, James (2003), 'Caroline Drama', in *The Cambridge Companion to English Renaissance Drama*, A. R. Braunmuller and Michael Hattaway (eds), 2nd edn, Cambridge: Cambridge University Press, pp. 344–71.

Burks, Deborah G. (1996), 'This sight doth shake all that is man within me': Sexual Violation and the Rhetoric of Dissent in *The Cardinal*', *Journal of Medieval and Renaissance Studies*, 2, 6, 153–90.

Burnett, Mark Thornton (2004), '*Tamburlaine the Great, Parts One and Two*', in *The Cambridge Companion to Christopher Marlowe*, Patrick Cheney (ed.), Cambridge: Cambridge University Press, pp. 127–43.

Bushnell, Rebecca (1992), 'Tyranny and Effeminacy in Early Modern England', in *Reconsidering the Renaissance*, Mario A. DiCesare (ed.), Binghamton, NY: Medieval and Renaissance Texts and Studies, pp. 339–54.

Butler, Martin (2003), 'Private and Occasional Drama', in *The Cambridge Companion to English Renaissance Drama*, A. R. Braunmuller and Michael Hattaway (eds), 2nd edn, Cambridge: Cambridge University Press, pp. 131–63.

— (2008), 'Romans in Britain: *The Roman Actor* and the Early Stuart Classical Play', in *Philip Massinger: A Critical Reassessment*, Douglas Howard (ed.), Cambridge: Cambridge University Press, pp. 139–70.

— (1984), *Theatre and Crisis, 1632–1642*, Cambridge: Cambridge University Press.

Callaghan, Dympna (ed.) (2000), *The Duchess of Malfi: Contemporary Critical Essays*, London: Macmillan.

Cary, Elizabeth, The Lady Falkland (1994), *The Tragedy of Mariam, the Fair Queen of Jewry*, Barry Weller and Margaret W. Ferguson (eds), Berkeley, Los Angeles and London: University of California Press.

Chadwick, Owen (1988), *The Reformation*, London, Penguin.

Chambers, Edmund Kerchever (1930), *William Shakespeare*, vols I–II, Oxford: The Clarendon Press.

— (1951), *The Elizabethan Stage*, vols I–IV, Oxford: The Clarendon Press.

— (1951), *William Shakespeare: A Study of Facts and Problems*, Oxford: The Clarendon Press.

Champion, Larry S. (1975), 'Ford's *'Tis Pity She's a Whore* and the Jacobean Tragic Perspective', *PMLA* 90, 78–87.

Chapman, Mathieu (2017), *Anti-Black Racism in Early Modern English Drama: The Other 'Other'*, London: Routledge.

Cinthio, Giovanni Battista Giraldi (1574), *Hecatommithi, onero centto novella di M. Giovanbattista Giraldi Cinthio*, Venice: Enea de Alaris.

Clare, Janet (1990), *'Art Made Tongue-Tied by Authority': Elizabethan and Jacobean Dramatic Censorship*. Manchester: Manchester University Press.

— (2006), *Revenge Tragedies of the Renaissance*, Tavistock: Northcote Publishing House.

— (2014), *Shakespeare's Stage Traffic: Imitation, Borrowing and Competition in Renaissance Theatre*, Cambridge: Cambridge University Press.

Clark, Ira (1993), *The Moral Art of Philip Massinger*, Lewisburg: Bucknell University Press.

— (2014), *Professional Playwrights: Massinger, Ford, Shirley and Brome*, Lexington: University Press of Kentucky.

Clark, Sandra (2013), *The Plays of Beaumont and Fletcher*, London: Routledge.

Clayton, Thomas (1994), '"That's She That was Myself': Not-so-Famous Last Words and Some Ends of *Othello*', *Shakespeare Survey* 46, 61–8.

Clerico, Terri, 'The Politics of Blood: John Ford's *'Tis Pity She's a Whore*', *English Literary Renaissance* 22, 3, 405–34.

Cogswell, T., and P. Lake (2006), 'Buckingham Does the Globe', *Shakespeare Quarterly* 60, 253–78.

Coleman, David (2010), *John Webster, Renaissance Dramatist*, Edinburgh: Edinburgh University Press.

Comensoli, Viviana (1999), *Household Business: Domestic Plays of Early Modern England*, Toronto, Buffalo and London: University of Toronto Press.

Cooper, Tarnya, et. al. (2006), *Searching for Shakespeare*, New Haven: Yale University Press.

Craik, Thomas W. (ed.) (1995), *Henry V*, The Arden Shakespeare, London and New York: Routledge.

Crawforth, Hannah, Sarah Dustagheer and Jennifer Young (2015), *Shakespeare in London*, London: Bloomsbury.

Croll, Morris W. (1903), *The Works of Fulke Greville*, Philadelphia: J. B. Lippincott Company.

Cummings, Brian (2002), *Literary Culture of the Reformation: Grammar and Grace*, Oxford: Oxford University Press.

Daalder, Joost (1988), 'Folly and Madness in *The Changeling*', *Essays in Criticism* 38, 1, 1–21.

Dent, R. W. (1981), *Shakespeare's Proverbial Language, An Index*, Berkeley: University of California Press.

— (2011), 'Learning and Teaching Resources: Mapping Texts, Spaces and Bodies', Andrew Hiscock (ed.), *Women Beware Women: A Critical Guide*, London: Continuum, pp. 77–98.

Dessen, Alan C. (1995), *Recovering Shakespeare's Theatrical Vocabulary*, Cambridge: Cambridge University Press.

Dillon, Janette (2007), *The Cambridge Introduction to Shakespeare's Tragedies*, Cambridge: Cambridge University Press.

Dollimore, Jonathan (1986), 'Subjectivity, Sexuality, and Transgression: The Jacobean Connection', *Renaissance Drama*, n.s., 17, 53–81.

— (1987), *Radical Tragedy: Religion, Ideology and Power in the Drama of Shakespeare and His Contemporaries*, New York and London: Harvester Wheatsheaf.

— (1999), *Death, Desire and Loss in Western Culture*, London: Penguin Books.

Donaldson, Ian (2013), *Ben Jonson: A Life*, Oxford: Oxford University Press.

Doob, Penelope B. R. (1973), 'A Reading of *The Changeling*', *English Literary Renaissance* 3, 1, 183–206.

Dryden, John (1971), *The Works of John Dryden, Volume XVII: Prose, 1668–1691*, Berkeley: University of California Press.

Dustagheer, Sarah (2014), 'Acoustic and Visual Practices Indoors', in *Moving Shakespeare Indoors: Performance and Repertoire in the Jacobean Playhouse*, Andrew Gurr and Farah Karim-Cooper (eds), Cambridge: Cambridge University Press, pp. 137–51.

Dutton, Richard (1991), *Mastering the Revels: The Regulation and Censorship of English Renaissance Drama*, London: Macmillan.

— (2009) (ed.), *The Oxford Handbook of Early Modern Theatre*, Oxford: Oxford University Press.

Eaton, Sara (1984), 'Beatrice-Joanna and the Rhetoric of Love in *The Changeling*', *Theatre Journal* 36, 3, 371–82.

Eccles, Christine (1990), *The Rose Theatre*, New York: Routledge.

Eliot, T. S. (1963 [1927]), 'Thomas Middleton', *Elizabethan Dramatists*, London: Faber, pp. 83–93.

— (1963 [1932]), 'John Ford', *Elizabethan Dramatists*, London: Faber, pp. 120–33.

Erne, Lukas (2010), '"Our other Shakespeare": Thomas Middleton and the Canon', *Modern Philology* 107, 3, 493–505.

— (2013), *Shakespeare as a Literary Dramatist*, 2nd edn, Cambridge: Cambridge University Press.

Farr, Dorothy M. (1979), *John Ford and the Caroline Drama*, London: Macmillan.

Foakes, R. A. (ed.) (1966), *The Revenger's Tragedy*, Cambridge: Harvard University Press.

— (1986), 'Tragicomedy and Comic Form', in *Comedy from Shakespeare to Sheridan*, A. R. Braunmuller and J. C. Bulman (eds), Newark: University of Delaware Press, pp. 74–88.

— (2003), 'Playhouses and Players', in *The Cambridge Companion to English Renaissance Drama*, A. R. Braunmuller and Michael Hattaway (eds), 2nd edn, Cambridge: Cambridge University Press, pp. 1–52.

Foley, Helene P., and Jean E. Howard (2014), 'The Urgency of Tragedy Now', *PMLA* 129:4, 617–633.

Ford, John (2002), *'Tis is Pity She's a Whore'*, in *English Renaissance Drama*, David Bevington et al. (eds), New York and London: W. W. Norton.

Forker, Charles R. (1986), *The Skull beneath the Skin: The Achievement of John Webster*, Carbondale and Edwardsville: Southern Illinois University Press.

Frye, Norhtrop (1991), *Fools of Time: Studies in Shakespearean Tragedy*, Toronto, Buffalo and London: The University of Toronto Press.

Fuchs, Barbara (2012), 'Middleton and Spain', in *The Oxford Handbook of Thomas Middleton*, Gary Taylor and Trish Thomas Henley (eds), Oxford: Oxford University Press, pp. 404–17.

Gair, Reavley (1982), *The Children of Paul's: The Story of a Theatre Company, 1553–1608*, Cambridge: Cambridge University Press.

Garrett, Martin (ed.) (1991), *Massinger: The Critical Heritage*, London: Routledge.

Gbadamosi, Gabriel (2012), 'Playwright to Playwright: *The Changeling*', in *The Oxford Handbook of Thomas Middleton*, Gary Taylor and Trish Thomas Henley (eds), Oxford: Oxford University Press, pp. 390–403.

Gibson, Colin (ed.) (1978), *The Selected Plays of Philip Massinger*, Cambridge: Cambridge University Press.

— (2008), 'Massinger's Theatrical Language', in *Philip Massinger: A Critical Reassessment*, Douglas Howard (ed.), Cambridge: Cambridge University Press, pp. 9–38.

Goldberg, Jonathan (1994), 'Romeo and Juliet's *Open Rs*', in *Queering the Renaissance*, Jonathan Goldberg (ed.), Durham, NC and London: Duke University Press, pp. 218–35.

Goodman, Henry (2004), 'King Richard III', in *Players of Shakespeare 6*, Robert Smallwood (ed.), Cambridge: Cambridge University Press, pp. 198–218.

Gossett, Suzanne (ed.) (2011), *Thomas Middleton in Context*, Cambridge: Cambridge University Press.

Graves, R. B. (1978), '*The Duchess of Malfi* at the Globe and Blackfriars', *Renaissance Drama* 9, 193–209.

Greenberg, Marissa (2015), *Metropolitan Tragedy: Genre, Justice, and the City in Early Modern England*, Toronto, Buffalo and London: University of Toronto Press.

Greville, Fulke (1939), *Poems and Dramas of Fulke Greville First Lord Brooke*, Geoffrey Bullough (ed.), vols I–II. Edinburgh and London: Oliver Boyd.

Griffith, Eva (2013), *A Jacobean Company and Its Playhouse: The Queen's Servants at the Red Bull*, Cambridge: Cambridge University Press.

Gurr, Andrew (1989), 'The Shakespearian Stages, Forty Years On', *Shakespeare Survey* 41, 1–12.

— (1989), '*The Tempest*'s Tempest at Blackfriars', *Shakespeare Survey* 41, 91–102.

— (1992), *The Shakespearean Stage, 1574–1642*, Cambridge: Cambridge University Press.

— (2004), *Playgoing in Shakespeare's London*, 3rd edn, Cambridge: Cambridge University Press.

— (2004), *The Shakespeare Company, 1594–1642*, Cambridge: Cambridge University Press.

— (1996), *The Shakespearean Playing Companies*, Oxford: Clarendon Press.

— (2010), 'The Move Indoors', in *Shakespeare in Stages: New Theatre Histories*, Christine Dymkowski and Christie Carson (eds), Cambridge: Cambridge University Press, pp. 7–21.

Gurr, Andrew and Farah Karim-Cooper (2014), *Moving Shakespeare Indoors: Performance and Repertoire in the Jacobean Playhouse*, Cambridge: Cambridge University Press.

Haber, Judith (2010), '*The Duchess of Malfi*: Tragedy and Gender', in *The Cambridge Companion to English Renaissance Drama*, Emma Smith and Garrett A. Sullivan, Jr. (eds), Cambridge: Cambridge University Press, pp. 236–48.

Hadfield, Andrew (2001), *The Elizabethan Renaissance, 1500–1620*, Oxford: Blackwell.

Hall, Kim F. (1995), *Things of Darkness: Economies of Race and Gender in Early Modern England*, Ithaca and London: Cornell University Press.

Hammond, Paul (2009), *The Strangeness of Tragedy*, Oxford: Oxford University Press.

Happé, Peter (1999), *English Drama Before Shakespeare*, London and New York: Longman.

Harbage, Alfred (1964), *Cavalier Drama: An Historical and Critical Supplement to the Study of the Elizabethan and Restoration Stage*, Kent: Russell & Russell.

Hattaway, Michael (1982), *Elizabethan Popular Theatre*, London: Routledge & Kegan Paul.

— (2006), 'Tragedy and Political Authority', in *The Cambridge Companion to Shakespearean Tragedy*, Claire McEachern (ed.), Cambridge: Cambridge University Press, pp. 110–31.

Hawkins, Harriet (1988), 'Mortality, Morality, and Modernity in *The Broken Heart*: Some Dramatic and Critical Counter-Arguments', in *John Ford: Critical Re-Visions*, Michael Neil (ed.), Cambridge: Cambridge University Press, pp. 129–52.

Heinemann, Margot (1980), *Puritanism and Theatre: Thomas Middleton and Opposition Drama under the Early Stuarts*, Cambridge: Cambridge University Press.

— (2003), 'Political Drama', in *The Cambridge Companion to English Renaissance Drama*, A. R. Braunmuller and Stanley Wells (eds), 2nd edn, Cambridge: Cambridge University Press, pp. 164–96.

Helgerson, Richard (1997), 'Murder in Faversham: Holinshed's Impertinent History', in *The Historical Imagination in Early Modern Britain: History, Rhetoric, and Fiction*, Donald R. Kelley and David Harris Sacks (eds), Cambridge: Cambridge University Press, pp. 133–58.

Henke, Robert (2012), 'John Webster: Collaboration and Solitude', in *The Cambridge Companion to Shakespeare and Contemporary Dramatists*, Ton Hoenselaars (ed.), Cambridge: Cambridge University Press, pp. 181–96.

Henslowe, Philip (2002), *Henslowe's Diary*, R. A. Foakes (ed.), Cambridge: Cambridge University Press.

Hill, Janet (2002), *Stages and Playgoers: From Guild Plays to Shakespeare*, Montreal and Kingston: McGill-Queen's University Press.

Hiscock, Andrew (2011) (ed.), *Women Beware Women: A Critical Guide*, London: Continuum.

Hoenselaars, Ton (2012), 'Shakespeare: Colleagues, Collaborators, Co-authors', in *The Cambridge Companion to Shakespeare and Contemporary Dramatists*, Ton Hoenselaars (ed.), Cambridge: Cambridge University Press, pp. 97–119.

Hogan, A. P. (1977), '*'Tis Pity She's a Whore*: The Overall Design', *Studies in English Literature, 1500–1600* 17, 2, 303–16.

Holbrook, Peter (2015), *English Renaissance Tragedy: Ideas of Freedom*, London: Bloomsbury.

Homem, Rui Carvalho (2012), 'Philip Massinger: Drama, Reputation, and the Dynamics of Social History', in *The Cambridge Companion to Shakespeare and Contemporary Dramatists*, Ton Hoenselaars (ed.), Cambridge: Cambridge University Press, pp. 212–25.

Honingmann, E. A. J. (2016) (ed.), *Othello*, New York: Bloomsbury Arden.

Hopkins, Lisa (1990), '"As tame as the ladies": Politics and Gender in *The Changeling*', *English Literary Renaissance* 20, 320–39.

— (1994), *John Ford's Political Theatre*, Manchester: Manchester University Press.

— (2000), *Christopher Marlowe: A Literary Life*, New York and Houndsmills, Basingstoke: Palgrave.

— (2012), 'John Ford: Suffering and Silence in *Perkin Warbeck* and *'Tis Pity She's a Whore*', in *The Cambridge Companion to Shakespeare and Contemporary Dramatists*, Ton Hoenselaars (ed.), Cambridge: Cambridge University Press, pp. 197–211.

Howard, Douglas (2008), 'Massinger's Political Tragedies', in *Philip Massinger: A Critical Reassessment*, Douglas Howard (ed.), Cambridge: Cambridge University Press, pp. 117–38.

— (ed.) (2008), *Philip Massinger: A Critical Reassessment*, Cambridge: Cambridge University Press.

Howard-Hill, T. H. (ed.) (1993), *The Trials of Frances Howard: Fact and Fiction at the Court of King James*, London: Routledge.

Hoxby, Blair (2015), *What Was Tragedy?: Theory and the Early Modern Canon*, Oxford: Oxford University Press.

Huebert, Ronald (1977), *John Ford: Baroque English Dramatist*. Montreal and Kingston: McGill-Queen's University Press.

Jardine, Lisa (1996), *Reading Shakespeare Historically*, London and New York: Routledge.

Jones, Emrys (1969), '*Othello*, *Lepanto* and the Cyprus Wars', *Shakespeare Survey* 21, 47–52.

Jones, Oliver (2014), 'Documentary Evidence for a Reimagined Indoor Jacobean Theatre', in *Moving Shakespeare Indoors: Performance and Repertoire in the Jacobean Playhouse*, Andrew Gurr and Farah Karim-Cooper (eds), Cambridge: Cambridge University, pp. 65–78.

Jonson, Ben (1996), *The Complete Poems*, George Parfitt (ed.), London: Penguin.

— (2012), 'To the Memory of My Beloved, the Author, Master William Shakespeare, And What He Hath Left Us', in *The Cambridge Edition of the Works of Ben Jonson*, vol. 5, David Bevington, Martin Butler and Ian Donaldson (eds), Cambridge: Cambridge University Press.

Jordan, Robert (1970), 'Myth and Psychology in *The Changeling*', *Renaissance Drama* 3, 157–65.

Kermode, Frank (2000), *Shakespeare's Language*, London: Allen Tate.

Kerrigan, John (1996), *Revenge Tragedy: Aeschylus to Armageddon*, Oxford: Clarendon Press.

Kiséry, András (2016), *Hamlet's Moment: Drama and Political Knowledge in Early Modern England*, Oxford: Oxford University Press.

Korda, Natasha (2011), 'Women in the Theatre', in *The Oxford Handbook of Early Modern Theatre*, Richard Dutton (ed.), Oxford: Oxford University Press, pp. 456–73.

Kowsar, Mohammad (1986), 'Middleton and Rowley's *The Changeling*: The Besieged Temple', *Criticism* 28, 2, 145–64.

Kyd, Thomas (1970), *The Spanish Tragedy*, J. R. Mulryne (ed.), London: A. C. Black and New York: W. W. Norton.

Lawrence, Jason (2005), *Who the Devil Taught Thee So Much Italian?: Italian Language Learning and Literary Imagination in Early Modern England*, Oxford: Oxford University Press.

Leech, Clifford (1970), *John Webster: A Critical Study*, New York: Haskell House.

Leggatt, Alexander (1988), *English Drama: Shakespeare to the Restoration, 1590–1660*, London: Longman.

— (1988), *Shakespeare's Political Drama: The History Plays and the Roman Plays*, London and New York: Routledge.

Lesser, Anton (1993), 'Richard of Gloucester in *Henry VI* and *Richard III*', in *Players of Shakespeare 3*, Russell Jackson and Robert Smallwood (eds), Cambridge: Cambridge University Press, pp. 140–59.

Lever, J. W. (1987), *The Tragedy of State: A Study of Jacobean Drama*, London: Methuen.

Levin, Harry (1965), *Christopher Marlowe: The Overreacher*, London: Faber & Faber.

Lindley, David (ed.) (1984), *The Court Masque*, Manchester: Manchester University Press.

Lomax, Marion (ed.) (2008), *'Tis Pity She's a Whore and Other Plays*, Oxford: Oxford University Press.

Luckyj, Christina (ed.) (2011), *The Duchess of Malfi: A Critical Guide*, London: Continuum.

MacKay, Ellen (2011), *Persecution, Plague, and Fire: Fugitive Histories of the Stage in Early Modern England*, Chicago and London: University of Chicago Press.

Madeleine, Richard (1988), '"Sensationalism" and "Melodrama" in Ford's Plays', in *John Ford: Critical Re-Visions*, Michael Neil (ed.), Cambridge: Cambridge University Press, pp. 29–54.

Maguire, Laurie and Emma Smith (2012), '"Time's comic sparks"; The Dramaturgy of *A Mad World, My Masters* and *Timon of Athens*', in *The Oxford Handbook of Thomas Middleton*, Gary Taylor and Trish Thomas Henley (eds), Oxford: Oxford University Press, pp. 181–95.

Malcolmson, Cristina (1990), "'As Tame as the Ladies': Politics and Gender in *The Changeling*', *English Literary Renaissance* 20, 2, 320–39.

Marcus, Leah S. (2000), 'Jonson and the Court', in *The Cambridge Companion to Ben Jonson*, Richard Harp and Stanley Stewart (eds), Cambridge: Cambridge University Press, pp. 30–42.

Marino, James (2011), *Owning William Shakespeare: The King's Men and their Intellectual Property*, Philadelphia: University of Pennsylvania Press.

Marlowe, Christopher (2003), *The Complete Plays*, Frank Romany and Robert Lindsey (eds), London: Penguin.

Marston, John (1978), *Antonio's Revenge*, W. Reavley Gair (ed.), Manchester: Manchester University Press and Baltimore: The Johns Hopkins University Press.

— (1986), *The Selected Plays of John Marston*, MacDonald P. Jackson and Michael Neill (eds), Cambridge: Cambridge University Press.

Massai, Sonia (ed.) (2011), *'Tis Pity She's a Whore*, London: Arden Early Modern Drama.

Massinger, Philip (2012), *The Roman Actor*, Martin White (ed.), Manchester: Manchester University Press.

Mateer, David (2009), 'Edward Alleyn, Richard Perkins and the Rivalry between the Swan and Rose Playhouses', *Review of English Studies* 60, 61–77.

Maus, Katharine Eisaman (1995) (ed.), *Four Revenge Tragedies*, Oxford: Oxford University Press.

McAdam, Ian (1999), *The Irony of Identity: Self and Imagination in the Drama of Christopher Marlowe*, Newark: University of Delaware Press and London: Associated University Presses.

McAlindon, Tom (1996), *Shakespeare's Tragic Cosmos*, Cambridge: Cambridge University Press.

— (2004), *Shakespeare 'Minus' Theory*, Aldershot and Burlington, VT: Ashgate.

McCabe, Richard A. (1993), *Incest, Drama, and Nature's Law, 1550–1700*, Cambridge: Cambridge University Press.

McCulloch, Diarmaid (1990), *The Later Reformation in England, 1547–1603*, New York: St. Martin's Press.

McEarchen, Claire (ed.) (2002), *The Cambridge Companion to Shakespearean Tragedy*, Cambridge: Cambridge University Press.

McLuskie, Kathleen (1981), 'Caroline Professionals: Brome and Shirley', in *The Revels History of Drama in English, 1613–1660*, Philip Edwards, G. E. Bentley and Lois Potter (eds), London: Methuen.

McMillin, Scott and Sally-Beth MacLean (1998), *The Queen's Men and Their Plays*, Cambridge: Cambridge University Press.

McMullan, Gordon (2007), *The Revenger's Tragedy*, in *Thomas Middleton: The Collected Works*, Gary Taylor and John Lavagnino (eds), Oxford: Clarendon Press, pp. 543–93.

— (2010), 'The Changeling and the Dynamic of Ugliness', in *The Cambridge Companion to English Renaissance Tragedy*, Emma Smith and Garret A. Sullivan Jr. (eds) Cambridge: Cambridge University Press, pp. 222–35.

— (2014), *Women Beware Women*, William C. Carroll (ed.), New York: Bloomsbury.

Middleton, Thomas, and William Rowley (2002), *The Changeling*, in *English Renaissance Drama*, David Bevington et al. (eds), New York and London: W. W. Norton, pp. 1593–659.

— (1958), *The Changeling*, N. W. Bawcutt (ed.), Manchester: Manchester University Press.

Mikesell, Margaret Lael (1983), 'Catholic and Protestant Widows in *The Duchess of Malfi*', *Renaissance and Reformation* 7,4, 265–79.

Montrose, Louis (1996), *The Purpose of Playing: Shakespeare and the Cultural Poetics of the Elizabethan Theatre*, Chicago and London: The University of Chicago Press.

Mooney, Michael E. (1986), '"Framing" as Collaborative Technique: Two Middleton-Rowley Plays', in *Drama in the Renaissance: Comparative and Critical Essays*, Clifford Davidson, C. J. Giankaris and John H. Stroupe (eds), New York: AMS Press, pp. 300–14.

Morton, Richard (1966), 'Deception and Social Dislocation: An Aspect of James Shirley's Drama', *Renaissance Drama* 9, 227–46.

Moulton, Ian Frederick (1996), '"A Monster Great Deformed": The Unruly Masculinity of *Richard III*', *Shakespeare Quarterly* 47, 3, 251–68.

— (2014), *Love in Print in the Sixteenth Century: The Popularization of Romance*, New York: Palgrave Macmillan.

Mullaney, Steven (1988), *The Place of the Stage: License, Play, and Power in Renaissance England*, Ann Arbor: The University of Michigan Press.

Mulryne, J. R., and Stephen Fender (1968), 'Marlowe and the "Comic Distance"', in *Christopher Marlowe*, Brian Morris (ed.), London: Ernest Benn, pp. 49–64.

Munro, Lucy (2005), *Children of the Queen's Revels: A Jacobean Theatre Company*, Cambridge: Cambridge University Press.

— (2010), 'Tragic Forms', in *The Cambridge Companion to English Renaissance Tragedy*, Emma Smith and Garrett A. Sullivan (eds), Cambridge: Cambridge University Press, pp. 86–101.

— (2012), 'Middleton and Caroline Theatre', in *The Oxford Handbook of Thomas Middleton*, Gary Taylor and Trish Thomas Henley (eds), Oxford: Oxford University Press, pp. 164–80.

Nashe, Thomas (1985), *Pierce Penniless His Supplication to the Devil*, in *The Unfortunate Traveller and Other Works*, J. B. Steane (ed.), London: Penguin, pp. 49–145.

Neill, Michael (1978), '"Wits most accomplished Senate": The Audience of the Caroline Private Theatres', *SEL* 18, 341–60.

— (ed.) (1988), *John Ford: Critical Re-Visions*, Cambridge: Cambridge University Press.

— (1991), '"Hidden malady": Death, Discovery, and Indistinction in *The Changeling*', *Renaissance Drama* 22, 95–121.

— (ed.) (2009), *Othello*, Oxford: Oxford University Press.

Nicoll, Allardyce (1968), *English Drama: A Modern Viewpoint*, New York: Barnes and Noble.

Nuttall, A.D. *Shakespeare the Thinker*, New Haven, CT: Yale University Press.

— (2001), *Why Does Tragedy Give Pleasure?*, Oxford: Clarendon.

Oakley Brown, Liz (2011), 'Learning and Teaching Resources: Mapping Texts, Spaces and Bodies', in *Women Beware Women: A Critical Guide*, Andrew Hiscock (ed.), London: Continuum, pp. 171–88.

O'Callaghan, Michelle (2009), *Thomas Middleton*, Edinburgh: Edinburgh University Press.

— (2012), 'Thomas Middleton and the Early Modern Theatre', in *The Cambridge Companion to Shakespeare and Contemporary Dramatists*, Ton Hoenselaars (ed.), Cambridge: Cambridge University Press, pp. 165–80.

Onions, C. T. (1986), *A Shakespeare Glossary*, Oxford: Oxford University Press.

Orell, John (1997), 'Designing the Globe, Reading the Documents', in *Shakespeare's Globe Rebuilt*, J. R. Mulryne and Margaret Shewring (eds), Cambridge: Cambridge University Press.

Orgel, Stephen, and Roy Strong (1973), *Inigo Jones: The Theatre of the Stuart Court*, Berkeley: University of California Press.

Palfrey, Simon and Tiffany Stern (2007), *Shakespeare in Parts*, Oxford: Oxford University Press.

Patterson, Annabel (1984), *Censorship and Interpretation: The Conditions of Writing and Reading in Early Modern England*, Madison: University of Wisconsin Press.

Peck, Linda Levy (1990), *Court Patronage and Corruption in Early Stuart England*, Boston: Unwin Hyman.

— (ed.) (1992), *The Intellectual Milieu of the Jacobean Court*, Cambridge: Cambridge University Press.

Perry, Curtis (1997), *The Making of Jacobean Culture*, Cambridge: Cambridge University Press.

Pincombe, Mike (2010), 'English Renaissance Tragedy: Theories and Antecedents', in *The Cambridge Companion to English Renaissance Tragedy*, Emma Smith and Garrett A. Sullivan (eds), Cambridge: Cambridge University Press, pp. 3–16.

Pollard, Tanya (2010), 'Tragedy and Revenge', in *The Cambridge Companion to English Renaissance Tragedy*, Emma Smith and Garrett A. Sullivan, Jr. (eds), Cambridge: Cambridge University Press, pp. 58–72.

Potter, Lois (2010), 'Tragedy and Performance', in *The Cambridge Companion to English Renaissance Tragedy*, Emma Smith and Garrett A. Sullivan Jr. (eds), Cambridge: Cambridge University Press, pp. 102–15.

Proudfoot, G. R. (1977) (ed.), 'Five Dramatic Fragments', *Collections*, vol. 9, The Malone Society, Oxford: Oxford University Press, pp. 52–7.

Rainolds, John (1609 [1597]), *A Defence of the Judgment of the Reformed Churches, that a man may lawfullie not onelie put away his wife for her adulterie, but also marrie another*, Dordrecht: [by George Walters?].

Randall, Dale B. J. (1986), 'Some New Perspectives on the Spanish Setting of *The Changeling* and Its Source', *Medieval and Renaissance Drama in England* 3, 189–216.

Ravelhofer, Barbara (2017), 'Shirley's Tragedies', in *James Shirley and Early Modern Theatre: New Critical Perspectives*, Barbara Ravelhofer (ed.), London: Routledge, pp. 86–107.

Rebholz, Ronald A. (1971), *The Life of Fulke Greville First Lord Brooke*, Oxford: Clarendon Press.

Rees, Joan (1971), *Fulke Greville, Lord Brooke, 1554–1628*, London: Routledge and Kegan Paul.

Revenger's Tragedy, The (1991), in Brian Gibbons (ed.), *The Revenger's Tragedy*, London: A. C. Black and New York: W. W. Norton.

Richardson, Catherine (2010), 'English Renaissance Tragedy', in *The Cambridge Companion to English Renaissance Tragedy*, Emma Smith and Garrett A. Sullivan Jr (ed.), Cambridge: Cambridge University Press, pp. 17–29.

Ricks, Christopher (1960), 'The Moral and Poetic Structure of *The Changeling*', *Essays in Criticism* 10, 3, 290–306.

Rochester, Joanne (2010), *Staging Spectatorship in the Plays of Philip Massinger*, Farnham: Ashgate.

Rose, Mary Beth (1988), *The Expense of Spirit: Love and Sexuality in English Renaissance Drama*, Ithaca and London: Cornell University Press.

Rossiter, A. P. (1969), *English Drama from Early Times to the Elizabethans*, London: Hutchinson University Library.

Rutter, Tom (2012), *The Cambridge Introduction to Christopher Marlowe*, Cambridge: Cambridge University Press.

Ryan, Kiernan (2002), *Shakespeare*, Houndsmills, Basingstoke and New York: Palgrave Macmillan.

Sackville, Thomas and Thomas Norton (1970), *Gorboduc: or, Ferrex and Porrex*, Irby B. Cauthen, Jr. (ed.), Lincoln: University of Nebraska Press.

Sanders, Julie (1999), *Caroline Drama: The Plays of Massinger, Ford, Shirley, and Brome*, Tavistock: Northcote House.

— (2011), *The Cultural Geography of Early Modern Drama, 1620–1650*, Cambridge: Cambridge University Press.

Schoenbaum, Samuel (1955), *Middleton's Tragedies: A Critical Study*, New York: Columbia University Press.

Scott, William (2013 [?1599]), *The Model of Poesy*, Gavin Alexander (ed.), Cambridge: Cambridge University Press.

Semenza Colón, Gregory M. (2010), 'The Spanish Tragedy and Metatheatre', in Emma Smith and Garrett A. Sullivan, Jr. (eds), *The Cambridge Companion to English Renaissance Tragedy*, Cambridge: Cambridge University Press, pp. 153–62.

Shakespeare, William (1994), *Anthony and Cleopatra*, Michael Neill (ed.), Oxford: Oxford University Press.

— (1998), *Hamlet*, G. R. Hibbard (ed.), Oxford: Oxford University Press.

— (1998), *Henry V*, Gary Taylor (ed.), Oxford: Oxford University Press.

— (2000), *Richard III*, John Jowett (ed.), Oxford: Oxford University Press.

— (2000), *Romeo and Juliet*, Jill L. Levenson (ed.), Oxford: Oxford University Press.

— (2006), *Othello*, Michael Neill (ed.), Oxford: Oxford University Press.

— (2016), *The New Oxford Shakespeare, The Complete Works*, Garry Taylor, John Jowett, Terri Bourus and Gabriel Egan (eds), Oxford: Oxford University Press.

Shapiro, James (2005), *1599: A Year in the Life of William Shakespeare*, London: Faber & Faber.

Shepherd, Simon (1986), *Marlowe and the Politics of Elizabethan Theatre*, Brighton: The Harvester Press.

Shirley, James (1966), *The Cardinal*, Charles Forker (ed.), Bloomington: Indianapolis University Press.

— (1986), *The Cardinal*, E. M. Yearling (ed.), Manchester: Manchester University Press.

Sidney Herbert, Mary (1998), vol. I, *Poems, Translations, and Correspondence*, in *The Collected Works of Mary Sidney Herbert, Countess of Pembroke*, Margaret P. Hannay, Noel J. Kinnamon and Michael G. Brennan (eds), Oxford: Clarendon Press.

Sidney, Sir Philip (1973), *An Apology for Poetry*, Geoffrey Shepherd (ed.), Manchester: Manchester University Press and New York: Barnes & Noble.

Sillitoe, Peter (2013), *Shakespearean London Theatres*, Leicester and London: ShaLT.

Simpson, James (2002), *Reform and Cultural Reformation*, vol. 2: 1350–547, *Oxford English Literary History*, Oxford: Oxford University Press.

Sinfield, Alan (1983), *Literature in Protestant England, 1560–1660*, London & Canberra: Croom Helm and Totowa, NJ: Barnes & Noble.

Smallwood, R. L. (1981), '*'Tis Pity She's a* Whore and *Romeo and Juliet*', *Cahiers Elizabethains* 20, 49–70.

Smith, Bruce R. (1994), *Homosexual Desire in Shakespeare's England: A Cultural Poetics*, Chicago and London: The University of Chicago Press.

— (1999), *The Acoustic World of Early Modern England: Attending to the O-Factor*. Chicago and London: University of Chicago Press.

Smith, Irwin (1964), *Shakespeare's Blackfriars Playhouse*, New York: New York University Press.

Snuggs, Henry (1960), *Shakespeare in Five Acts: Studies in a Dramatic Convention*, New York: Vantage.

Spivack, Bernard (1958), *Shakespeare and the Allegory of Evil*, New York: Columbia University Press.

Stapleton, Michael, J. (2013), 'Ovid in *The Jew of Malta*', in *The Jew of Malta: A Critical Reader*, Robert Logan (ed.), London and New York: Bloomsbury.

Stavig, Mark (1968), *John Ford and the Traditional Moral Order*, Madison: University of Wisconsin Press.

Steiner, George (1996), 'Tragedy, Pure and Simple', in *Tragedy and the Tragic: Greek Theatre and Beyond*, M. S. Silk (ed.), Oxford: Clarendon Press, pp. 534–46.

Stern, Tiffany (2004), *Making Shakespeare: From Stage to Page*, Abington and New York: Routledge.

— (2010), 'The Theatre of Shakespeare's London', in *The New Cambridge Companion to Shakespeare*, Margreta de Grazia and Stanley Well (eds), Cambridge: Cambridge University Press, pp. 45–60.

Stopes, C. C. (1970), *Burbage and Shakespeare's Stage*, 1913, New York: Haskell House.

Straznicky, Marta (2004), *Privacy, Playreading, and Women's Closet Drama, 1550–1700*, Cambridge: Cambridge University Press.

Streete, Adrian (2010), *Protestantism and Drama in Early Modern England*, Cambridge: Cambridge University Press.

Sturgess, Kieth (ed.) (1985), *John Ford: Three Plays*, London and New York: Three Plays.

Styan, J. L. (1994), *Shakespeare's Stagecraft*, Cambridge: Cambridge University Press.

Sullivan, Garret A. (2005), *Memory and Forgetting in English Renaissance Drama*, Cambridge: Cambridge University Press.

Syme, Holger Schott (2016), 'The Theater of Shakespeare's Time', in *The Norton Shakespeare*, 3rd edn, Stephen Greenblatt et al. (eds), New York: W. W. Norton, pp. 93–118.

Tacitus ([1931], 1998), *The Histories, Books IV–V, The Annals, Books I–III*, Clifford H. Moore and John Jackson (trans.), Cambridge, MA: Harvard University Press.

Tanner, Tony (2010), *Prefaces to Shakespeare*, Cambridge, MA and London: The Belknap Press of Harvard University Press.

Taylor, Gary (1993), 'The Structure of Performance: Act Intervals in the London Theatres, 1576–1642', in *Shakespeare Reshaped, 1601–1623*, Gary Taylor and John Jowett (eds), Oxford: Oxford University Press, pp. 3–50.

— (1994), 'Forms of Opposition: Shakespeare and Middleton', *ELR* 24, 283–314.

— (2012), 'History – Plays – Genres – Games', in *The Oxford Handbook to Thomas Middleton*, Gary Taylor and Trish Thomas Henley (eds), Oxford: Oxford University Press, pp. 47–63.

Taylor, Gary, and Rory Loughnane (2017), 'The Canon and Chronology of Shakespeare's Works', in *Authorship Companion*, The New Oxford Shakespeare, Gary Taylor and Gabriel Egan (eds), Oxford: Oxford University Press, pp. 416–602.

Taylor, Gary and Michael Warren (1983), *Division of the Kingdoms: Shakespeare's Two Versions of 'King Lear'*, Oxford: Oxford University Press.

Thompson, Ayanna (2016), 'Introduction', in E. A. J. Honingmann (ed.), *Othello*, New York: Bloomsbury Arden, pp. 1–118.

Thomson, Leslie (1986), '"Enter Above": The Staging of *Women Beware Women*', *Studies in English Literature* 26, 331–43.

Thomson, Peter (1992), *Shakespeare's Professional Career*, Cambridge: Cambridge University Press.

Tricomi, Albert (1989), *Anticourt Drama in England, 1603–1642*, Charlottesville: University Press of Virginia.

Trussler, Simon (2006), *The Faber Pocket Guide to Elizabethan and Jacobean Drama*, London: Faber & Faber.

Turner, Henry S. (2006), *The English Renaissance Stage: Geometry, Poetics, and the Practical Spatial Arts, 1580–1630*, Oxford: Oxford University Press.

Underdown, David (1985), *Revel, Riot and Rebellion: Popular Politics and Culture in England, 1603–1660*, Oxford: Clarendon Press.

Van Es, Bart (2013), *Shakespeare in Company*, Oxford: Oxford University Press.

Vickers, Brian (2012), 'Identifying Shakespeare's Additions to *The Spanish Tragedy* (1602): A New(er) Approach', *Shakespeare* 8:1, 12–43.

Vitkus, Daniel (2003), *Turning Turk: English Theater and the Multicultural Mediterranean, 1570–1630*, New York and Houndsmills, Basingstoke: Palgrave Macmillan.

Waller, Gary (1986), *English Poetry of the Sixteenth Century*, New York and London: Longman, 1986.

Watson, Robert N. (2003), 'Tragedy', in *The Cambridge Companion to English Renaissance Drama*, A. R. Braunmuller and Michael Hattaway (eds), Cambridge: Cambridge University Press, pp. 292–343.

— (2006), 'Tragedies of Revenge and Ambition', in Claire McEachern (ed.), *The Cambridge Companion to Shakespearean Tragedy*, Cambridge: Cambridge University Press, pp. 160–81.

Webster, John (2002), *The Duchess of Malfi*, in *English Renaissance Drama*, David Bevington (ed.), New York and London: W. W. Norton, pp. 1749–1832.

— (2002), *The White Devil*, in *English Renaissance Drama*, David Bevington (ed.), New York and London: W. W. Norton, pp. 1659–748.

Weimann, Robert (1987), *Shakespeare and the Popular Tradition in the Theater: Studies in the Social Dimension of Dramatic Form and Function*, Robert Schwartz (ed.), Baltimore and London: Johns Hopkins University Press.

Weis, René (1996) (ed.), *The Duchess of Malfi and Other Plays*, Oxford: Oxford University Press.

Wentersdorf, Karl P. (1977), 'The Repertory and Size of Pembroke's Company', *Theatre Annual* 33, 71–85.

Wells, Stanley (2015), *Great Shakespearean Actors: Burbage to Branagh*, Oxford: Oxford University Press.

Whetstone, George (1593), *Avrelia, the paragon of pleasure and princely delights*, London: by [Thomas Orwin] for Richard Johnes.

Whigman, Frank (1983), 'Sexual and Social Mobility in *The Duchess of Malfi*', *PMLA* 100, 2, 167–86.

White, Martin (ed.) (1982), *Arden of Faversham*, London and New York: Norton.

Wickham, Glynne (1963), *Early English Stages, 1300–1660*, vol. II, *1576 to 1660*, Part I, New York: Columbia University Press.

Wickham, Glynne, Herbert Berry and William Ingram (eds) (2000), 'Stephen Gordimer to Matthew Parker, 12 May 1545', *English Professional Theatre, 1530–1660*, Cambridge: Cambridge University Press, p. 28.

Wiggins, Martin (ed.) (1998), *Four Jacobean Sex Tragedies*, Oxford: Oxford University Press.

— (2000), *Shakespeare and the Drama of His Time*, Oxford: Oxford University Press.

— (ed.) (2008), *A Woman Killed with Kindness and Other Domestic Plays*, Oxford: Oxford University Press.

Wiggins, Martin, in association with Catherine Richardson (2012), *British Drama 1533–1642: A Catalogue*, vol. II: 1567–1589, Oxford: Oxford University Press.

— (2013), *British Drama, 1533–1642: A Catalogue*, vol. II: 1590–1597, Oxford: Oxford University Press.

— (2014), *British Drama, 1533–1642: A Catalogue*, vol. III: 1598–1602, Oxford: Oxford University Press.

— (2015), *British Drama, 1533–1642: A Catalogue*, vol. V: 1603–1608, Oxford: Oxford University Press.

Wilkes, G. A. (1988) (ed.), *Ben Jonson: Five Plays*, Oxford: Oxford University Press.

Wilks, John S. (1990), *The Idea of Conscience in Renaissance Tragedy*, London: Routledge.

Wilson, F. P. (1969), *The English Drama, 1485–1585*, Oxford: The Clarendon Press.

Wiseman, Susan (1998), *Drama and Politics in the English Civil War*, Cambridge: Cambridge University Press.

Womack, Peter (2006), *English Renaissance Drama*, Oxford: Blackwell Publishing.

Woodcock, Matthew (2008), *Shakespeare, Henry V*, Basingstoke and Macmillan: Palgrave Macmillan.

Wymer, Rowland (1995), *Webster and Ford*, London: Macmillan.

Young, Karl (1933), 'Honorius of Autun's "De Tragoediis", *Gemma Animae*, Lib. I, Cap. LXXXII', in *The Drama of the Medieval Church*, vol. I, Oxford: The Clarendon Press.

Zucker, Adam, and Alan B. Farmer (eds) (2006), *Localizing Caroline Drama: Politics and Economics of the Early Modern English Stage, 1625–1642*, Basingstoke and New York: Palgrave Macmillan.

Index